A Guide to EU Environmental Law

A Guide to EU
Environmental Law

JOSEPHINE VAN ZEBEN AND ARDEN ROWELL

UNIVERSITY OF CALIFORNIA PRESS

University of California Press
Oakland, California

University of California Press
Oakland, California

Library of Congress Cataloging-in-Publication Data

Names: Zeben, Josephine A. W. van, 1984– author. |
    Rowell, Kristen Arden, 1982– author.
Title: A guide to EU environmental law / Josephine van
    Zeben and Arden Rowell.
Description: Oakland, California : University of
    California Press, [2020] | Includes bibliographical
    references and index.
Identifiers: LCCN 2020011737 (print) | LCCN 2020011738
    (ebook) | ISBN 9780520295216 (cloth) |
    ISBN 9780520295223 (paperback) |
    ISBN 9780520968059 (ebook)
Subjects: LCSH: Environmental law—European Union
    countries. | Environmental policy—European Union
    countries.
Classification: LCC KJE6242 .Z43 2020 (print) |
    LCC KJE6242 (ebook) | DDC 344.2404/6—dc23
LC record available at https://lccn.loc.gov/2020011737
LC ebook record available at https://lccn.loc.
gov/2020011738

Manufactured in the United States of America

29   28   27   26   25   24   23   22   21   20
10   9   8   7   6   5   4   3   2   1

For our families—past, present, and future

Contents

List of Illustrations ix

List of Spotlight Boxes xi

Preface xiii

**PART ONE. BUILDING BLOCKS OF
EU ENVIRONMENTAL LAW**

1. Regulating Environmental Impacts

3

2. Key Actors

12

3. Types of Law

36

4. Regulatory Instruments

57

PART TWO. EU ENVIRONMENTAL LAW

5. Contextualizing EU Environmental Law

77

6. Pollution Control

92

Air Pollution   99
Water Pollution   112
Soil Pollution   122
Chemical Substances   129
Waste Management   134

7. Ecosystem Management

156

Biodiversity   163
Wildlife   169
Special Ecosystems Management: Habitats   177
Agriculture   183

8. Climate Change

193

Mitigation   209
Adaptation and Natural Hazards   229

Conclusions   245
Acknowledgments   247
Appendix 1. Time Line of EU Environmental Law   249
Appendix 2. Membership of the EU   251
Additional Resources   257
Glossary   261
Index   269

Illustrations

FIGURES

1. EU Legislative, Executive, and Judicial Branches *13*

2. Conferral *18*

3. EU Infringement Procedures *23*

4. AQFD Assessment Thresholds *104*

5. Time Line of EU Water Legislation *114*

6. Conservation Trends by Habitat Type *181*

7. Historical Greenhouse Gas Emissions *199*

8. Annual Greenhouse Gas Emissions (Total Emissions in Billions of Metric Tons per Year, 2017) *200*

9. Greenhouse Gas Emissions per Capita (Metric Tons per Person per Year, 2014) *201*

10. Projected Impacts of Climate Change in the EU by the 2080s *202*

A1. Time Line of EU Environmental Law *250*

A2. Membership of the EU *252*

TABLES

1. Characteristics of Environmental Impacts *6*

2. Comparing Regulations and Directives *45*

3. EU Environmental Principles *49*

4. Strengths and Weaknesses of Regulatory Instruments *64*

5. AQFD Quality Thresholds, Levels, and Values *105*

6. Soil-Related EU Legislation *126*

7. EU Law on Solid Waste *141*

8. EU Law on Hazardous Waste *143*

9. EU Law on Radioactive Waste *145*

10. Important EU Laws Related to Ecosystem Management *161*

11. EU Biodiversity Targets for 2020 *167*

12. CITES Appendices *175*

13. Aims and Financing of the Common Agricultural Policy *186*

14. Important International Climate Change Agreements *207*

15. EU Legislation on Climate Change Mitigation *213*

Spotlight Boxes

1. Distribution of Environmental Impacts in the EU *8*

2. The Role of Agencies in the EU *17*

3. Private Enforcement in EU Environmental Law *24*

4. The Internal Market and EU Environmental Law *79*

5. Impact Assessments *86*

6. Key Air Pollutants Regulated under EU Law *103*

7. The Ozone-Depleting Substances Regulation *107*

8. Water Quality Standards in the Water Framework Directive (WFD) *117*

9. Bathing Water *118*

10. Right2Water and European Citizens' Initiatives *120*

11. The Doomed Soil Framework Directive *125*

12. Soil Sealing *127*

13. Defining "Waste" *138*

14. Single-Use Plastics *139*

15. Euratom *144*

16. Convention on Biological Diversity *165*

17. Natura 2000 Network *172*

18. Environmental Impact Assessments *179*

19. Climate Science *195*

20. Key Challenges in Climate Change Policy *197*

21. Member State and Local Climate Change Policies *208*

22. Discounting *211*

23. Emissions Trading *215*

24. Gases and Industries Regulated by the EU ETS *218*

25. Carbon Leakage *220*

26. Energy Union *225*

Preface

How should humans shape the world in which they live? Countries around the world have crafted different answers to this question. This volume summarizes the ways in which the European Union (EU) has answered this question through the vehicle of environmental law.

Most resources on environmental law are written for lawyers who are already well versed in the legal system of a particular country. While those resources are valuable for specialists, we believe they have two important limitations.

First, by limiting their audience to law students or lawyers, traditional environmental law resources exclude many stakeholders of environmental law. Environmental problems affect everyone: scientists and social scientists, policymakers and activists, citizens and students, all of whom have important roles to play in how the environment is governed and protected. One fundamental purpose of this book is to reach these audiences by explaining the environmental law of the EU without assuming that the reader has any prior legal training in EU law.

Second, because environmental problems—such as pollution, ecosystem degradation, and climate change—share many similarities regardless of where they are located, there is much to be learned from comparative approaches to environmental law. Yet traditional environmental law resources are optimized for domestic legal specialists, not comparative scholars. This book is different. Distinctively, it was written contemporaneously with its companion volume on the environmental law of the United States. Both volumes seek to distill the essential elements of environmental law, and both volumes follow the same modularized structure, which was designed to facilitate comparisons.

Both books begin with the building blocks of domestic environmental law: an overview of key legal actors, types of law, and regulatory tools that the EU (or the United States) uses to address environmental problems. The second part of each book delves into specific environmental issues that environmental law regulates: pollution, ecosystem management, and climate change. In future, this structure will be echoed in other books in this series, allowing for easy comparisons between how the EU deals with environmental problems through law and how other jurisdictions tackle the same issues.

We believe this book provides a long-overdue resource on environmental law for those who work in environmental policy or environmental science. It can also act as a brief textbook for an undergraduate or foreign course on environmental law, and as a starting point for comparative environmental scholars. Readers intent on in-depth study of particular environmental laws will find the book helpful for orientation and context, and will find suggestions for more traditional specialized resources at the end of the book.

Environmental law is a diverse, complex, and ever-changing area of law that addresses some of society's biggest challenges. By boiling down the essentials of environmental law, we hope to encourage meaningful dialogue across disciplinary and national borders, between environmental lawyers and other environmental practitioners, and among environmental lawyers in different jurisdictions. Humans necessarily affect the environments in which they live. By sharing ideas and improving the understanding of how laws around the world shape the environment, we hope to help in identifying strategies for increasing environmental quality and, in turn, for promoting human flourishing.

PART ONE

Building Blocks of EU Environmental Law

CHAPTER ONE

Regulating Environmental Impacts

Environmental law regulates human behavior in light of its environmental impacts. Environmental impacts affect the surroundings or conditions in which humans, plants, and animals function. Every country around the world has developed its own legal and nonlegal approaches to addressing environmental impacts. These responses are partly based on normative choices about what a good environment would look like, and are informed by historical, natural, cultural, and political conditions that tend to vary widely within and between countries.

To understand how the European Union approaches environmental law, it is important to understand the distinctive challenges that are presented by regulating the environment. Environmental impacts affect the environment in which people live, rather than affecting people directly. While humans can directly change their environments—by taking actions that affect environmental quality, such as littering or picking up litter, emitting or reducing air pollutants, cutting down or planting trees—any effect of those actions on human well-being will be indirect, as a result of subsequent human exposure to the degraded or improved environment. Some environmental impacts may have very few implications for humans, while others may have profound implications for human health, well-being, and flourishing. Understanding the implications of human actions for environmental quality, and the implications of environmental quality for human ends, thus presents special challenges to environmental regulation.

This chapter begins by introducing the core challenges to environmental law that are created by the fundamental characteristics of environmental impacts: namely, that those impacts tend to be diffuse through space and time, complex, and nonhuman in character. It then flags key normative values and choices that the EU has made regarding environmental impacts. Understanding these background normative choices can help readers in approaching the remainder of the book, which further develops the key actors, types of law, and specific strategies the EU has deployed to address particular environmental problems.

KEY CHALLENGES IN REGULATING ENVIRONMENTAL IMPACTS

Many challenges in environmental regulation can be traced back to three characteristics of environmental impacts. First, because the environment is both durable and dynamic, many environmental impacts are diffuse through space and time. A person who tosses a plastic bottle on the ground does not merely affect that space in that moment; the bottle may be washed away to a distant spot, or even a distant ocean, and it may take hundreds of years to degrade into microplastics, which then may affect the environment for hundreds of years more. Few, if any, of these impacts may be apparent to the person who threw the bottle on the ground in the first place, and even experts may have a difficult time predicting exactly where and when the plastic will generate environmental impacts.

Second, the impacts of human action on the environment tend to be complex. Natural environmental systems are already complex before humans become involved; it should not be surprising that it is still more complicated to predict the full implications of human action on natural environments, and to predict the follow-on effects of environmental quality on human well-being. Only in recent years have scientists started to understand the multiple implications of plastic waste, and of degraded microplastics, on natural environments and human health. Most likely, the extent of environmental and human impacts of plastic waste depends significantly on the scope and interaction of that waste—on how many people use and dispose of plastics, and in what ways, with what frequency, and in what locations. The environmental impacts of plastic disposal are therefore obscure, technical, and dependent upon knowledge—which will often be unavailable—about other human actions that may also affect the environment.

Third, consider that environmental impacts affect the natural environment, and that they therefore relate to the nonhuman animals, plants, and processes that make up much of human surroundings. Natural processes will eventually lead to the dispersion and decomposition of a plastic bottle that is thrown on the ground—but understanding those natural processes presents challenges on its own. Understanding the implications of those processes, and of the plastic's decomposition, on the environment presents additional scientific and informational challenges: How will the plastic affect the particular ecosystem(s) into which it degrades? What plants, animals, or fungi might be affected, how, and how acutely? What other plants, animals, or fungi might be affected, in turn, by the direct impacts of environmental plastics on prey species or food sources? Which, if any, of these nonhuman effects impact human well-being? Understanding the environmental impacts of human actions requires answering questions like these, and thus carries a special kind of informational burden. And it may also trigger difficult questions about the extent to which nonhuman impacts should matter for their own sake.

Moreover, knowledge about an environmental impact does not guarantee legal action to remedy that impact. The environment cannot speak for itself, but depends on humans to do so on its behalf. The likelihood of a legal or social response differs depending on the perceived economic and social value of the environment to (a group of) individuals. This means that there are situations in which environmental impacts can go unnoticed, and unchecked, for long periods. At the same time,

TABLE I

Characteristics of Environmental Impacts

	Impact	Regulatory Challenge
Diffusion	Environmental consequences are often *geographically and spatially distant* from the human activities that caused those consequences.	Detecting and predicting the environmental impacts of human (in)action.
Complexity	Environmental consequences tend to be *obscure, technical, and interactive.* Many small individual actions may combine in complicated ways to create a single impact; a single action may have multiple impacts; and the type(s) of those impacts may be difficult to measure, understand, and/or solve.	Gathering and interpreting information about environmental impacts.
		Tracing causal connections between human actions and consequences.
Nonhuman	Environmental consequences tend to relate to the *nonhuman animals, plants, and processes* that make up much of human surroundings.	Identifying (or creating) a nexus between human behavior and the nonhuman environment.
		Challenging to meaningfully represent nonhuman interests.

human law is able to directly regulate only human behavior. Environmental law must therefore create a nexus between human behavior and the nonhuman environment, both to understand the impact of current human behaviors and to shape human behavior in directions that reflect a preferred relationship with the nonhuman environment.

THE ROLE OF NORMATIVE VALUES

Decisions about how to approach environmental problems are, explicitly or implicitly, decisions about how people want to shape the environment in which they live. This means that reasonable people might disagree as to whether the EU's strategies, as detailed in the second part of this book, work well or poorly when measured against specific environmental problems. Societies and individuals often disagree on these normative decisions, which should be unsurprising, given that they implicate important personal and social values. The choice of legal structures to respond to environmental impacts has equally important normative implications.

The EU's powers to regulate the environment are set out in the European Union treaties (see chapters 2 and 3). The priorities that the EU should set in regulating environmental impacts—which ones to prioritize, how to view risks, how to relate environmental goals to other economic and social goals—are also informed, in part, by the EU treaties. The treaties detail that in relation to general EU goals, the EU must strive for "a high level of protection of the environment and improvement of the quality of the environment."[1] EU environmental policy specifically must pay attention to principles such as the precautionary principle and the "polluter pays" principle.[2] Moreover, the EU is meant to achieve "social justice and protection," "solidarity between generations," and "solidarity among Member States"[3]—normative goals that indirectly also relate to choices regarding environmental sustainability and protection.

The operationalization of these aims varies between environmental problems, as there is no uniform tool for the prioritization of these aims. It can be difficult, or even impossible, to make good on all of these aims within one policy or piece of legislation. Generally speaking, the combination of the precautionary and preventative principles makes the EU's environmental policies aim toward the prevention of environmental harm, even if that harm is temporally distant. In other words, the EU is relatively risk averse when it comes to accepting the possibility of environmental harm. For example, the use of genetically modified organisms continues to be extremely limited in the EU as compared to, for instance, the United States.[4] The fact that EU environmental law originates from the European Commission, a body made up of highly expert civil servants who are insulated from political pressures, further aids in facilitating long-term approaches to environmental policymaking.

Another important normative question that is answered differently across jurisdictions relates to environmental justice, which concerns the fairness of how environmental impacts are distributed. The diffuse, complex, and nonhuman character of environmental impacts makes managing the distribution of environmental impacts more challenging even than the already normatively charged task of determining questions of classic compensation for civil wrongs, such as the ones that arise when one individual person takes an acute action that directly harms one other person. The challenge of determining who can fairly be harmed—and harmed in diffuse, complex, and indirect ways via environmental impacts—is therefore ethical as well as practical.

SPOTLIGHT 1. DISTRIBUTION OF ENVIRONMENTAL IMPACTS IN THE EU

In some jurisdictions, such as the United States, *environmental justice*—the distribution of environmental consequences among different population groups—is an important discussion point in environmental policymaking and public debates surrounding it. Given the EU's restrictive competence in social policy, environmental justice has been a less prominent feature of EU environmental policy and related debates. This does not, however, mean that the distribution of environmental harm is equal or fair in the EU.

In 2018, the European Environment Agency published the first-ever report on the distribution of environmental impacts in the EU. The report shows that the distribution of air pollution, noise, and extreme temperatures tends to more negatively affect groups of lower socioeconomic status. This is particularly true in urban areas. At a regional level, regions with affected groups can mostly be found in eastern and southeastern Europe. The uneven impact on these groups is partially due to higher exposure levels and partially caused by the greater vulnerability of people in these groups, such as elderly, children, and people in generally poor health.

The EU's ability to provide a complete answer to the question of environmental justice is restricted by the Member States' competence in many areas of social policy. Depending on how environmental justice is categorized—as an environmental or a social issue—the competence may be understood to lie with the Member States rather than the European legislature. The EU Member States have increasingly started to acknowledge and confront the issue of environmental justice, but this has yet to lead to a European-level approach to the issue.[5] Notwithstanding the EU's expanding influence over environmental law, this dynamic highlights the continuing importance of all actors in the EU's multilevel governance system in addressing environmental problems.

SUMMARY

This chapter described the key characteristics of environmental impacts and how they can complicate environmental regulation. It also flagged the importance of identifying the normative choices that are made in deciding on how to address environmental impacts through law.

TAKEAWAYS

✓ Regulating environmental quality is challenging because environmental impacts tend to be diffuse, complex, and nonhuman in character.

✓ Different countries regulate environmental impacts differently. Many of the choices that countries make in regulating the environment reflect normative values.

KEY TERMS

COMPLEX IMPACTS Environmental impacts that are obscure, technical, and/or interactive. These can be difficult to measure, understand, and regulate.

DIFFUSE IMPACTS Environmental impacts that are geographically and/or spatially distant from the human actions that caused them.

ENVIRONMENT The surroundings or conditions in which humans, plants, and animals function.

ENVIRONMENTAL IMPACTS Consequences (generally of human actions) for the surroundings or conditions in which humans, plants, and animals function.

ENVIRONMENTAL JUSTICE Concerns about the fair distribution of environmental impacts.

ENVIRONMENTAL LAW The use of law to regulate human behaviors with environmental impacts.

EXTERNALITIES Costs and benefits related to an activity that are experienced by someone other than the person engaged in the activity.

NONHUMAN IMPACTS Environmental impacts that relate primarily or exclusively to nonhuman animals, plants, and processes.

NORMATIVE Relating to or deriving from a standard or norm.

PRECAUTIONARY PRINCIPLE An EU principle related to risk management, which provides that if there is the possibility that a given policy or action might harm the public or the environment, and there is an absence of scientific consensus, the action should not be pursued.

DISCUSSION QUESTIONS

1. What are examples of diffuse environmental impacts? Which is harder to effectively address: impacts that are diffuse through space or impacts that are diffuse through time?

2. What should be the role of science and scientific information when considering environmental impacts? Can science alone solve complex problems?

3. How do nonhuman processes and humans interact to create environmental problems?

4. Should nonhuman animals have rights in the same way that humans do?

5. What do you think is the most challenging feature of environmental impacts for the law: diffusion, complexity, or nonhuman character? Why?

6. What role should environmental justice play in environmental legal strategies?

NOTES

1. Article 3(3) Treaty on European Union (TEU).

2. Article 191(1) Treaty on the Functioning of the European Union.

3. Article 3(3) TEU.

4. For detailed information on the EU's policy in this area, visit http:// ec.europa.eu/food/plant/gmo_en.

5. See spotlight 1; see also the European Environment Agency report "Unequal exposure, unequal impacts," available at www.eea.europa.eu/publications /unequal-exposure-and-unequal-impacts/.

CHAPTER TWO

Key Actors

In order to contextualize the environmental laws discussed in part II of this book, it is important to know the actors who create, implement, and enforce the law. It is helpful to consider who has the power to fill in the gaps when laws are ambiguous, or to change policy. This chapter therefore introduces key actors in the European legal landscape and describes how those actors work together (or not!) to create EU environmental law.

The EU legal system is created through complex interactions between the EU institutions, the Member States and their subnational authorities, and private actors. Understanding these interactions is a crucial first step to understanding EU environmental law. This chapter will create that context by discussing several elements and processes of the EU legal system: the institutions of the EU, the powers of the EU, the enforcement of EU law, and the EU's role as an international actor. This discussion will touch on issues beyond environmental law, but their relevance for environmental law will be highlighted throughout.

THE INSTITUTIONS OF THE EUROPEAN UNION

The EU is a multilevel system of governance made up of constituent nation-states—called Member States.[1] The EU grew out of an agreement among a group of sovereign nation-states to combine some of their powers, with the goal of better achieving shared goals, such as peace and prosperity. Although the EU is composed of nation-states, it is not a nation-state itself; it is an intergovernmental and supranational organization with limited sovereignty.

The EU is made up of seven main institutions: the European Parliament, the European Council, the Council of Ministers (often referred to simply as "the Council"), the European Commission, the Court of Justice of the European Union (CJEU), the European Central Bank, and the Court of Auditors.[2] The powers and features of these institutions are set out in the EU treaties. In this chapter, we will focus on the four institutions that are directly involved in the creation and enforcement of EU environmental law: the Parliament, the Council of Ministers, the Commission, and the CJEU.

Loosely speaking, these institutions can be analogized to the legislative, executive, and judicial functions in a traditional tripartite system of government. Under this rough analogy, the Council and the Parliament serve a legislative role, the Commission serves an executive role, and the CJEU functions as a judiciary.

The structure of the EU reflects a normative commitment to the rule of law[3] and an ambition to adhere to many of the constitutional principles followed by national democracies. As a result, the EU's institutional makeup reflects the principle of separation of powers—resulting in the division of tasks among three branches of government that can act as checks and balances for each other—and the principle of representative

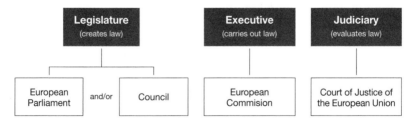

Figure 1. EU Legislative, Executive, and Judicial Branches.

democracy, which holds that power should be exercised by leaders whose authority is granted by the people.[4] While these principles are important to the EU's structure, the supranational and multilevel character of the EU necessitates differences in the implementation of these principles as compared to their traditional national settings. An exhaustive discussion of those differences goes beyond the scope of this book. However, one such difference should be noted here, since it is central to the identity of the EU and a nice starting point for our discussion on the conceptual/defining distinctions between these institutions: namely, the difference in the interests represented by each EU institution, particularly national and/or European interests. The Parliament, the Commission, and the CJEU are "European" institutions insofar as they are meant to represent the European interest, as directly elected representatives of the European electorate or as European civil servants or judges, respectively. The Council of Ministers votes in line with Member States' interests, which may or may not overlap with the European interest at any given time. In what follows, we will briefly discuss the key features of these four institutions, paying specific attention to those relevant for environmental regulation.

The European Parliament has 751 members,[5] who are directly elected by EU citizens every five years. Elections are held nationally and representation is proportional, based on Member State population, with a minimum of six and a maximum of ninety-six members of Parliament (MEPs) per Member State. Although MEPs are elected nationally, they are meant to represent the interests of all European citizens while in Parliament. As a result, MEPs sit together with MEPs from other Member States who represent similar political interests, rather than with MEPs from the same Member State. The Greens/European Free Alliance is an example of such a group, composed of seventy-four MEPs representing "green" and progressive interests.[6] These provisions are aimed at ensuring that the Parliament is both "directly" democratic (that is, directly elected by the European people) and "European" in its legislative decisions. When the Parliament votes, it does so by simple majority.

By contrast, the Council of Ministers is composed of Member State representatives at the ministerial level.[7] These representatives are assumed to vote on behalf of their Member States and to be able to bind the latter to decisions made in the Council. Unlike the other EU institutions, the composition of the Council is not static. Member States may decide to send a different representative depending on the Council's agenda. For example, if the Council is voting on an environmental proposal, a Member State may decide to send its environmental minister instead of its trade minister. Other Member States may decide to have one minister who sits in on all Council meetings, such as the minister for external relations or even a minister specifically for European affairs.[8] When the Council votes, it typically does so by qualified majority, which can be obtained only through support of at least 55 percent of Member State votes (total of twenty-seven votes), representing at least 65 percent of the EU's population.[9] The exception to this is during special legislative procedures, where unanimity is often required.

The Commission is the EU's executive, responsible for drafting, implementing, and enforcing EU law. It is divided into a number of topic-specific Directorates-General, each of which has specific mandates (including "energy," "environment," and "climate action"), and each of which is headed by a single Commissioner.[10] In all its actions, the Commission is meant to "promote the general interest of the Union."[11] In order to ensure this, all members of the Commission are supposed to be chosen "on the ground of their general competence and European commitment" and to be completely independent.[12] Interestingly, this means that even though the Member States control the nomination of Commissioners, the Commissioners are not meant to represent national interests. The intended separation between Commissioners and the interests of their home Member State is underscored in the procedure for their appointment: Member States have no control over the specific Directorate-General that their Commissioner is chosen to head. Germany, for example, can propose a Commissioner but cannot ensure that its Commissioner is chosen to run, for example, the Directorate-General of Energy or of Trade.

More generally, the President of the Commission is elected by the European Parliament by an absolute majority. The Council then adopts a list of candidate Commissioners, one for each Member State, together with the Commission President-elect. These candidates have to appear before parliamentary committees in their prospective fields of responsibility. Assuming all candidates receive a positive assessment, the Parliament votes on the full Commission, including the President and the High Representative of Foreign Affairs and Security Policy, in a single vote of consent. The Council then formally appoints them through qualified majority.

Commissioners are supported by civil servants, who are selected through a centralized system called the *concours*. In order to qualify for employment by the Commission, these civil servants have to pass a gauntlet of merit-based tests and must be proficient in at least two EU languages (with one of them being English, German, or French). The Commission employs around twenty-five thousand civil servants, making it by far the biggest of the EU institutions. At the same time, the size of the Commission looks startlingly small when compared to the executive departments of many countries. The US federal government, for example, employs around 1.8 million civil servants, while the federal government of Germany employs 2.2 million people.

The Commission has positioned itself as a body of particular expertise in environmental legislation. This expertise is reflected in the high level of technicality of its legislation and its use of increasingly complex regulatory methods, such as emissions trading.[13] Problematically, Member States' ability to implement these policies has not always kept pace with the Commission's ability to regulate. As a result, faulty implementation or non-implementation of environmental directives has become increasingly widespread within the EU. Simultaneously, EU environmental law is often adopted by countries outside of the EU that lack similar regulatory expertise and/or want to obtain greater access to the EU market for their products.[14] The so-called REACH Regulation on the registration, evaluation, authorization, and restriction of chemicals, for example, is an 849-page law that is considered one of the most complex pieces of legislation ever passed by the EU.[15] Despite its complexity, it is the authoritative legal framework for the regulation of chemicals and has been voluntarily adopted by countries worldwide.

Finally, the judicial branch of the EU, the CJEU, is made up of two courts: the Court of Justice and the General Court.[16] The General Court includes at least one judge of each Member State, typically two. Judgments by the General Court can be subject to appeal to the Court of Justice. The Court of Justice is the highest judicial authority on matters of EU law and has sole jurisdiction over questions that concern the interpretation and validity of EU law.[17] The Court of Justice is composed of twenty-seven judges, one from each Member State. One structural challenge of the EU was to decide how to manage the multiple different languages (currently twenty-four) spoken in Member States. The main language of the Court of Justice is French, but most judgments are issued in several EU languages, which at a minimum include the languages of the parties.

SPOTLIGHT 2. THE ROLE OF AGENCIES IN THE EU

The EU's regulatory power does not depend on administrative agencies in the same way that many other jurisdictions do. In the United States, agencies have become so important that they have been described as "the fourth branch" of government. The powers of EU agencies tend to be much more restricted than their US counterparts and typically only facilitate coordination of other actors under a specific regulation or directive, such as the European Chemicals Agency, which is meant to assist in the implementation of the REACH Regulation. There are also more general environmental agencies, such as the European Environment Agency. The latter agency's role is restricted to gathering information and providing support to Member States in implementing EU environmental laws.

POWERS OF THE EUROPEAN UNION

The ability of the EU to legislate or to make legally binding decisions on a specific topic is framed in terms of *competence*. Competences are powers that are conferred, in whole or in part, by the Member States to the EU (principle of conferral). This marks a key difference between the EU and nation-states: the EU's sovereignty—and therefore its competence to act in a certain policy area—is not intrinsic or complete; it must be expressly conferred by the Member States and is limited to those expressly conferred powers.[18]

There are three types of competence: exclusive, shared, and supportive.[19] In areas of exclusive competence, the EU is the only actor empowered to legislate; in areas of shared competence, both the EU and the Member States may legislate. Supportive competences allow the EU to facilitate and coordinate action between the Member States but do not empower the EU to legislate or take any independent actions.[20] Once the EU has exercised its competence in a shared area, Member States are preempted from acting.

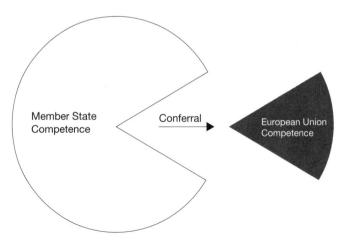

Figure 2. Conferral.

Environmental policy is an area of shared competence in which the EU is very active, and the preemption of Member State action on environmental issues is common. The main exceptions to this are situations in which the Member States want to take more ambitious action regarding environmental protection than the EU. In most cases, this remains possible even when the EU has already acted, provided that these protection measures do not create any problems for the EU internal market and/or are based on a demonstrable environmental need supported by scientific evidence.[21]

The exercise of EU competence in environmental policy, while widespread, is not automatic. Before the EU can act in this area, or any other area of shared or supportive competence, it has to show that the principle of subsidiarity is respected. Subsidiarity imposes a dual burden on the EU legislature; it has to show that the objectives could not be (sufficiently) achieved by the Member States, and that it would be better achieved through EU action.

The subsidiarity principle is enforced through political controls (during the legislative process) and legal controls (after the legislative process). The political controls require the European Commission to provide a reasoned view on how the subsidiarity principle is fulfilled, which is reviewed by the Council of Ministers, the European Parliament, and national parliaments.[22] If legislation is passed but a Member State, European institution, or other interested party still feels that subsidiarity was not properly observed, it can bring a case before the Court of Justice—a legal control. Very few of these cases have been brought and none of them have been successful.[23]

It has proven easy to fulfill the principle of subsidiarity for most environmental issues. This can be directly traced back to the geographic diffusion of environmental impacts: as soon as an environmental impact can be felt in more than one Member State—or is caused by one Member State but materializes in another—the regulation of that impact is considered better achieved at the EU level. A different way of

TREATY ON EUROPEAN UNION, ARTICLE 5(3):
THE SUBSIDIARITY PRINCIPLE

"Under the principle of subsidiarity, in areas which do not fall within its exclusive competence, the Union shall act only if and in so far as the objectives of the proposed action cannot be sufficiently achieved by the Member States, either at central level or at regional and local level, but can rather, by reason of the scale or effects of the proposed action, be better achieved at Union level."

looking at this is to say that EU regulation of environmental impacts is aimed at overcoming the problem of externalities that Member States may impose on each other. Because the EU can regulate the environment in the entire EU territory, it cannot externalize environmental effects on others (or, at least, on others within the EU).

Once it has been established that the EU is empowered to adopt a particular environmental law, the Commission also has to show that the principle of proportionality has been respected. This means that the EU should take only those actions "necessary to achieve the objectives of the Treaties."[24] The effect of this principle is primarily observable through the types of secondary EU law that the EU may adopt to regulate the issue in question: regulations and directives.[25] Regulations are binding in their entirety on the Member States and do not require any transposition or implementation by the Member States; they immediately become law and the Member States do not have any discretion as to their transposition into national law. Directives are equally binding, but only as to the result that must be achieved; it is left to the Member States to decide on the method of implementation.[26]

The relationship between the EU and its Member States depends on a fine balance between the need for effective cooperation and the safeguarding of national sovereignty in a supranational system. The principles of conferral, subsidiarity, and proportionality—and their political and legal protection mechanisms—are key in maintaining this balance. In the field of environmental law, the balance often tips in favor of the EU legislature due to the transboundary effects of most environmental issues.

ENFORCEMENT OF EU LAW

The EU differs from international organizations in many ways. Much of this difference is expressed through the types of laws that the EU can adopt (as explained in chapter 3). Another key difference lies in the way that EU law can be enforced. The EU has various legal mechanisms to ensure that its supranational laws are implemented and enforced.[27] The focus in this chapter will be on enforcement by EU institutions against Member States, and on enforcement actions against EU institutions, at the European level. There are two additional ways in which EU law is enforced, both extremely important. One is through private enforcement (see spotlight 3) and the other is through national courts. Enforcement through national courts can be both private (initiated by private actors) and public (initiated by public actors). The enforcement of EU law in national courts is made possible through the direct effect of EU law, which is explained in detail in chapter 3.

EU-level enforcement actions against Member States take two main forms: an infringement procedure started by the Commission[28] and/or a pecuniary penalty imposed by the CJEU.[29] A single enforcement action can involve both procedures. Pecuniary penalties can be used together with an infringement procedure, as well as separately.

In infringement procedures, the Commission is alerted to a breach of EU law. This alert can come from a complaint by an individual, the European Parliament, the press, the Office of the European Ombudsman, or monitoring by the Commission itself. If the Commission finds that the complaint has merit, the Member State in question will be invited to explain its behavior and to settle the issue with the Commission (the pre-contentious stage). If this fails, the Commission will send an official letter to the Member State with formal notification of the complaint. The Member State has two months to reply to this letter, after which the Commission has one year to decide whether to proceed with or close the case. If the Commission decides to proceed, it will issue a reasoned opinion. This opinion sets out the grounds of the alleged infringement and the time period for complying with the measures proposed. If the Member State fails to comply within that period, the Commission will refer the matter to the CJEU.

The aim of the infringement procedure is to ensure an amicable solution to these situations without the need for litigation.[30] Perhaps unsurprisingly, this is not always possible. To manage situations where infringement procedures are insufficient, the Maastricht Treaty introduced the possibility of imposing a pecuniary penalty on Member States. This pecuniary penalty can either be imposed as part of an infringement procedure—the result of a referral to the CJEU—or be a stand-alone action in the specific situation where a Member State has failed to notify measures for the transposition of an EU directive.[31] The latter type of violation is so common that a specific procedure was created. In both cases, either a lump sum or a daily penalty can be imposed, and if the penalty follows an infringement procedure, there is no upper limit to the awarded amount.[32]

In addition to these two processes, Member States can bring actions against other Member States.[33] Interestingly, the complaining Member State does not have to contact the other Member State before starting official proceedings (as the Commission would do in the pre-contentious stage). Rather, it has to inform the Commission of its intention to bring the action. After this, the process is much the same as the infringement procedure brought by the Commission, with the Commission mediating between the two states. However, even if the Commission finds that there is no breach, the complaining Member State may bring a case before the CJEU. These types of actions are extremely rare, as Member States tend to strongly prefer political solutions over judicial disputes.

All the mechanisms described above suffer from similar flaws. Perhaps the most important one is that these processes are extremely time consuming; in 2008, the Commission estimated that it took around fifty months to go through an infringement process from the reasoned option until referral.[34] Another concern is the level of discretion that the Commission has in (not) pursuing certain cases, and the fact that there is no systematic way to detect violations by Member States can make enforcement seem arbitrary. This is further complicated by the fact that inadequate implementation of EU law is the most common Member State breach of EU law.[35] At times, this type of breach can be difficult to establish, as what constitutes "inadequate" implementation may not be self-evident, especially when it involves the implementation of directives.

A final form of enforcement action applies only to actions by EU institutions. The tripartite system of separation of powers to which the EU institutions loosely conform suggests that there should be a form of checks and balances among the EU legislature, executive, and judiciary. The main expression of this is the CJEU's power to review the legality of "acts"

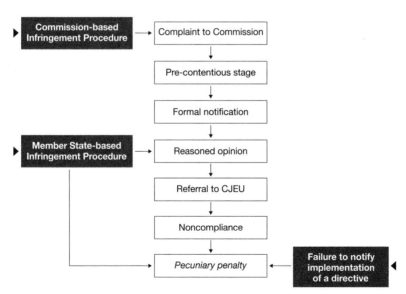

Figure 3. EU Infringement Procedures.

SPOTLIGHT 3. PRIVATE ENFORCEMENT
IN EU ENVIRONMENTAL LAW

The European Court of Justice has created distinct European legal doctrines to facilitate the enforcement of EU law by private actors. Although private enforcement of EU law is far more advanced than, for example, the private enforcement of international law, it continues to face significant challenges.

First, EU environmental law is primarily adopted through directives addressed to Member States. Directives allow Member States significant discretion in how to achieve EU environmental goals, so as to accommodate the differences in environmental circumstances in the Member States. Private actors can only bring actions against Member States for faulty or negligent implementation that goes beyond acceptable discretion. Such actions can be brought only once the transposition period of the directive has expired. Moreover, private actors have to demonstrate that the provision(s) of the relevant directive meant to convey claimable rights to individuals, which is not always the case.

Second, the complex, diffuse, and nonhuman nature of environmental impacts can make it harder for individual private actors to gather the information needed to establish both causation and a legitimate interest in bringing a case.

Finally, litigation can be very costly and success is often uncertain. Even when successful, private actors may not receive financial compensation in environmental cases if they have not suffered individual harm.

(primarily legislative acts but not exclusively) of the EU institutions. This includes acts of the Council of Ministers, the European Parliament, and the Commission but also those of the European Council, the European Central Bank, and any other EU body or agency that can adopt actions that can create legal effects vis-à-vis third parties.[36]

The CJEU's power of judicial review of these acts is limited by several factors. First, the review can happen only on the basis of certain grounds (lack of competence, infringement of an essential procedural requirement, infringement of the treaties, misuse of powers),[37] and the applicant bringing the case must prove standing. Some applicants—such as Member States or the EU institutions—automatically have standing. Other applicants—such as individuals—have to show "direct and individual concern" with respect to the contested action.[38] Meeting this threshold can be very difficult, which means that enforcement by individuals is limited and arguably undermines the CJEU's ability to act as a check on other EU institutions. An often-cited counterargument in favor of limited possibility of review is that these acts enjoy a presumption of democratic legitimacy and therefore should be shielded from judicial review (see spotlight 3).

THE EU AS AN INTERNATIONAL ACTOR

Environmental processes are not limited by jurisdictional boundaries and can therefore affect, and be affected by, actions beyond national borders. The majority of EU environmental laws deal with exactly this type of environmental issue, as these are the areas in which EU competence is most easily claimed—the subsidiarity principle is fulfilled because it would be difficult for EU Member States to effectively address these problems by themselves. In addition to these "European" environmental issues, there are many environmental problems that extend beyond the territory of the EU. In order to deal with geographic diffusion beyond EU borders, the EU has espoused a strong commitment to multilateralism with non-EU countries and international organizations.

The EU strives to be an international "green leader." Unlike the United States, which has generally been reluctant to sign international environmental treaties (including the Kyoto Protocol and the Paris Agreement), the EU invests heavily in multilateral solutions to environmental problems, relying on its market power to export its normative position on issues such as democracy, environment, and human rights.

Since the Treaty of Lisbon, the EU enjoys legal personality,[39] which means that the EU is able to acquire legal rights and obligations and become a party to international treaties and organizations. Prior to the Treaty of Lisbon, many of the external powers of the EU were only "implied"—based on the EU's internal powers and what these might logically require the EU to be able to do. The explicit grant of legal personality in the EU treaties has thus clarified some of the issues surrounding the EU's authority to act internationally (or "externally").

Environment is a leading theme in the EU's general external policy: "[T]he Union's action on the international scene shall work to a high degree of cooperation ... in order to ... help develop international measures to preserve and improve the quality of the environment."[40] In addition, the EU's environmental competence has an external component: "Union policy on the environment shall contribute to ... promoting measures on the international level to deal with regional or worldwide environmental problems, and in particular combating climate change."[41] Notwithstanding these strong statements on the EU's role in international environmental action, environmental policy is an area of shared competence, which means that the powers to act "internationally" also remain shared between the Member States and the EU.[42] In these situations, the EU establishes a shared negotiation position and takes the lead in negotiations; Member States continue to be involved in determining negotiation strategy, in the negotiations themselves and, at times, in the signing and ratification of resulting treaties.

This structure can lead to several problems. First, it may be difficult for third countries to identify who speaks for the EU. Henry Kissinger famously stated, "I do not know who to call when I want to speak to 'Europe.'" That situation has improved since the adoption of the Treaty of Lisbon, which created the European External Action Service, which brings together diplomats from the Commission, the Council of Ministers, and Member States.[43] In most international negotiations, the EU adopts a common policy beforehand, which sets out the priorities and strategies of the EU and its Member States. Second, it is not always clear—especially if both the EU and the Member States are party to an international treaty—who is primarily responsible for fulfilling the obligations imposed by the relevant treaty.

The latter has led to some innovative constructions under international law, such as the one under the Kyoto Protocol. Part of the United Nations Framework Convention on Climate Change, the Kyoto Protocol imposes on its parties binding commitments to reduce greenhouse gas emissions; it was signed by both the EU and its Member States.[44] As part of the negotiations, the EU secured agreement that the Member States would be allowed to achieve their reduction targets collectively through the so-called bubble provision.[45] This would allow some Member States to increase their emissions without there being a violation of their international obligation, since others would be simultaneously reducing their emissions. The EU has adopted internal legislation to operationalize this agreement.[46] This is particularly significant given the relatively strong enforcement mechanisms available to the EU with respect to its Member States (including the ability to impose penalties and withhold support from noncompliant Member States), which contrast with the lack of strong enforcement mechanisms under international law. The internalization of international commitments by the EU thus tends to strengthen the international regime in question, as compliance is more likely and more easily enforced for the EU Member States.

The EU invests heavily in fulfilling its international obligations and generally tries to respect international law where possible. However, there are instances where international legal norms and EU law are in conflict. In these situations, the CJEU has been clear on the relative strength of international laws versus EU norms: EU law—particularly norms that protect fundamental rights of EU citizens—cannot be set aside in favor of international laws. In one important case, this led the CJEU to invalidate an EU regulation that had been adopted to give effect to a UN Security Council resolution—the most authoritative and binding form of international law—because the regulation violated a "constitutional principle" of the EU.[47] While the EU is an advocate of multilateralism and aims to be a leader in the area of international environmental law, the EU also limits its adherence to international law in reference to its own norms regarding democracy and human rights.

SUMMARY

The question of who creates, implements, and enforces EU environmental law is at least as complex and important as what constitutes EU environmental law. This chapter has provided an overview of the EU institutions, the powers of the EU, the enforcement of EU law, and the EU's relationship to international law. These combine to form the institutional structure on which EU environmental law is built.

TAKEAWAYS

✓ The European Union is a multilevel system of governance made up of constituent nation-states, called Member States.

✓ The EU's multilevel governance structure divides competences between the EU's institutions and its Member States. EU institutions have only those powers conferred to them in the EU treaties. All other authority is reserved to the Member States. Even when competence to legislate is in the hands of the EU, the Member States are tasked with the implementation of EU law.

✓ Environment is an area of shared competence between the EU and Member States, meaning that both are empowered to legislate to promote and address environmental quality. The subsidiarity principle is used to determine which of the two is better placed to adopt environmental regulation. Once the EU has regulated, Member States' power to do so becomes very restricted.

✓ The EU institutions roughly function through three separate branches: the legislative (Council of Ministers and Parliament), the executive (European Commission), and the judiciary (CJEU). Agencies play a very limited role in EU (environmental) law.

✓ EU environmental law is influenced by, and influences, international action on environmental issues. Multilateralism is a key principle of EU governance, and the EU tries to influence international processes where possible.

KEY TERMS

CHECKS AND BALANCES A model of governance that limits the concentration of power by giving each of the branches of government the authority to limit the power of the other(s).

COMPETENCE The EU's authority to act within a certain policy area in order to achieve set objectives. This authority can be exclusive (i.e., the EU is the only actor empowered to legislate), shared (i.e., subject to the subsidiarity principle), or supportive (i.e., the EU can facilitate and coordinate action between Member States but cannot legislate or take any independent actions).

COUNCIL OF MINISTERS The EU legislative body composed of government ministers of the Member States (its formal name is the Council of the European Union).

COURT OF JUSTICE OF THE EUROPEAN UNION The EU's judicial body and ultimate authority on the interpretation of EU law, made up of the General Court and the Court of Justice.

DIRECTIVE A type of EU law aimed at achieving a certain effect, leaving open to Member States how to implement and achieve that effect.

DIRECTORATE-GENERAL A branch of the European Commission responsible for the drafting, implementation, and enforcement of EU law in a specific area.

EUROPEAN COMMISSION The EU institution responsible for proposing legislation, implementing decisions, and managing the day-to-day business of the EU.

EUROPEAN COUNCIL The EU institution that sets out the general political direction of the EU. Consists of heads of states or government of the Member States, as well as its President and the President of the European Commission.

EUROPEAN PARLIAMENT The elected EU body that exercises legislative and budgetary powers.

EXCLUSIVE COMPETENCE Areas in which the EU is the only actor empowered to legislate.

INFRINGEMENT PROCEDURE A procedure aimed at establishing and ensuring that an EU Member State fulfills its obligations under EU law.

INTERGOVERNMENTAL LAW Processes and laws that are created by states and aimed at states (e.g., international law).

JUDICIAL REVIEW The power of a court to review actions taken by the other branches of government, often by testing those actions against constitutional norms.

JURISDICTION The authority to make legally binding decisions within a given territory or subject area.

LEGAL PERSONALITY The capacity to have legal rights and duties within a certain legal system.

LEGISLATIVE PROCEDURE The process through which legislative proposals (or "bills") are made into binding laws (or "acts").

>   ORDINARY LEGISLATIVE PROCEDURE In the EU, a procedure involving several actors, most importantly the European Parliament and the Council of Ministers.

>   SPECIAL LEGISLATIVE PROCEDURE In the EU, this legislative procedure can vary but typically excludes the European Parliament and involves only the Council of Ministers.

MEMBER STATE A nation-state that is a signatory (or "member") of the EU treaties.

PREEMPTION A process whereby the law of one level of government displaces the law of another. In the United States, this is most commonly preemption of state law by federal law.

PRIMARY EU LAW Foundational EU law, such as the EU treaties, resulting from an intergovernmental process between the Member States (a type of intergovernmental law).

PRINCIPLE OF CONFERRAL An EU legal principle stipulating that the EU has only those competences that are explicitly conferred to it by the Member States via the EU treaties.

PRINCIPLE OF PROPORTIONALITY An EU legal principle aimed at limiting the EU's exercise of competence to that which is strictly necessary to achieve the EU's objectives.

PRINCIPLE OF SUBSIDIARITY An EU legal principle meant to regulate the division of competence between the Member States and the EU in areas of shared competence.

QUALIFIED MAJORITY VOTING The method of voting within the EU, whereby both a majority of countries and a majority of the EU's population has to vote in favor of a legislative proposal in order for it to pass.

REGULATION A type of EU law that is binding in terms of both its substance and its objective; Member State implementation is restricted to translating the regulation into national law.

REPRESENTATIVE DEMOCRACY Democracy exercised through elected officials representing a group of people.

SECONDARY EU LAW Supranational law resulting from the legislative process between the EU institutions.

SEPARATION OF POWERS An organizational principle of government whereby the legislative, executive, and judicial functions of the government are assigned to separate actors.

SHARED COMPETENCE Areas in which the EU and its Member States share the responsibility to legislate.

SOVEREIGNTY The power to make laws and impose police power on people within a certain territory.

STANDING The legal right to bring a case before a court.

SUPPORTIVE COMPETENCE Areas in which the EU can act only
when explicitly requested to do so by the Member States.

SUPRANATIONAL LAW Processes and laws that are made by international bodies that can bind states (e.g., EU law).

DISCUSSION QUESTIONS

1. Does it make sense for the environment to be an area of shared
   competence between the EU and Member States? What challenges might arise if the environment were instead an exclusive
   competence of the EU? What challenges might arise if it were
   instead an exclusive competence of Member States?

2. Are there any actors that you think should play a bigger role in
   EU environmental law?

3. Which actor in EU environmental law are you most familiar
   with? Why?

4. Should the Member States play a larger or smaller role in EU
   environmental law?

5. What do you think about the role of international law in EU
   environmental law?

6. How does this structure differ from that in your country
   (if at all)?

NOTES

1. Since 1958, the European project has taken the shape of the European
Economic Community, the European Atomic Energy Community, and the
more recent European Community, all of which had different institutional
structures and powers. The EU as we know it now is the more recent iteration
of these institutions and has existed since the Lisbon Treaty (adopted in 2007,
in force since 2009).

2. Article 13(1) Treaty on European Union (TEU).

3. Article 2 TEU.

4. Article 10(1) TEU ("The functioning of the Union shall be founded on representative democracy").

5. This was the number of MEPs at the start of the 2019–24 term, and the maximum number allowed under the Lisbon Treaty. When the United Kingdom left the EU in 2020, the number of MEPs was reduced to 705.

6. The Ninth European Parliament (2019–24) has seven such groups and a residual category of non-inscrit MEPs. The composition of these groups (also listing nationality of MEPs) can be found at www.europarl.europa.eu/meps /en/crosstable.html.

7. The Council of Ministers (formally the Council of the European Union, but often referred to simply as "the Council") must be distinguished from the European Council, which consists of the heads of state or government of the Member States. The European Council, though extremely important, plays no official role in the legislative process. Rather, it sets out the general policy and priorities of the EU. The President of the Commission and the High Representative of the Union for Foreign Affairs and Security Policy also participate in European Council meetings. See also Article 15 TEU.

8. Some federal Member States, such as Germany, may even decide to send a representative of one of its federated states (Länder in Germany) rather than a representative of the federal government if the topic of discussion is one that falls within that state's competence.

9. Article 16(4) TEU.

10. For a full list, visit http://ec.europa.eu/info/departments_en.

11. Article 17(1) TEU.

12. Article 17(3) TEU.

13. See also chapter 5.

14. Anu Bradford, "The Brussels Effect" (2015) 107 *Northwestern University Law Review* 1.

15. Regulation (EC) No 1907/2006 concerning the Registration, Evaluation, Authorisation and Restriction of Chemicals (REACH).

16. There are also several specialized courts, but they fall outside the scope of our discussion.

17. National courts may, and often have to, apply EU law but are not allowed to decide on the meaning of EU law in cases where its meaning is unclear. They must refer to the Court of Justice in those cases.

18. The principle of conferral can be found in Article 5(2) TEU and reads: "Under the principle of conferral, the Union shall act only within the limits of the competences conferred upon it by the Member States in the Treaties to attain the objectives set out therein. Competences not conferred upon the

Union in the Treaties remain with the Member States." This underlines that the EU cannot claim any competences as being implicitly conferred on it based on necessity or other criteria.

19. See Article 2(1)(2) and (5) Treaty on the Functioning of the European Union (TFEU).

20. This is an important role for the EU in areas that are otherwise considered important for national identity and sovereignty and therefore *not* part of EU competences, such as educational policy (see Article 6 TFEU).

21. The scope for Member States' unilateral environmental action has been subject to much litigation and discussion. See chapter 5, spotlight 4.

22. See Protocols 1 (on the role of national parliaments) and 2 (on the application of the principles of subsidiarity and proportionality) to the EU treaties.

23. See, for example, Case C 84/94 *United Kingdom v. Council* [1996] ECR I-5755.

24. Article 5(4) TEU (this principle applies to all categories of competence).

25. Article 288 TFEU.

26. These types of law are discussed in detail in chapter 4.

27. There are also various nonlegal ways in which EU law is enforced, such as the EU's SOLVIT program (see http://ec.europa.eu/solvit/what-is-solvit/index_en.htm) and the EU Pilot system (see http://ec.europa.eu/internal_market/scoreboard/performance_by_governance_tool/eu_pilot/index_en.htm).

28. Article 258 TFEU.

29. Article 260 TFEU.

30. The process is detailed in Article 258 TFEU.

31. In case of the latter, the Court has to follow the guidance of the Commission as to the amount of the penalty. This is not true for the former.

32. The Court may also impose interim measures after an infringement procedure; see Article 278 TFEU.

33. Article 259 TFEU.

34. In 2009 this was reduced to twenty-four months, but this is still considerable; see Communication from the Commission on implementing European Community Environmental Law, COM (2008) 773 final.

35. Other grounds for breach include violations of the duty of sincere cooperation, interference with EU external relations, and actions taken by the courts of a Member State.

36. See Article 263 TFEU.

37. Article 263 TFEU, para 2.

38. Article 263 TFEU, para 4.

39. See Article 47 TEU and Article 335 TFEU.

40. Article 21(2)(f) TEU.

41. Article 191(1) TFEU.

42. See, especially, Article 191(4) TFEU (the EU's power to cooperate with third countries and international organizations is "without prejudice to Member States' competence to negotiate in international bodies and to conclude international agreements").

43. See https://eeas.europa.eu/headquarters/headquarters-homepage_en.

44. At the time of signing, there were fifteen Member States.

45. Article 4 of the Kyoto Protocol.

46. See Council Decision 2002/358/EC concerning the approval, on behalf of the European Community, of the Kyoto Protocol to the United Nations Framework Convention on Climate Change and the joint fulfillment of commitments thereunder, OJ L 130, 15.5.2002, at 1–3.

47. Case C–402/05 P and C–415/05, *P. Kadi and Al Barakaat International Foundation v. Council and Commission* [2008] ECR I–6351.

CHAPTER THREE

Types of Law

This chapter sets out the types of EU law available to legal actors in creating, implementing, and enforcing environmental legal strategies. Knowing about the different types of law that make up EU environmental law is valuable for several reasons. First, different types of law are made through different processes and often involve different key actors. Understanding the processes that underlie different types of law can also be useful in predicting future laws, and in advocating legal change. Second, different types of law require different strategies for researching and understanding what the law is.

In understanding EU environmental law, it is helpful to know both about the legal systems of the Member States and the EU, and about the relationship between these systems, as this is the context in which EU legal instruments and EU legal principles operate.

LEGAL SYSTEMS IN THE EU

To a European lawyer, *law* typically refers to law made by the European institutions in the form of regulations or directives, and/or to EU treaty provisions.[1] However, EU environmental law is closely interrelated with the laws of the Member States and relies on them for most implementation and enforcement. It is therefore helpful to briefly consider the different legal systems that exist within the EU.

The EU incorporates twenty-eight legal systems: those of the twenty-seven Member States and that of the EU as a whole. Some of these systems are based on common law, and others on civil law.[2] This categorization affects both how the law operates and how a citizen (or researcher) can find out what the law is. Most Member States are part of the civil law tradition; after the United Kingdom left the EU in 2020, Ireland and the Republic of Cyprus are the only Member States that are part of the common law family. In civil law systems, core legal principles are systematically codified into referable systems, or codes. These are meant to essentially stand on their own, with court judgments serving only to clarify uncertain terms. This means that, in a civil law system, it is often possible to develop a reasonable understanding of the law by searching through the codes.

In common law systems, there is no comprehensive compilation of legal rules in a codified form. Even particular rules that have been at least partially codified—such as those found in constitutions, statutes, and regulations—are subject to interpretation by courts. In adjudicating cases, common law courts give precedential authority to prior court decisions and base their decisions on judge-made common law principles that were developed in prior cases. In other words, common law courts are bound by precedent, in a principle known as *stare decisis* (Latin: "to stand by things decided"). This means that courts defer to prior, similar decisions from superior courts (vertical stare decisis, or binding precedent) and often defer to their own prior decisions (horizontal stare decisis). Because common law relies on lines of precedent created by judges, it is often necessary to read and interpret lines of precedential judicial opinions to understand what the law is likely to be in any particular scenario.

The Court of Justice of the EU has frequently emphasized the unique nature of the European legal system as positioned between national and international law.[3] Analogously, the EU's legal system can perhaps best be described as a mix of common and civil law principles. Most EU law is adopted in the form of written laws that are easily accessible and meant to be understood without formal training in common law precedent. However, the interpretation of these laws by the CJEU is absolutely crucial to their scope and meaning, making the role of European judges more comparable to that in a common law system. At the same time, when EU law is made, representatives of all Member States weigh in (for example, through the Council of Ministers). This means that some principles of EU law reflect values often found in civil law countries, while others reflect common law principles.

In both civil and common law systems, different types of law apply depending on whose behavior is being addressed. *Private law* applies to interactions between private parties—for example, to individuals entering into contracts (governed by contract law) or individuals who harm other individuals (governed by tort law). *Public law,* by contrast, applies to public actors acting in their public capacity—for example, to regulators (whose behavior is governed by administrative law) or legislators (whose ability to legislate is governed by the constitution). Because the actions of private individuals and the actions of public servants can affect environmental quality, both private and public law can play important roles in regulating environmental quality.

RELATIONSHIP BETWEEN EU AND NATIONAL LAWS

The hierarchy between the EU's legal system and the Member States' legal systems is a source of ongoing debate.[4] For the purposes of environmental law, it is widely accepted that environmental laws adopted by the EU trump national laws, environmental or otherwise.[5] However, European law depends on the Member States for the bulk of its implementation and enforcement. This means that European law must be integrated with the preexisting national legal systems of the Member States. Given that environmental law has ties to many other areas of law—such as property law, tort law, and criminal law—this integration can be time-consuming and complicated. Adding to the complexity, many of these areas are not regulated by the EU in the same way that environmental law is: property law, for example, is almost entirely regulated by Member States. Moreover, the EU highly values, and frequently interacts with, international law. As a result, one would have to look far beyond "EU environmental law" proper in order to fully appreciate all the laws that are relevant to environmental regulation in the EU.

The Court of Justice of the EU has developed two legal doctrines that are of particular relevance to the relationship between EU and national law: primacy of EU law and direct effect. It is important to have a basic understanding of these doctrines, especially if you are to understand the advantages and disadvantages of using, inter alia, a regulation or a directive as a means to regulate the environment.

Primacy—also referred to as supremacy—of EU law was created by the Court of Justice in response to a clash between EU and national law. In the 1964 case *Flaminio Costa v. ENEL,* the question was raised whether an EU law can be changed or repealed by a more recent national law—as would be the case for most national laws if a newer, conflicting, national law were adopted.[6] The Court decided that in order for the EU to function as the treaties envisaged—namely as a new legal system, which became an integral part of the legal systems of the Member States and which their courts are bound to apply—it would be necessary for EU law to take supremacy over national law, even if these laws were more recent, or perhaps "more fundamental" (such as the provisions of a national constitution). The alternative—that unilateral changes made by one Member State could overrule EU law—would create a situation where the agreements that lead to EU law would not be absolute and where the Member States would be unequal, since those who did not want to be bound could simply adopt a different law. In order to strengthen its position, the Court referred to the fact that the Member States chose to limit their sovereignty by signing the EU treaties—even though the primacy of EU law is not explicitly mentioned in those treaties.

The scope of primacy has been, and continues to be, heavily debated between the European courts and their national counterparts, and in academic writing on EU law. Some constitutional courts maintain the position that the primacy of EU law is conditional on national law and could therefore be overruled under certain conditions—for example, if a constitutional court believes that its own constitution provides better human rights protection than the EU's Charter of Fundamental Rights. Situations in which a national court has overruled EU law in case of a clash between EU and national law have been extremely rare, and this has not yet happened to EU secondary legislation, such as a directive or regulation.[7]

In order to be able to enforce the primacy of EU law, you need to find a judge who is empowered to decide on whether EU law is indeed applicable, and if so, how EU law should be interpreted and applied. If EU law were enforceable only before EU courts, there would be many practical difficulties for individuals in relying on and enforcing EU law—so much so that it might prove impossible, as is often the case for international law. In another crucially important case—the 1963 *van Gend en Loos* case—the Court of Justice had to decide whether individuals had the right to rely on EU law against another party in their national court. The Court answered that they did because the "[European] Community [now the EU] constitutes a new legal order of international law ... the subjects of which comprise not only Member States but also their nationals."[8] In order for this new order to work, the enforcement of EU law could not only be in the hands of the European Commission or the Member States; individuals should also have the right to enforce EU law against their Member State or other individuals. The Court believed that this would greatly add to the "effet utile" of European law: the idea that the goals of EU law are in fact achieved through its enforcement.[9]

The parameters of the direct effect of EU law continue to be contested and there is a rich body of case law on this topic.[10] For the purposes of EU environmental law, the following is important to keep in mind: *direct effect* of all types of EU secondary law is not the same. In all cases, certain conditions have to be fulfilled in order for direct effect to be achieved, namely that the provision of EU law must be sufficiently clear and precise, must be capable of conferring rights to an individual, and is not dependent on a national implementing measure. The result of these conditions is that most treaty provisions and regulations have horizontal and vertical direct effect, meaning that they can be enforced against private actors and against a public authority or Member State, respectively. Directives only have vertical direct effect. As already noted, there are many ifs and buts related to this area of EU law, and the doctrine of direct effect is still developing through case law. The key implication of this is that in many cases, individuals can rely on EU law in their national courts, which greatly increases its enforceability, including in the area of environmental law. However, since many environmental laws are adopted in the form of directives, as discussed in the next section, and the direct effect of directives is limited, the private enforcement of EU environmental law can be difficult, especially as between individuals.

TYPES OF EU ENVIRONMENTAL LAW

The European Commission, which is responsible for drafting all European legislation,[11] may choose the form of EU environmental law, except in rare circumstances where the EU treaties explicitly provide otherwise. There are five types of EU acts: *regulations, directives, decisions, recommendations,* and *opinions.*[12] Regulations, directives, and decisions are legally binding; recommendations and opinions are *soft law,* meaning that they cannot be enforced by a court of law.

The European environmental *acquis*—the collection of all EU environmental laws—amounts to more than three hundred regulations and directives.[13] The adoption of this acquis, together with the rest of EU law, is a very costly condition of EU membership, and much is invested by the EU and candidate countries to facilitate this process. Similarly, compliance with the acquis, and the monitoring of this compliance, is an important responsibility of the Member States and the Commission, respectively.

The Legislative Process

EU secondary law can be created through two types of legislative procedures: the ordinary legislative procedure and the special legislative procedure.[14] The European Commission, although not part of the legislature, plays a pivotal part in all legislative processes. The Commission has exclusive right of legislative initiative, which means that any legislation has to start with a proposal from the Commission. Member States, EU institutions, and even EU citizens may petition the Commission to put together such proposals, but the shape and substance of the proposal is within the discretion of the Commission.[15]

EU secondary law has to be in line with primary European law in order to be valid law. For example, the EU cannot legislate on issues outside its competence, which would violate Article 5(1) of the Treaty on European Union,[16] or adopt discriminatory laws, which would violate Article 10 of the Treaty on the Functioning of the European Union (TFEU).[17] These legal acts of the EU are binding on the Member States and/or any other parties they address, and can be enforced by the Court of Justice.

All legal acts adopted through the ordinary or special legislative procedure are European law, regardless of what they are called or what their content is.[18] Acts that are not adopted through these processes are *not* EU law, regardless of whether the rules they create may look or sound like laws. This means that the legal force of European law comes from the process through which it is created, not (only) from the institutions that create it. An example of EU acts that are not legislation, even though they may look like it, are delegated and/or implementing acts adopted by the Commission in order to give expression to more general goals set out in secondary EU law. These acts represent a third category of EU acts, which are not legislation but can be very important in specifying the responsibilities of Member States or individuals affected by secondary

EU law. In order to understand EU environmental policy, knowledge of these specific acts is often not necessary, but awareness of the Commission's important role in implementation through such acts is.

In the ordinary legislative procedure, the Commission submits a proposal for legislation to the Parliament and the Council of Ministers. The proposed legislation then goes through several readings before it is approved or rejected.[19] Throughout this process, either the Parliament or the Council has the power to reject the proposed legislation. Special legislative procedures can either have the Council acting as the sole legislator, with the Parliament's role limited to consultation, or vice versa.[20]

Most environmental legislation is adopted through the ordinary legislative procedure. The exceptions to this are any rules of a fiscal nature (for example, taxes) and any measures affecting town and country planning, quantitative management of water resources, land use, or energy supply. In these situations, a special legislative procedure applies, which requires unanimity in the Council and consultation of (not voting by) the Parliament.[21] The special legislative procedure gives extra weight to Member State interests: Member State representatives decide on the adoption of a legislative measure to the exclusion of the European voice of the Parliament. From this it may be inferred that the measures listed above are considered particularly pertinent to national interests, and that even though environmental policy is generally a shared competence, certain legislative safeguards have been adopted to ensure the primacy of national interests on these issues.

Types of EU Law

Regulations are arguably the "strongest" legal acts the EU can adopt: they have general application, are legally binding in their entirety, and are directly applicable. The latter is particularly important because it means that even without any additional implementing measures taken by the Member States, the provisions of a regulation can be relied upon by, and applied to, actors within the EU. This means that private actors can be forced to act in accordance with a regulation by Member State governments or by other private actors;[22] conversely, private actors can hold their Member State accountable for not fulfilling their obligations under a regulation. Even though regulations are directly applicable, Member States may still have to adopt additional laws to ensure compliance with the regulation. Common examples of this include laws that ensure the creation of new institutions or processes, as under the Regulation on the EU Ecolabel.[23]

The use of regulations in EU environmental law is relatively rare; in 1992, there were forty environmental regulations, as compared to 196 directives. The main strength of regulations is their ability to create uniformity in legislation across Member States. In most environmental situations, uniformity is undesirable because of the variability in circumstances of the Member States. Regulations are, however, commonly used for the transposition of international environmental obligations into EU law. Many international treaties make the EU and Member States jointly liable for any breach of international obligations, which in turn empowers the EU to adopt stringent regulation to ensure compliance by the Member States.

Directives are by far the most common type of legal act within EU environmental law and are strongly preferred by Member States.[24] They are also legally binding, but only to the Member States to which they are addressed and only "as to the result to be achieved."[25] This means that directives set out an environmental aim and leave Member States free to choose the method through which that aim is achieved. As a consequence, directives are very flexible mechanisms, allowing for a range of implementation strategies tailored to national circumstances.

At times, this variety in implementation can make it difficult to distinguish incompetent implementation from non-implementation. Not all Member States have the same capacity to put in place new processes and laws to achieve EU aims. As a result, the Commission—tasked with ensuring the implementation of and compliance with EU law—is heavily burdened with supervising all national implementation processes, in terms of both transposition ("translating" EU law to national law) and practical implementation (creating new processes and institutions) (see table 2).

Decisions are the third type of legally binding act. Unlike regulations and directives, they can be directed at any natural or legal person, not only Member States. When a decision specifies the addressee—for example, "Commission Decision concerning a questionnaire for Member States' reports on the implementation of Council Directive on waste"[26]—it is binding only for them; decisions do not have general application. Delegated and implementing acts of the Commission often take the form of decisions. When used in this way, the Commission can adopt decisions without going through a legislative process involving the Council and the Parliament (as you'll remember from earlier: this also means these decisions are not EU law proper and their impact is formally more limited, even if in practice they are very important). Decisions taken by the Council of Ministers and/or by Parliament tend to be more "powerful" because they usually are not limited to certain addressees; they are most commonly used to ratify international treaties that the EU is party to, such as the Council decision on the conclusion of the convention on long-range transboundary air pollution.[27]

The EU can also use recommendations and opinions in shaping EU environmental law. Soft law instruments are a popular tool of international environmental law;[28] they send a strong moral and political

TABLE 2

Comparing Regulations and Directives

Regulation	Directive
General application	Application to addressees
Binding in entirety	Binding as to aim
Implementation used for operationalization	Implementation essential for functioning

statement but do not legally bind countries to any enforceable commitments. The EU rarely uses soft law. The most common way that recommendations and opinions are used is to clarify criteria of implementation or to "translate" differences between legal traditions of the Member States.[29] *Guidelines, communications,* and *resolutions* fulfill similar roles and are used more frequently by the Commission for environmental matters.

Finally, there are two types of nonlegal acts that directly and indirectly affect European environmental law: Environmental Action Programmes (EAPs) and financial instruments. EAPs set out the general policy aims of EU environmental law, as formulated by the European Council[30] and the Parliament, and were around even before the EU had competence to regulate the environment directly.[31] Financial instruments are also a key part of the EU's toolkit; a large part of its budget is committed to "regional development," which aims to reduce the socioeconomic differences and increase cohesion within and between Member States through development of less affluent regions. There are five so-called structural funds, which have a combined worth of 351.8 billion euros.[32] Between 2007 and 2013, around 100 billion euros was allocated to environmental programs, although none of these funds were explicitly aimed at environmental protection.[33] Alongside these funds is the LIFE Programme, which is intended to be the central financial instrument for environmental, nature conservation, and climate change projects. LIFE (L'Instrument Financier pour l'Environment, or financial instrument for the environment) was established in 1992 and has thus far financed around 4,171 projects amounting to 3.4 billion euros.[34] The aims and criteria of the LIFE Programme are linked to those set out in EAPs. Nevertheless, there have been concerns about the method of selection of projects and their integration with other projects.[35] Unsurprisingly, the use of well-resourced EU funds is often controversial. With respect to the environment, the integration principle suggests that environmental concerns should be considered for each EU project. However, this is not always reflected in the aims of the funds or the deliberations on their spending. Many financial policies, such as the

Common Agricultural Policy, were not designed to prioritize environmental protection and have had to be updated over time.

LEGAL PRINCIPLES

Legal principles play an important role in EU environmental law. Some of these principles are specific to environmental policy, while others are general principles of EU law that also affect EU environmental policy. Some important general principles have already been discussed, such as subsidiarity and proportionality. Principles of this kind are "systemic"; they are essential to the constitutional structure of the EU and aim to protect fundamental rights and values, such as equality, legal certainty, and the right to a defense.[36] The Court of Justice has had an important role in developing—and creating—these principles; today, most of them can be found in the EU treaties or in the Charter of Fundamental Rights.

The EU's environmental principles are listed in Article 191(2) TFEU, which states that EU environmental policy must be based on "the precautionary principle and on the principles that preventative action should be taken, that environmental damage should as a priority be rectified at source and that the polluter should pay."[37] These environmental principles play a role at every stage of the legislative process.

Article 191(2) TFEU states that EU environmental policy must aim at a "high level of protection of the environment, taking into account the diversity of situations in the various regions of the Union."[38] This seemingly straightforward aim hides two difficult questions: What is a sufficiently "high" level of environmental protection in any particular situation? And how should the EU's duty to ensure a high level of protection be balanced against Member States' specific environmental, economic, social, and cultural circumstances? The legal principles in the remainder of Article 191(2) TFEU help answer these questions by identifying the considerations that are meant to guide environmental decisions.

In preparing legislation, the Commission has to show how the legislative proposal respects the principles in Article 191(2) TFEU. Every

TREATY ON THE FUNCTIONING OF THE EUROPEAN UNION,
ARTICLE 191(2): ENVIRONMENTAL PRINCIPLES

"Union policy on the environment shall aim at a high level of protection taking into account the diversity of situations in the various
regions of the Union. It shall be based on the precautionary principle
and on the principles that preventative action should be taken, that
environmental damage should as a priority be rectified at source
and that the polluter should pay."

proposed directive or regulation is accompanied by an impact assessment (see spotlight 5 in chapter 5) that answers these questions, as well
as questions on general EU principles such as subsidiarity, proportionality, and nondiscrimination. If a legal act is found to violate any of
these principles, it should not be adopted; the violation of a general
principle of EU law can be grounds for invalidating the legal act. Once
a legal act has come into force, legal principles guide parties that try to
interpret the law in order to align it with their specific environmental
reality. The Court of Justice plays a crucial role as the final arbiter in
cases where the interpretation of the law and/or the application of legal
principles is unclear or disputed.

It is impossible to legislate in a way that covers all potential situations
or individual acts. Legal principles help guide the EU in situations that
are not explicitly referenced by the law but that it was clearly intended
to cover, without having to create a new rule for each factual variation.
The substantive outcome of the application of an environmental principle will therefore vary depending on the particulars of a given situation,
even if the reasoning remains the same (see also table 3).

Two final principles, the integration principle and sustainable development, occupy a special position. Neither of these principles is mentioned in Article 191(2) TFEU, despite their clear environmental roots.

TABLE 3
EU Environmental Principles

Principle	Definition	Legal Source
Precautionary principle	Seeks to minimize harm from *unknown* environmental risks	Article 191(2) TFEU & secondary EU law
Preventative principle	Seeks to minimize harm from *known* environmental problems	Article 191(2) TFEU & secondary EU law
"Rectification at source" principle	Tries to prevent further harm by addressing the course of the environmental problem	Article 191(2) TFEU & secondary EU law
"Polluter pays" principle	Aims to ensure that costs are internalized by those engaged in polluting activity	Article 191(2) TFEU & secondary EU law
Integration principle	"Environmental protection requirements shall be taken into account in defining and implementing other Union policies and activities, in particular with a view to promoting sustainable development"	Article 11 TFEU
Sustainable development	Balances economic, social, and environmental development; sustainable management of global natural resources	Several relevant articles (e.g., Article 3 and 21 TEU)

The explicit aim of these principles is to ensure that environmental considerations are incorporated into non-environmental policies. They are applicable to all EU policies, not only environmental policies. In a way, they are a species of general EU principles founded on environmental values, underlining that the EU's ambitions for achieving its environmental aims go beyond its environmental policies.[39]

SUMMARY

Environmental law is a critical part of the effective management of environmental impacts. The EU environmental acquis is an enormous body of laws adopted at the European level, dependent on national implementation, and heavily influenced by the EU's international environmental commitments. Apart from legally binding acts, EU environmental law is also heavily influenced by nonlegal acts and legal principles, which can determine the interpretation of EU law.

TAKEAWAYS

- ✓ EU environmental law is a collection of EU legal acts, principles, national laws, and international law. Legal acts adopted by the institutions of the EU are binding on the Member States, making them a type of supranational law.
- ✓ The most common legal acts in EU environmental policy are directives. Directives leave discretion to the Member States to tailor laws to their specific environmental, economic, and social circumstances.
- ✓ The effectiveness of EU environmental law relies heavily on national implementation. The EU does not have the competence or the manpower necessary to implement and enforce all EU law by itself.
- ✓ Legal principles help to bridge gaps between environmental law and practical implementation. Their creation and interpretation are mainly in the hands of the Court of Justice. Many of them have now been codified within the treaties.

KEY TERMS

ADMINISTRATIVE LAW Law that governs governmental bodies, such as administrative agencies.

ADMINISTRATIVE PROCEDURE Rules that govern procedures used by agencies and in agency proceedings.

CIVIL LAW A legal system that codifies core principles into referable systems, such as statutes.

CIVIL PROCEDURE The rules that must be followed in noncriminal judicial courts.

COMMON AGRICULTURAL POLICY (CAP) A European policy creating a system of subsidies and support programs for agriculture. The CAP has environmental impacts but was not designed specifically to manage those impacts.

COMMON LAW Law made by judges, published in the form of judicial opinions, which gives precedential authority to prior court decisions (can be both public and private law).

CONSTITUTIONAL LAW Law that provides for the structure and functioning of a government—for how the government is "constituted"—and how the government is supposed to interact with individuals (a form of public law).

CONTRACT LAW Law that governs how promises between individuals are enforced (a form of private law).

CRIMINAL LAW Law that governs the punishment and behavior of those who commit crimes—behaviors that are considered so socially damaging that they are punishable by law (a form of public law).

CRIMINAL PROCEDURE Rules that govern criminal legal procedures.

DIRECTIVE A type of EU law aimed at achieving a certain effect, leaving open to Member States how to implement and achieve that effect.

ENVIRONMENTAL ACTION PROGRAMME (EAP) An articulation of the EU's goals for environmental policy development.

ENVIRONMENTAL PRINCIPLES Principles on environmental policy that are listed in the Treaty on the Functioning of the European Union, which provides that such policy "shall be based on the precautionary principle and on the principles that preventative action should be taken, that environmental damage should as a priority be rectified at source and that the polluter should pay."

GUIDELINE A type of EU law that is not binding on third parties (i.e., it is binding only on the party issuing the guidelines).

IMPLEMENTING/DELEGATED ACTS Type of delegated EU law adopted by the European Commission.

INTEGRATION PRINCIPLE A principle that provides that environmental protection requirements should be taken into account in defining and implementing EU policies and activities, particularly with a view to promoting sustainable development.

INTERGOVERNMENTAL LAW Processes and laws that are created by states and aimed at states (e.g., international law).

LIFE PROGRAMME A financial instrument for funding environmental, nature conservation, and climate change projects.

OPINION A nonbinding policy document aimed at clarifying the interpretation of legal acts and/or other policy documents.

"POLLUTER PAYS" PRINCIPLE A principle that aims to ensure that costs are internalized by those engaged in polluting activity.

PRECAUTIONARY PRINCIPLE An EU principle related to risk management, which provides that if there is the possibility that a given policy or action might harm the public or the environment, and there is an absence of scientific consensus, the action should not be pursued.

PREVENTATIVE PRINCIPLE A principle that seeks to minimize harm from known environmental problems.

PRIMARY EU LAW Foundational EU law, such as the EU treaties, resulting from an intergovernmental process between the Member States (a type of intergovernmental law).

PRIVATE LAW Law that governs relationships between individuals (e.g., contract law, tort law, and property law).

PROPERTY LAW Law about the relationships between people and things.

PUBLIC LAW Law that governs issues that affect the general public or state (e.g., constitutional law, administrative law, and criminal law).

RECOMMENDATION A legally nonbinding act from the EU.

REGULATION A type of EU law that is binding in terms of both its substance and its objective; Member State implementation is restricted to translating the regulation into national law.

SECONDARY EU LAW Supranational law resulting from the legislative process between the EU institutions.

SUPRANATIONAL LAW Processes and laws that are made by international bodies that can bind states (e.g., EU law).

SUSTAINABLE DEVELOPMENT PRINCIPLE A principle that seeks to balance economic, social, and environmental development in managing global natural resources.

TORT LAW Law that governs how people can use law to receive compensation for harms or injuries that other individuals have caused them (a form of private law).

DISCUSSION QUESTIONS

1. What downsides are there to using regulations to address environmental problems? Do directives address these downsides?

2. Is it wise to have an integration principle that requires consideration of environmental protection requirements when implementing other goals? What downsides are there to this requirement, if any? Are there other issues or problems (poverty, education, national security, fairness, etc.) that also deserve to be integrated into all policies?

3. What role should criminal law play in regulating the environment?

4. How important is it for environmental law to be able to change quickly, in response to changing circumstances or improving information? Which types of law are most likely to be able to respond quickly to changes, and which would you expect to be slower to change?

NOTES

1. For more detail, see the sections "Relationship between EU and National Laws" and "Types of EU Environmental Law" later in this chapter.

2. Scotland has a mixed legal system, which means that it combines principles of civil and common law.

3. Case 26/62 *van Gend en Loos* [1963] ECLI:EU:C:1963:1.

4. See Ana Bobić, "Constitutional Pluralism Is Not Dead: An Analysis of Interactions between Constitutional Courts of Member States and the European Court of Justice" (2017) 18 *German Law Journal* 1395.

5. This also means that in case of a clash between EU environmental law and national constitutional law (constitutional law is traditionally considered the most important and powerful source of law in a legal system), EU environmental law will be upheld over national constitutional law. See, e.g., Case 106/77 *Simmenthal* [1978] ECLI:EU:C:1978:49.

6. Case 6/64 *Costa v. ENEL* [1964] ERC 585.

7. See Danish Supreme Court Case 15/2014 *Ajos,* Judgment of 6 December 2016 (rejecting the horizontal application of general principle of EU law); and Czech Constitutional Court Case Pl. ÚS 5/12 *Slovak Pensions,* Judgment of 31 December 2012 (stated that the Court of Justice was acting *ultra vires* and disapplied the latter's *Landtová* judgment).

8. Case 26/62 *van Gend en Loos* [1963] ECLI:EU:C:1963:1.

9. Case 14/83 *Sabine von Colson and Elisabeth Kamann v. Land Nordrhein-Westfalen* [1984] ECLI:EU:C:1984:153.

10. For a good overview, see Craig and de Burca, chapter 7.

11. Moving forward, the only type of European law discussed is secondary law, unless stated otherwise.

12. Article 288 TFEU.

13. Latest estimate made in 2001; see http://ec.europa.eu/environment/archives/enlarg/pdf/benefit_short.pdf.

14. Article 289 TFEU.

15. Article 17(2) TEU.

16. "The limits of Union competences are governed by the principle of conferral. The use of Union competences is governed by the principles of subsidiarity and proportionality."

17. "In defining and implementing its policies and activities, the Union shall aim to combat discrimination based on sex, racial or ethnic origin, religion or belief, disability, age or sexual orientation."

18. Article 289(3) TFEU.

19. Article 294 TFEU.

20. Article 289(2) TFEU.

21. Article 192(2) TFEU.

22. The horizontal enforcement of regulations (i.e., between private parties) is subject to a relatively few conditions; see Josephine van Zeben, "The Untapped Potential of Horizontal Private Enforcement within EC Environmental Law" (2010) 22 *Georgetown International Environmental Law Review* 241.

23. Regulation (EC) No. 66/2010 of the European Parliament and of the Council on the EU Ecolabel, OJ 2010 L27/01–19.

24. Andrew Jordan, "The Implementation of EU Environmental Policy: A Policy Problem without a Political Solution?" (1999) 17 *Environment and Planning C: Government and Policy* 69–90.

25. Article 288 TFEU.

26. Commission Decision OJ 1997 L 256/13–19.

27. Council Decision 81/462/EEC.

28. Geoffrey Palmer, "New Ways to Make International Environmental Law" (1992) 86 *American Journal of International Law* 259–283.

29. Recommendation 2001/331/EC of the European Parliament and of the Council providing for minimum criteria for environmental inspections in the Member States, OJ 2001 L 118/41.

30. Recall from chapter 2 that the European Council is distinct from the Council of Ministers. The European Council is constituted by the heads of government of all EU Member States and does not form part of the legislative process. The Council of Ministers includes ministerial representatives of all EU Member States and, with the Parliament, is part of the legislative process.

31. All EAPs are available at http://ec.europa.eu/environment/action-programme/.

32. Budget 2014–2020; see http://ec.europa.eu/regional_policy/en/funding/available-budget/.

33. "Working for the Regions: EU Regional Policy 2007–2013," EU Commission DG Regional Policy, January 2008, http://ec.europa.eu/regional_policy/sources/docgener/presenta/working2008/work_en.pdf, at 16.

34. See http://ec.europa.eu/environment/life/index.htm.

35. See "Final Evaluation of LIFE+: Summary of Conclusions and Recommendations," 14 December 2012, https://ec.europa.eu/environment/archives/life/about/documents/121214_conclusions.pdf.

36. This distinction is based on work by Tadis Tridimas, *The General Principles of EU Law* (2nd ed., Oxford University Press 2007), 4.

37. Article 191(2) TFEU.

38. Article 191(2) TFEU.

39. The Court of Justice has also referred to the precautionary principle as a "general principle of EU law," but clearly the precautionary principle can still be traced back to Article 191(2) TFEU, unlike the integration and sustainable development principles that are found outside of the Environmental Title of the TFEU. See Case T-74/00 etc. *Artegodan* [2002] ECLI:EU:T:2002:283, para 184.

CHAPTER FOUR

Regulatory Instruments

A regulatory instrument is a set of rules and restrictions that govern a certain activity, including directions on what happens if people undertake too much, or too little, of that activity. Different types of regulatory instruments work like different tools in a regulator's tool belt. For example, regulators who wanted to promote energy conservation could use several different tools—regulatory instruments—to accomplish that goal. They might ban energy-hungry industrial activities, or permit new factories to be built only when they are outfitted with energy-efficient technologies; they might tax energy use, or subsidize purchase of energy-efficient home appliances; or they might nudge high-use consumers to reduce their usage by informing them of average use rates. Any of these approaches might successfully further the policy goal of reducing energy use, but each relies on a different instrument to achieve that end.

In principle, policymakers have access to the same legal tools and regulatory instruments regardless of the area or type of law in which they are regulating. In practice, the "fit" between the regulatory instrument and the regulatory problem is crucial for its effectiveness. In this regard, the diffuse, complex, nonhuman character of environmental impacts can pose a real challenge to policymakers; a regulatory instrument that may work very well for fighting crime could prove very ineffective for improving air quality. Similarly, some actors and some types of law are better suited to deploying some regulatory instruments.

This chapter sets out the most common types of regulatory instruments and how they are used to address specific environmental impacts. Particular attention will be paid to their strengths and weaknesses in terms of addressing the diffuse, complex, and nonhuman nature of environmental impacts.

HOW DO REGULATORY INSTRUMENTS WORK?

There are many different regulatory instruments, and new ones are continuously developed and tested to deal with new types of activities and better manage familiar ones. The common core of all regulatory instruments is that they seek to influence an actor—typically an individual or a business—to make the "right" decision, or at least to behave as the policymaker prefers. In the context of environmental impacts, the preferred decision may be to do more or less of something, or to stop doing something entirely. In order to achieve this, regulation provides incentives. These incentives can take multiple forms: they may be financial—for example, taxing an environmentally costly activity; penal—when someone is imprisoned for creating environmental harm; or sometimes only psychological—for example, structuring decisions to make it easier for people to behave in ways that have pro-environmental impacts. They can also be positive or negative—the so-called "carrots versus sticks" approach—by either rewarding "good" behavior or punishing "bad" behavior. These incentives interact with one another: when someone receives a prison sentence for dumping toxic waste, there often will be a social consequence as well.

The deterrent effect of a specific regulatory instrument—the extent to which the regulation is able to discourage someone from acting in a certain way—depends on many factors, including the type of actor, the type of consequence, and the actor's perceived likelihood that their behavior will be recognized and penalized. The same is true for any positive effect that regulation may create to encourage preferred behaviors.

Policymakers' assumptions regarding people's motivations and decision making are not always accurate. Sometimes this is because policymakers assume that people will behave "rationally," making decisions that optimize their personal well-being. Empirical research into people's actual behavior is increasingly showing the limitations of the rationality assumption, demonstrating instead that there are many—very strong, subconscious, and arguably irrational—psychological processes that drive many behaviors. These findings have led to the creation of new regulatory instruments and are especially promising for the regulation of environmental actions, which have proven particularly sensitive to intuitive rather than rational motivators. Behavioral insights are also changing the use of traditional instruments, as is further discussed below.

Finally, *social norms* play an important role vis-à-vis regulatory instruments. Social norms tend to develop through frequent social interactions, not through top-down regulatory processes. As such, they are not a regulatory instrument per se. Nevertheless, their interaction with regulatory instruments is important: people's perception of a law, and their likelihood of compliance, will change depending on whether the law—and the regulatory instrument tasked with enforcing it—is considered consistent with or contrary to social norms. Unjust laws—however defined—are very difficult to enforce, and voluntary compliance with such laws will be limited. Conversely, laws that simply reiterate preexisting social norms need little or no separate legal enforcement, as the social norms themselves will drive people toward compliance. In societies, or areas of society, where there are few laws, social norms ensure that people's interactions have a measure of predictability. Norms that are never translated into law can be so effective that, for example, sustainable exploitation of natural resources can take place even in the absence of individual property rights and/or an enforcement system like the judiciary.[1]

TYPES OF INSTRUMENTS

Four types of instruments play a particularly important role in environmental policy: traditional instruments of command-and-control regulation, which work through mandating or banning behaviors; economic instruments, which rely on adjusting prices for behaviors upward or downward; information-based instruments, which rely on disclosure and information provision; and emerging behavioral instruments, such as nudges, which work through purposefully shaping people's decision-making processes.

As a group, *command-and-control regulation* broadly covers all regulation that is founded in the prohibition or prescription of specific behavior, for instance through permits or bans. Command-and-control regulation is easily the most widespread type of regulation, used in various forms in most areas of regulation. Despite its ubiquity, the use of command-and-control regulation is often criticized as "inefficient." To prescribe or prohibit behavior, a lot of information is needed that the government may not be in the best place to obtain or interpret.[2] Command-and-control regulation is also being changed by increased behavioral insights; for example, bans have proven far more effective when combined with messaging that suggests moral or social disapproval of the action.

Economic instruments do not prohibit or mandate specific behavior. Instead, they provide "prices" on behavior and rely on individuals' private cost-benefit analysis as to whether they wish to continue with their behavior once it becomes costlier. Environmental taxes, for example, do not prohibit the use of heavily polluting products, but they make their use less economically viable or appealing. Another way to phrase this would be to say that the regulation forces people to "internalize the negative externalities of their actions." Economic instruments have also been affected by behavioral insights. For example, increased awareness of loss aversion has taught us that a small tax of five cents on disposable bags used at a grocery store is likely to be perceived as a loss from the status quo, whereas a "rebate" of five cents for each reusable bag used is likely to be perceived as a gain. Because people value losses more strongly than equivalent gains, behavioral research suggests that the loss—the tax—is more effective at reducing disposable bag use.

An important application of economic instruments to environmental policy comes with cap-and-trade systems, such as the European Union Emissions Trading Scheme (EU ETS).[3] These schemes create tradeable permits that individuals engaged in a certain activity need to purchase in order to continue their production of environmentally harmful substances. In the EU ETS, producers of energy-intensive products that create high levels of CO_2 and other greenhouse gases need to monitor their emissions and "pay" a certain number of allowances each year that corresponds with their emission levels. Because allowances tend to be assigned on the basis of historical emissions, lowering emissions through technological progress or less production will result in an excess of emission allowances that can then be sold to others. This means that there is both an absolute *cap* on environmental harm and the potential for economic efficiency in achieving reductions by allowing for *trade*.

Economic instruments are generally considered more cost-effective than command-and-control regulation because they allow the "market" to price the actions that people want to engage in. This means that those with the most information about the regulated behavior can make informed decisions about what is an efficient level of activity, keeping in mind their private costs and broader public costs (which are theoretically internalized because of the economic instrument). An important limitation of these instruments is that their implementation still relies on good information in order to get the basic price, or trading scheme, "right." When regulators have poor information, it can undermine economic instruments. For example, under the EU ETS approach to greenhouse gases, limited data about historical emissions meant that participants were awarded far more allowances than they needed, which meant there was no economic incentive to reduce emissions.[4] As a result, the economic instrument struggled to work as policymakers had planned. Economic instruments sometimes also meet with moral objections, as some consider the monetization of certain environmental processes to be wrong. For example, when Namibia auctioned a permit to hunt an endangered black rhino for $350,000—with the plan of using the proceeds to protect surviving rhino populations—the decision was met with controversy and protests, as some saw the choice to sell the right to kill an endangered animal as immoral.[5]

Information-based instruments seek to inform people's behavior. Two common forms of information-based instruments are labels and disclosure regimes. Importantly, these instruments do not prescribe a certain type of behavior but rather require people to inform others (or be informed) about the behavior they (or others) engage in. They are often used together with other, possibly more prescriptive, instruments. An example of this type of regime is the European Pollutant Release and Transfer Register, which collects and disseminates information on environmental releases and transfers of toxic substances.[6] The Nature Protection and Environmental Impact Assessment procedure, based on the process in the US National Environmental Policy Act, also serves an informational function, ensuring that the environmental implications of decisions are taken into account before the decisions are made.

Building on behavioral research in the social sciences, *behavioral instruments* have emerged as a separate category of regulatory instrument over recent years. The basis for behavioral instruments is the concept of "choice architecture," developed by Nobel Prize–winning economist Richard Thaler and law professor Cass Sunstein, and popularized in their book *Nudge*.[7] Choice architecture relies on the purposeful structuring of decision-making contexts to shape people's behavior toward selected ends.

The two main applications of choice architecture in the environmental context arise through *default rules* and *framing*. Researchers have found, across multiple legal and nonlegal contexts, that default rules are remarkably "sticky," such that once a rule is identified as the status quo, people have a strong tendency to stick with that rule. Successful environmental applications have included automatically enrolling consumers in green energy programs and/or recycling programs; setting default printer settings to print double-sided instead of single-sided; adopting packaging and sales practices that encourage consumers and businesses to generate less waste, such as providing disposable straws to diners only upon request; and hotel policies to wash linens and towels only upon guest request.[8]

Framing, on the other hand, uses people's reliance on heuristics for quick decision making and the importance of context in our ability to process information. Small changes in how contextual cues are presented or framed can be strategically used to shape people's behaviors. For example, the same option is typically evaluated more favorably when it is seen as the middle or intermediate in the set of options considered than when it is seen as extreme.[9] Thus, an option for regulatory stringency that is contrasted with two other options—one more stringent and one less stringent—is likely to generate more intuitive support than if the same option were included in a list of all less stringent alternatives. Or consider that framing can be used to associate environmental actions with positive or negative emotions—"smiley" and "frowny" emoticons, for example, have been used effectively to encourage people to use less energy than their neighbors.[10]

Although behavioral instruments continue to gain traction worldwide, they are not uncontroversial. Some commentators worry that use of behavioral research can be manipulative. Others are concerned that using behavioral instruments to encourage people to act in preferred ways is paternalistic; still others think that behavioral instruments are insufficiently strong responses when people are making bad or damaging decisions. Where such objections are persuasive, other instruments may be preferable.[11]

In light of the complexity of today's regulatory problems, particularly in the environmental sphere, the most effective regulatory instrument is often not *one* instrument, but a combination of regulatory approaches. For example, using default rules and framing together tends to be more

TABLE 4

Strengths and Weaknesses of Regulatory Instruments

Regulatory Instrument	Strengths	Weaknesses
Command and control • Bans • Permits	• Easy to enforce • Familiar to regulators and society	• Requires a lot of information to be effective • Bans may stop potentially positive innovation
Economic instruments • Taxes • Subsidies • Market-based instruments	• Flexible • Internalizes previously external costs and benefits of activity	• Pricing must be accurate • Moral objections to pricing
Information-based instruments • Labels • Disclosure regimes	• Flexible • Information creation • Possibility for private enforcement • Cheap to implement	• Less coercive • Puts a decision-making burden on private parties
Behavioral instruments • Framing • Default rules	• Builds on preexisting psychological processes • Low enforcement costs	• Can be seen as paternalistic or manipulative • May not account for cultural and social differences

effective than using either one separately: informing homeowners about standard energy use (setting a default usage rate) *and* including an emoticon related to their use (triggering a framing effect) has been found to more effectively reduce energy consumption than just informing people about status quo usage rates.[12] Similarly, using framing alongside command-and-control regulation can improve people's perception of the regulation's requirements, make compliance more likely, and reduce enforcement needs. Finally, policymakers must also consider that the combination of instruments may itself lead to increased costs, inefficiencies, or other unintended consequences (see table 4).[13]

CHOOSING AMONG REGULATORY INSTRUMENTS

Ideally, to regulate most effectively, policymakers—often legislators—tailor the choice of regulatory instrument to the features of behavior they are regulating. Admittedly, this does not always happen, for a variety of reasons. The policymakers may be unfamiliar with new regulatory techniques—such as behavioral nudges—or may misunderstand the complex environmental problem, or the behavior, they are attempting to regulate. Or they may be focused on protecting industry or private interests, which can be in conflict with public interests, or may be interested only in short-term goals, which can lead to myopic instrument choices. These possibilities suggest the importance of making both policymakers and those who can influence policy aware of the range of instruments that are available for regulating environmental quality. The process of choosing an instrument that presents the best fit between regulatory instrument and problem is generally referred to as *instrument choice.*

Instrument Choice

Scholars and policymakers have invested heavily in the technical skill of instrument choice. This has produced important insights that help policymakers determine the best fit between instrument and regulatory problem. Take, for example, the problem of greenhouse gas emissions, which (as discussed further in chapter 8) presents a series of regulatory challenges. In responding to those challenges, policymakers have a number of choices to make about which legal instruments to use to address the problem. They might use command-and-control regulation in the form of an emission standard, which tells specific actors how much they are allowed to emit; an economic mechanism, such as a cap-and-trade scheme or a tax; or a behavioral instrument that attempts to shape behavior by nudging people toward reduced emissions or that merely informs them about how their emissions compare to their neighbors'. All these instruments might lead to a reduction in emissions. But the actual amount of the reduction, and the cost at which it is achieved, varies hugely between the instruments. In order to determine the best fit, therefore, policymakers need to carefully recognize their own goals with respect to the regulatory problem.

It is almost never the case that policymakers want to put an absolute stop to polluting activities; environmental law tends to try and balance environmental protection with other societal goals such as economic growth, human health, and scientific development. Instrument choice is thus not only about regulating the activity that leads to the environmental impact, but also about regulating the effects of the regulation itself.

For instrument choice in environmental contexts, chief challenges are presented by the diffuse, complex, and nonhuman character of the impacts the policymaker seeks to regulate. Regulatory instruments often can address only one or two such elements at a time, leaving it to policymakers to determine which of their priorities are most important and/or to cobble together multiple instruments to address a single problem. To complicate things further, there are typically institutional, legal, and practical limitations on the policymakers' discretion that can take priority over the fit between the regulatory instrument and the environmental impact.

Restrictions on Instrument Choice

Policymakers must manage their instrument choice within a number of institutional, legal, and practical constraints. Institutionally, policymakers are often constrained by the constitutional structure of their government and by their place within it. Most constitutional democracies around the world reserve legislative power—the power to make laws—to elected legislatures. As a result, for either constitutional or political reasons, legislators are often the policymakers who must select the instrument(s) to be used to accomplish legislative goals.

The regulation of environmental impacts can generally be divided into two stages: goal setting during the legislative process that results in environmental laws, followed by instrument choice by expert policymakers in order to create regulation that implements those laws. Broadly speaking, decisions that set goals that will affect the distribution of costs and benefits, in the present and over time, between different groups of people—and between people and the environment—are reserved for the legislature. Decisions regarding the achievement of those legislative goals through instrument choice tend to be delegated to policymakers. However, the level of discretion given to policymakers regarding instrument choice and design again varies between jurisdictions and regulatory problems.

In the EU, it can be difficult to draw a hard line between these two stages. The competence of the EU to regulate certain impacts is limited—in terms of the types of issues it can address (as compared to those that are the responsibility of the Member States)[14] and in the types of measures it can take to do so. Specifically, in regard to the second point, environmental regulation is expected to be *proportionate*—that is, it should not be more invasive or burdensome than is absolutely necessary to achieve the policy aim. Moreover, the EU cannot (easily) make use of certain types of regulatory instruments—for example, it is not empowered to adopt taxation of any kind. There is an exception for environmental taxation, which *may* be proposed by the EU, but any such proposal would be subject to a Member State veto.[15]

A great deal of environmental regulation around the world is adopted by administrative agencies or other bodies that exercise *delegated powers*. These powers often come with limitations on the tools or instruments that delegatees may use to achieve the goals of the delegating body. Many statutes specifically enumerate the instruments that agencies are required to use for particular problems; in such cases, agencies are limited to those choices. An administrative agency that is required to promulgate command-and-control emissions standards for new vehicles, for example, may not choose to rely on social norms instead of command-and-control. Moreover, while the powers of these agencies can be very far-reaching, they remain subject to review by higher bodies, such as the legislature and the judiciary.

Other restrictions on the powers of the regulator are practical, such as lack of budget or expertise. These can also influence the choice among regulatory instruments. If a jurisdiction already has an intricate tax system in place, adding another tax will appear to be a relatively low-cost move, since no new institutions or even processes for collection would have to be created. The creation of a cap-and-trade system, on the other hand, will almost always present significant start-up costs, including monitoring of previously unmonitored (or undermonitored) activities, setting up a trading space, ensuring the reliability of information on which trades are based, and so on. Many of these restrictions do not technically preclude the choice of an instrument, but they do provide constraints that may sometimes lead regulators to choose easier or cheaper instruments over more complex or expensive ones. Sometimes, political factors may play a role in these practicalities: for example, cutting an agency's budget will affect its ability to monitor certain activities and/or adopt certain regulatory instruments. It is therefore important to consider the laws that shape instrument choice—and the actors empowered to adopt such laws—alongside the specific strengths and weaknesses of specific regulatory instruments.

Finally, policymakers are sometimes limited by cognitive and historical processes that make it difficult for them to shift away from past instrument choices. Most environmental regulation in force today is command-and-control regulation, which is often criticized as being costly (for the regulator and regulated), inflexible, and dependent on only partially available information. Why, then, is it still so pervasive? One of the answers to this question is *path dependency*, which causes people to continue existing practices even when better ones could be adopted. Path dependency is caused mainly by the transaction costs that a shift from existing to new practices would entail. A real-life example is the continued use of the QWERTY keyboard, despite the fact that it has long been proven that another ordering of keys would lead to more efficient and faster typing. However, the costs of having to replace all existing keyboards and retrain all current typists to a new keyboard weigh more heavily than any potential efficiency gains.

In some situations, path dependency is a logical outcome of a cost-benefit analysis. But in many situations, the form that existing legislation has taken will determine the shape of future legislation and regulatory instruments regardless of the cost-benefit analysis of change. The US Clean Air Act of 1970—itself the product of path dependency—has remained unaltered through every subsequent major amendment, including those in 1974, 1977, and 1990, despite the addition of new programs and some changes to preexisting parts of the statute. This is also true for the US Clean Water Act and other pollution-control statutes, none of which have been meaningfully changed for nearly a half-century.[16] The historical developments that lead to the adoption of one instrument can thus also influence many future instrument choices through path dependency. Within the EU, the use of directives adds another layer to this issue, insofar as Member States are free to choose their method of implementation but, in doing so, are often confronted with their preexisting national regulation (or lack thereof). While it is impossible to provide a comprehensive overview of the presence of path dependency in these instances, it is interesting to note that research into the national implementation of the EU's Birds and Habitats Directives showed many Member States using new instruments, rather than building on existing ones, when implementing these directives.[17] This, of course, leaves open the question of how sticky these new instruments were, once adopted.

Apart from high transition costs, the adoption of new instruments, or the change of existing ones, also presents *compliance costs* to the actors affected by the regulatory instrument. Furthermore, policymakers may sometimes be subject to political pressure and influence, which can affect the substance of their decisions. Often the simple act of gathering the necessary information for instrument design and implementation requires exchanges with industry representatives and environmental NGOs, both of which will try to influence the regulatory process through the informational advantages they have vis-à-vis the policy-maker. This *regulatory capture* can lead to less *and* more stringent environmental regulation. Counterintuitively, it is not always the case that an economically powerful firm engaged in environmentally damaging behavior will push for *less* stringent regulation; more stringent and costly regulation can create a competitive advantage against smaller firms, or even a barrier to entry to the market, which would be in the larger firm's interest. Budget restraints and/or lack of expertise on the side of the policymaker make regulatory capture more likely, which in turn can have an important impact on instrument choice and design.

SUMMARY

Environmental law sets out societal goals with respect to the management of environmental impacts. In order to incentivize individuals, companies, and other actors involved in environmentally impactful activities, policymakers are tasked with designing regulatory instruments. These instruments harness financial, penal, and psychological motivations in order to change behaviors.

The choice between these instruments—which include command-and-control regulation, economic instruments, information-based instruments, and behavioral instruments—should prioritize the fit between environmental impact and regulatory instrument. Proper fit is most likely to produce changes in the behavior leading to environmental impacts. However, there are important restrictions to instrument choice, such as legal and practical restrictions on the available tools, as well as historical and cognitive processes that restrain policymakers' ability to choose freely between instruments.

TAKEAWAYS

✓ Regulatory instruments are used to incentivize individuals, companies, and other actors to act to further environmental goals.

✓ Instrument choice is aimed at choosing the "best" instrument in order to achieve certain types of behavior. What the best choice is depends on one's view of the relative importance of cost of regulation, cost of enforcement, cost of compliance, and stringency of goals.

✓ Instrument choice can also be restricted by legal, institutional, historical, or practical concerns regarding the power of the regulator and the rights of the party that is being regulated.

✓ Commonly used instruments include command-and-control instruments, economic instruments, information-based instruments, and behavioral instruments.

KEY TERMS

BEHAVIORAL INSTRUMENTS Instruments for regulating behavior that build on social science research, particularly in psychology and economics.

CAP-AND-TRADE SYSTEM A regulatory instrument that sets a maximum cap on a certain activity (e.g., emitting activities) and allows participants to trade permits with each other to engage in more or less of that activity.

CHOICE ARCHITECTURE Purposeful structuring of decision-making contexts to shape people's behavior toward selected ends.

COMMAND-AND-CONTROL REGULATION A group of regulatory instruments that rely on standard setting in order to permit or ban certain types of behavior.

COMPLIANCE COST The cost of complying with a regulatory standard.

DEFAULT RULES A preset course of action that takes effect automatically, unless decision makers provide an alternative specification.

ECONOMIC INSTRUMENTS Regulatory instruments that rely on economic incentives in order to achieve compliance.

EXTERNALITIES Costs and benefits related to an activity that are experienced by someone other than the person engaged in the activity.

FRAMING A behavioral instrument that uses small changes in how contextual cues are presented to strategically shape people's behaviors.

INSTRUMENT CHOICE Selection among different types of regulatory instruments with a view to create the "best" fit between the regulated behavior and the method of regulation.

MARKET-BASED REGULATION A regulation that makes use of economic incentives created by markets.

NUDGE A behavioral instrument that is meant to alter people's behavior in predictable ways, without forbidding any options or significantly changing economic incentives.

PATH DEPENDENCY A phenomenon whereby people continue existing practices even where better ones could be adopted, because of the costs associated with shifting to new "paths" or practices.

REGULATORY INSTRUMENT A tool that a regulator uses to achieve regulatory goals.

DISCUSSION QUESTIONS

1. Should the choice about regulatory instruments be made by legislators or agencies? On what basis?

2. Do economically powerful firms always want less environmental regulation? When might they push for more regulation?

3. How much should cost considerations (compliance and/or enforcement costs) weigh in the choice of instrument?

4. What are the best ways to ensure flexibility in regulatory instruments? What kind of flexibility is most important in

addressing environmental impacts? Link your answer to specific examples.

5. If people do not realize that they are being "regulated" (for instance, through the use of nudges), is this problematic? If so, why?

6. A regulatory instrument that was not discussed in this chapter is voluntary self regulation, whereby companies or industries create rules for themselves. What might be the advantages and disadvantages of such regulation with respect to environmental impacts?

7. How important do you think it is that something is considered morally wrong as well as legally wrong, especially with respect to the regulation of environmental impacts? Give an example from your personal experience.

NOTES

1. Elinor Ostrom, *Governing the Commons: The Evolution of Institutions for Collective Action* (Cambridge University Press 1990).

2. For more detail, see the section "Choosing among Regulatory Instruments" later in this chapter.

3. See also chapter 8.

4. See Harro van Asselt, "The Design and Implementation of Greenhouse Gas Emissions Trading" in Kevin Gray et al. (eds.), *Oxford Handbook of International Climate Change Law* (Oxford University Press 2016); Edwin Woerdman, "The EU Greenhouse Gas Emissions Trading Scheme" in Edwin Woerdman et al. (eds.), *Essential EU Climate Change Law* (Edward Elgar 2015) at 43–75; Josephine van Zeben, *The Allocation of Regulatory Competence in the European Emissions Trading System* (Cambridge University Press 2012).

5. See Jon Herskovitz, "Permit to Hunt Endangered Rhinoceros Sells for $350,000 despite Protests," Reuters (11 January 2014), www.reuters.com /article/us-usa-rhino-auction-idUSBREA0B02720140112.

6. See https://prtr.eea.europa.eu/.

7. See Richard Thaler and Cass Sunstein, *Nudge: Improving Decisions about Health, Wealth and Happiness* (Yale University Press 2008); see also Richard Thaler and Cass Sunstein, "Libertarian Paternalism Is Not an Oxymoron" (2003) 70 *University of Chicago Law Review* 1159.

8. See Hilary Byerly et al., "Nudging Pro-environmental Behavior: Evidence and Opportunities" (2017) 16 *Frontiers in Ecology and the Environment* 159; see also Cass Sunstein and Lucia Reisch, "Automatically Green: Behavioral Economics and Environmental Regulation" (2013) 38 *Harvard Environmental Law Review* 127–158.

9. See Mark Kelman et al., "Context-Dependence in Legal Decision Making" (1996) 25 *Journal of Legal Studies* 287. This phenomenon is sometimes called the "compromise effect."

10. See Wesley Shultz et al., "The Constructive, Destructive, and Reconstructive Power of Social Norms" (2007) 18 *Psychological Science* 429; see also Elisha Frederiks et al., "Household Energy Use: Applying Behavioral Economics to Understand Consumer Decision-Making and Behavior" (2015) 41 *Renewable and Sustainable Energy Reviews* 1385.

11. See Arden Rowell, "Behavioral and Psychological Instruments in Environmental Law" in Ken Richards and Josephine van Zeben (eds.), *Policy Instruments in Environmental Law* (Edward Elgar 2020).

12. See Shultz et al., Constructive, Destructive, and Reconstructive Power of Social Norms."

13. See, e.g., Christopher Böhringer et al., "Efficiency Losses from Overlapping Regulation of EU Carbon Emissions" (2008) 33 *Journal of Regulatory Economics* 299–317.

14. See chapter 2 for a more detailed discussion of shared competence in the area of environmental policy.

15. Article 192(b) Treaty on the Functioning of the European Union.

16. Daniel Cole, "Explaining the Persistence of 'Command-and-Control' in US Environmental Law" in Ken Richards and Josephine van Zeben (eds.), *Policy Instruments in Environmental Law* (Edward Elgar 2020).

17. See Irene Bouwma et al., "Following Old Paths or Shaping New Ones in Natura 2000 Implementation? Mapping Path Dependency in Instrument Choice" (2016) 18 *Journal of Environmental Policy & Planning* 214–233.

PART TWO

EU Environmental Law

CHAPTER FIVE

Contextualizing
EU Environmental Law

This chapter highlights three key features of the European legal system that—although most were not developed specifically to deal with environmental impacts—nevertheless respond to, and interact with, the challenges created by those impacts. In order to contextualize these features, this chapter starts with a short introduction to the history of European environmental regulation. It then expands on the roles of multilevel governance, the role of technocracy in regulation, and the role of risk analysis in EU environmental law.

Readers who are already familiar with the EU legal system may choose to begin the book here. Readers who are new to the EU legal system will find it helpful to first review the material included in part I.

A SHORT HISTORY OF EUROPEAN ENVIRONMENTAL REGULATION

When the EU was created, there was no (explicit) environmental competence, which meant that the EU was not empowered to create any laws directly aimed at regulating or protecting the environment. Any environmental regulation had to be justified by reference to other competences that had been explicitly conferred on the EU. In the period until 1987, there were therefore two main pathways to European environmental regulation: by linking environmental regulation to the EU's competence over the European economic market (the internal market) or to the general project of European integration.

One important example of environmental regulation on the basis of the EU's control over the internal market was the Directive on the classification, packaging, and labeling of dangerous substances, adopted in 1967.[1] Although this Directive clearly had environmental impacts by controlling dangerous substances, it was adopted on the grounds that the EEC had the competence to regulate the internal market as well as rules related to trade within that market. Importantly, European actions like this were generally supported by the Court of Justice of the European Union, which has exclusive jurisdiction over the validity and interpretation of European laws. In the 1970s and '80s, the CJEU handed down several landmark judgments that allowed for the lawful pursuit of environmental objectives in common market measures, and even stated that environmental protection is one of the "[European] Community's essential objectives."[2] These decisions played a key part in the development of European environmental competence.

The second important step toward a European environmental competence occurred through the development of Environmental Action Programmes (EAPs), which set out the EU's medium- to long-term environmental priorities. The first EAP was adopted in 1973 in response to the United Nations' Stockholm Conference on Sustainable Development. It was based on a new premise that provided a strong basis for European action on the environment: the idea that economic development, prosperity, and the protection of the environment were mutually interdependent. On the basis of this reasoning, environmental protection came to be viewed as "one of the essential tasks of the [European] Community," in line with the Court's earlier reasoning.[3] EAPs continue to be an important vehicle for environmental action in the EU, and a total of seven have been adopted since 1973.

SPOTLIGHT 4. THE INTERNAL MARKET AND
EU ENVIRONMENTAL LAW

States often change their environmental laws as a means of competing with other states' economies. Consider a state banning meat products that contain certain hormones. A state may choose to do this, at least partially, to accommodate domestic customer preferences. However, if this preference is a long-standing one, it is likely that domestic products did not contain these hormones to begin with, meaning that the ban will primarily affect imported products.

One of the cornerstones of the EU is the free movement of goods within its internal market. Product requirements related to environmental standards can restrict this free movement and therefore have a negative effect on the integration of the internal market. In this type of situation, the harmonization of national environmental laws through European legislation is common. For example, regulations on vehicle emissions set a uniform standard for vehicles produced in all Member States and create a level playing field while protecting environmental goals; these regulations serve an environmental as well as economic purpose. The harmonization of environmentally related product requirements reduces regulatory diversity within the EU. Because the EU's environmental protection standards tend to be high, this is often a net positive for the environment.

One long-standing and controversial question is how much space Member States (should) have to adopt more protective environmental regulation once the EU has regulated on a specific topic by means of a directive. In principle, a Member State would be allowed to adopt more stringent protection measures (see Article 193 TFEU), but it would have to provide new scientific evidence or show conditions specific to its national environment that necessitate this change from EU standards (Article 114(4) and (5) TFEU).

The aforementioned developments led to the inclusion of an environmental competence in the European treaties when the Single European Act was adopted in 1987. Today, the Treaty on European Union refers explicitly to the EU's competence in creating a "high level of protection and improvement of the quality of the environment."[4] This aim is detailed further in Articles 191–194 of the Treaty on the Functioning of the European Union (TFEU), which set out the scope of the EU's environmental competence. These Articles detail the objectives of EU environmental policy,[5] the principles that should be observed when the EU engages in environmental policy making,[6] the EU's duty to foster multilateral cooperation with non-EU countries and international organizations,[7] and the legal procedures that should be used to make environmental laws.[8]

Importantly, in addition to these specific environmental objectives, the EU has adopted the integration principle, an overarching principle that dictates that environmental protection must be integrated into the definition and implementation of all EU policies and activities.[9] The significance and scope of this commitment helps illustrate how the environment has gone from a collateral aim related to economic integration to a leading objective for all EU activities.

THREE DISTINCTIVE FEATURES OF EU ENVIRONMENTAL LAW

This section describes three distinctive features of EU environmental law: multilevel governance, technocracy, and risk analysis. These features give EU environmental law its unique flavor and present one of many potential formulas for managing the puzzling question of how humans should shape the world in which they live.

Multilevel Governance

Environmental consequences are often geographically and temporally distant from the human actions that caused those consequences.

Environmental impacts can also manifest differently depending on their location, often making it difficult and undesirable to impose a "one size fits all" solution. This is particularly true in a jurisdiction as vast and diverse as the EU. Multilevel governance, a core feature of the European legal system, accommodates some of the challenges caused by the geographic dispersal of environmental impacts.

The functioning of the EU as a system of multilevel governance is reflected in the division of labor regarding the legislation, implementation, and enforcement of laws between actors operating on different levels of governance. These levels tend to be divided through geographical jurisdictions. For example, Member States are empowered to act within their territory, while the EU can adopt measures that span the territory of all Member States. The division of power between these actors is complex and is partly based on the allocation of competence between the EU and its Member States. For environmental policy (a shared competence), two principles are particularly important: subsidiarity and proportionality. The principle of subsidiarity states that the EU should act only when (1) goals cannot be sufficiently achieved by the Member States and (2) when the EU would be more effective than Member States, while the principle of proportionality states that the EU should take only those actions necessary to achieve the goals of the treaties.[10]

As noted in chapter 2, it has proven easy to fulfill the principle of subsidiarity for most environmental issues. This can be traced back directly to the geographic diffusion of environmental impacts: as soon as an environmental impact can be felt in more than one Member State—or is caused by one Member State but materializes in another—the regulation of this environmental impact is considered better achieved at the EU level. A different way of looking at this is to say that EU regulation of environmental impacts is aimed at overcoming the problem of externalities that Member States may impose on each other. Because the EU can regulate the environment in the entire

EU territory, it cannot externalize environmental effects on others (or, at least, on others within the EU). In order to deal with geographic diffusion beyond EU borders, the EU has espoused a strong commitment to multilateralism with non-EU countries and international organizations.

Directives are an important expression of the multilevel nature of the EU legal system and a crucial means to accommodate geographic diffusion of environmental impacts. By leaving the implementation of directives in the hands of Member States, the use of directives allows for the achievement of the same environmental standards throughout the EU, while accommodating the significant variation of environmental conditions in the Member States. The so-called Bathing Water Directive is a good example of this.[11] It sets minimum standards for water quality in bathing spots throughout the EU by reference to the detectible levels of two types of bacteria. Member States are also tasked with informing the public about water quality and beach management. These standards apply to all Member States equally but require very different implementation measures in Italy, which has a vast number of coastal beaches, and Austria, where all bathing happens in inland lakes.[12]

Additional benefits of the use of directives are that they allow for experimentation and a degree of regulatory competition between the Member States. At the same time, because directives provide a minimum standard that must be attained regardless of the method of implementation, the risk of a race to the bottom is much reduced. Instead, races to the "top" are more common, as Member States compete for the most efficient and effective environmental regulation through national implementation. The potential drawback of giving Member States broad discretion in the implementation of EU environmental laws is that some Member States may fail to adequately implement the relevant directives. In this regard, the supranational nature of European law is very important because it allows for the enforcement of EU law in ways that would not be possible if EU law were more akin to international law.[13]

Technocracy

The diffuse and complex nature of environmental impacts can be particularly challenging for democratic legislatures, because environmental issues may be more complex than voters can easily understand, and the timelines needed to assess and regulate environmental impacts often do not align with the timelines of elections. This can lead to environmental commitments being abandoned, or not adopted in the first place, due to the limited political gain for elected officials in addressing long-term environmental issues. The EU's institutional makeup is relatively successful in dealing with this problem, although arguably this comes at the expense of other democratic values. In contrast to most national environmental law, EU environmental law is almost entirely incremental and unidirectional, leading to ever-greater environmental protection. This can partially be explained by the leading role of the European Commission in EU environmental policymaking.

The Commission and its technocratic staff are responsible for the drafting of EU secondary law and for ensuring that Member States fulfill their obligations to implement and enforce these laws. The Commission is made up entirely of career bureaucrats with high levels of policy-specific expertise and without political affiliations. Over the years, the Commission has built up a vast amount of expertise in environmental matters and is relatively insulated from political change, both in the EU and in the Member States. This is not to say that politics does not play a role in the EU's environmental policies. The Commission can only propose draft legislation, which then has to be approved by the Council of Ministers and the Parliament, both of which are political bodies. Furthermore, with the expansion of the EU, the interests of the Member States have become increasingly diverse, making it more challenging to reach political agreement on most issues, including the environment. Nevertheless, the pivotal role of the Commission in creating legislation ensures continuity of institutional knowledge regarding environmental issues and allows for the development of longer-term environmental agendas, such as the EAPs. The institutional buildup of the EU is therefore central in its ability to deal with the temporal diffusion of environmental impacts.

Importantly, each of these approaches plays out against a backdrop of key theoretical principles and concepts, which have been central to the development and application of EU environmental law. Many of these principles were initially developed, and continue to be developed, by the CJEU. Most have now been codified in the EU treaties, including the precautionary principle, the principle of preventive action, the "rectification at source" principle, the "polluter pays" principle, and the integration principle.[14] The precautionary principle has proven particularly important in how the EU views the acceptability of environmental risks under conditions of uncertainty, as will be highlighted in the next section.

Risk Analysis

Environmental consequences tend to be obscure, technical, and interactive. Many small, individual actions may combine in complicated ways to create a single impact; a single action may have multiple impacts; and the type(s) of those impacts may be difficult to measure, understand, and solve. In addition, full information regarding these processes may not be available, and, when it is, regulation can be fiendishly difficult.

Risk analysis is the key building block for managing the complexity of environmental impacts within EU environmental law. Risk analysis is a systemized method for identifying, assessing, quantifying, and evaluating risks. The European Commission is tasked with risk analysis as part of its decision-making and legislative drafting process and has adopted a three-stage process for risk analysis consisting of (1) risk assessment, (2) risk management, and (3) risk communication.[15]

Risk assessment involves assessing and quantifying the probabilities and magnitudes of hazards associated with particular behaviors and policies. Risk management, by contrast, involves policy-based decisions about which and how risks will be reduced or tolerated. Finally, risk communication is aimed at providing the public and other EU and Member State institutions with information about risks and their management. The processes of risk assessment and management, as well as their final outcomes, are subject to scrutiny by individuals and governmental actors, which makes this a crucial part of the EU's risk analysis process.

Risk analysis explicitly links scientific research and environmental policy. The systemization of this relationship tends to increase the transparency of environmental decision making, rendering it more susceptible to review by courts and the public. The Commission has developed detailed guidelines on risk analysis in its "Communication on the Precautionary Principle."[16] This communication underlines that judging the "acceptable level of risk for society is an eminently political responsibility."[17] In reaching these political decisions, the leading goal is that of scientific rigor: risk assessment procedures should be based on objective scientific information.

The formalist separation between science and policy on which risk analysis is based is sometimes hard to maintain, and some critics believe that continued attempts to segregate scientific and political processes obscure areas of politicized science.[18] Furthermore, while risk analysis is aimed at addressing the complexity of environmental impacts, unquantifiable or uncertain risks also pose particular challenges for the use of risk analysis in contexts like climate change or the development of new chemical substances. The EU fills this gap by recourse to the precautionary principle, which is understood to guide policy decisions in situations of scientific uncertainty where there are "reasonable grounds for concern that the potentially dangerous effects on the environment, human, animal or plant health may be inconsistent with the high level of protection chosen by the [EU]."[19] However, when the limits of scientific inquiry are met and/or when scientific evaluation does not give a conclusive answer regarding the preferable level of protection, the precautionary principle

SPOTLIGHT 5. IMPACT ASSESSMENTS

Environmental law must create a nexus between human behavior and the nonhuman environment, both to understand the impact of current human behaviors and to shape those behaviors in directions that reflect a preferred relationship with the nonhuman environment.

The EU responds to the challenges inherent in managing nonhuman impacts through the requirement that every regulatory initiative that is expected to have significant economic, social, or environmental impacts must be preceded by an impact assessment. The goal of an impact assessment is not exclusively environmental but does require the discussion of any environmental impacts. Impact assessments are undertaken by the European Commission, which is obliged to publish them together with the relevant proposal for the scrutiny of the Council of Ministers, the European Parliament, and any other affected parties.

Other jurisdictions—most notably the United States—combine requirements for impact analyses with quantitative cost-benefit analysis, used to establish monetary values for nonhuman and nonmarket impacts. In the EU, impact assessments are also meant to incorporate quantitative estimates where possible. However, this is not an absolute requirement: qualitative methods are also acceptable, as long as a clear methodology is adopted. Crucially, an impact assessment does not need to identify a preferred policy option; the comparison of options against common criteria is the key goal of the impact assessment. Much-used criteria include effectiveness, efficiency, and coherence with the overarching objectives of the EU (which include environmental objectives). The results of risk analysis also feature prominently in impact assessments.

Two strengths of impact assessments are that they allow for the inclusion of a broad range of considerations and require a high level of transparency in terms of the methods and data used. Moreover,

> they offer flexibility in allowing for different methods and different classifications of costs and benefits depending on the problem at hand. This can be particularly helpful for environmental problems. However, the lack of a unifying method can also reduce the comparability of assessments.

should be applied at the risk management stage. As a result, the precautionary principle can affect both the decision of whether to act with respect to risks and, if acting, which measures to take.

SUMMARY

This chapter has set out three key features of the European legal system that affect the EU's response to the challenges created by environmental impacts: multilevel governance, the role of technocracy, and the role of risk analysis. In order to contextualize these features, the chapter included a short introduction to the history of European environmental regulation.

TAKEAWAYS

✓ EU environmental law has developed rapidly and grown exponentially since the 1970s and is currently one of the richest areas of EU law.

✓ The EU's approach to environmental law relies on multilevel governance, technocracy, and risk analysis.

KEY TERMS

COMPLEX IMPACTS Environmental impacts that are obscure, technical, and/or interactive. These can be difficult to measure, understand, and regulate.

COST-BENEFIT ANALYSIS A decision procedure for quantifying (and typically monetizing) the expected positive and negative impacts of a proposed policy.

DIFFUSE IMPACTS Environmental impacts that are geographically and/or spatially distant from the human actions that caused them.

DISCOUNTING The process of making future (monetary) amounts comparable to current amounts.

ENVIRONMENT The surroundings or conditions in which humans, plants, and animals function.

ENVIRONMENTAL IMPACTS Consequences (generally of human actions) for the surroundings or conditions in which humans, plants, and animals function.

ENVIRONMENTAL JUSTICE Concerns about the fair distribution of environmental impacts.

ENVIRONMENTAL LAW The use of law to regulate human behaviors with environmental impacts.

EXTERNALITIES Costs and benefits related to an activity that are experienced by someone other than the person engaged in the activity.

MULTILEVEL GOVERNANCE A regulatory system in which several levels of authority compete and coordinate with each other.

NONHUMAN IMPACTS Environmental impacts that relate primarily or exclusively to nonhuman animals, plants, and processes.

PRECAUTIONARY PRINCIPLE An EU principle related to risk management, which provides that if there is the possibility that a given policy or action might harm the public or the environment, and there is an absence of scientific consensus, the action should not be pursued.

"RECTIFICATION AT SOURCE" PRINCIPLE The idea that pollution is best addressed at the source rather than at the site of pollution (if geographically and/or temporally distinct).

RISK ANALYSIS A systemized method for identifying, assessing, quantifying, and evaluating risks.

RISK ASSESSMENT The scientific and technical first "stage" of risk analysis where the probabilities and magnitudes of hazards associated with particular behaviors and policies are identified and quantified.

RISK COMMUNICATION The communication of risk with the goal of enabling people to make informed decisions and exchange information on risk.

RISK MANAGEMENT The second "stage" of risk analysis, in which policy-based decisions are made about which and how risks will be reduced or tolerated.

STRATEGIC IMPACT ASSESSMENT A type of environmental impact assessment that applies to plans and programs proposed by state actors.

TECHNOCRACY A bureaucracy that is run by technologists and/or is heavily reliant on technical expertise.

DISCUSSION QUESTIONS

1. What do you think is the most challenging feature of environmental impacts for the law: diffusion, complexity, or nonhuman character? Why?

2. How should society balance the values of democratic government and the importance of informing environmental policy with high-quality information and science? Is it more important for environmental law to reflect the best science, and the judgment of experts, or to reflect the values of the human population who must live under the environmental laws?

3. Is it appropriate to "monetize" environmental quality? Why or why not? If environmental quality is not monetized, what is the best way to decide how much money should be spent on environmental quality? What should we do if people attach different monetary values to environmental quality?

4. Which EU legal strategies in environmental law could be used by other jurisdictions? Which would be difficult to imitate? Why?

NOTES

1. Council Directive of 27 June 1967 on the approximation of laws, regulations and administrative provisions relating to the classification, packaging and labelling of dangerous substances, OJ 196, 16.8.1967, at 1.

2. See, e.g., Case 240/83 *Association de défense des brûleurs d'huiles usages* (ADBHU) [1985] ECR 531.

3. Declaration of the Council of the European Communities and of the representatives of the Governments of the Member States meeting in the Council of 22 November 1973 on the programme of action of the European Communities on the environment, OJ C112/1 from 20.12.1973.

4. Article 3(3) Treaty on European Union.

5. Article 191(1) Treaty on the Functioning of the European Union (TFEU).

6. Article 191(2) TFEU.

7. Article 191(4) TFEU.

8. Article 192 TFEU. These processes are discussed in detail in chapter 3.

9. Article 11 TFEU.

10. See chapter 2 for more detail.

11. Directive 2006/7/EC of the European Parliament and of the Council of 15 February 2006 concerning the management of bathing water quality and repealing Directive 76/160/EEC, OJ L 64/37.

12. For a detailed map of bathing water quality, visit www.eea.europa.eu /themes/water/interactive/bathing/state-of-bathing-waters.

13. On specific types of enforcement actions, see "Enforcement of EU Law" in chapter 2.

14. All principles can be traced back to Article 191(2) TFEU, except for the integration principle, which is defined in Article 11 TFEU.

15. This is in line with the EU's commitment to "better regulation"; see https://ec.europa.eu/info/law/law-making-process/better-regulation-why-and-how_en.

16. European Commission, "Communication on the Precautionary Principle" COM (2000) 1 final.

17. Ibid., at 3.

18. A significant literature has grown up around Alvin Weinberg's idea that some risk issues are "trans-scientific," in that they can be posed to science but not resolved by science alone. See Alvin Weinberg, "Science and Trans-Science" (1972) 10 *Minerva* 209. See also Wendy Wagner, "The Science Charade in Toxic Risk Regulation" (1995) 95 *Columbia Law Review* 1613, arguing that trans-scientific issues can be exploited for political purposes.

19. COM (2000) 1 final, at 2.

CHAPTER SIX

Pollution Control

This chapter provides a primer on the EU's legal approach to pollution control. It begins by defining the general problem of pollution. It then describes the fundamentals of the EU approach to controlling pollution, before providing snapshots of individual legal strategies used for particular types of pollution: air pollution, water pollution, soil pollution, chemicals and dangerous substances, and waste.

POLLUTION AS AN ENVIRONMENTAL PROBLEM

Pollution is the presence of higher-than-normal concentrations of unwanted materials in the air, water, or soil that may have adverse effects on humans or on nonhuman organisms.

Pollution control laws aim to (1) control human activities that lead to pollution and (2) limit the harms caused by human and nonhuman pollution. These goals are often pursued through two general strategies: *source reduction* and *exposure reduction*. Source reduction involves reducing the amount of pollution created in the first place (at the "source")—for example, by requiring industry to adopt technologies that generate less waste or by encouraging consumers to recycle. Exposure reduction involves amending behaviors so that there is less exposure to pollution—for example, by encouraging people to evacuate after a toxic waste spill or by identifying products that contain dangerous substances.

Pollution can occur through depositing of unwanted materials in the air, water, and soil. Some of these materials, such as toxic substances, are purposefully created because they offer benefits as well as potential dangers. Other substances, such as hazardous materials, are waste byproducts of daily life or of industrial processes without intrinsic value. Each type of pollution—air pollution, water pollution, soil pollution, toxic substances, and waste—presents its own challenges and opportunities for regulation, often related to the specific characteristics of the medium of pollution. Air pollution, for example, tends to be far more mobile— and thus far more likely to create diffuse and distant impacts—than soil pollution, the impact of which tends to be relatively local.

Although each medium of pollution has its own characteristics, pollution control regimes also face common challenges, which can be traced back to the diffuse, complex, and nonhuman nature of environmental impacts. In particular, polluting activity is often distant in space and time from the pollution exposures that cause harm. Tracing the causal relationships between pollution exposure and harm is therefore often difficult. Furthermore, the same pollutant can create different impacts depending on its concentration, the form of exposure, and even its location. Scientists attempt to track the relationship between amount of pollution exposure (the "dose") and the harm (the "response") it causes through what are called dose-response relationships; understanding such relationships is research intensive, however, and can be highly uncertain, particularly at low levels of exposure. The location of a pollutant can also matter. An interesting example of this is ozone, which poses significant risks to human health when found at the ambient or ground level, but which shields against ultraviolet radiation at the atmospheric level, protecting humans from sunburn and skin cancer. Furthermore, pollution affects nonhuman animals, plants, and ecosystems as well as human populations. At atmospheric levels, for example, ozone protects humans, but it also reduces plankton growth in the oceans, leading to diminished fish stocks and stunted plant growth. The complexity of pollution's impacts thus necessitates a strong connection between pollution control policy and scientific research.

An additional challenging aspect of pollution control comes from the interaction between pollution types and media. To effectively control pollution, policymakers must consider how pollution control regimes interact with one another, as well as with other regulatory and legal requirements. One important aspect of this challenge is cross-media pollution, which arises when pollutants are transferred from one environmental medium (such as air) to another (such as water): waste practices that allow for incineration may affect air pollution, for example, and contaminated water may end up depositing pollution into soil. As a result, policymakers must consider not only the best stringency for particular pollution control regimes, but also how those regimes may impact other polluting behaviors.

Finally, competing normative and political values also create challenges for pollution control, as different people and different institutional actors often differ on how much pollution is tolerable, how clean is clean enough, how to balance nonhuman and human interests, and whether the distribution of harms (and profit) from pollution is fair.

KEY CHARACTERISTICS OF POLLUTION CONTROL IN THE EU

The cost of pollution to the EU is enormous. For example, between 2008 and 2012, air pollution from industrial facilities alone was estimated to have created harm costing 329 billion to 1,053 billion euros; by comparison, the entire EU budget for 2014 was 143 billion euros.[1]

The geography of the EU is such that the impacts of most types of pollution are transboundary: the main waterways of Europe run through multiple Member States, and air pollution is a quintessentially transboundary problem, because of the high mobility of airborne pollutants. As a consequence, the case for EU action on the basis of subsidiarity has been relatively straightforward. In addition, pollution control affects economic activities, drawing in the EU via its regulation of the internal market. Despite these clear justifications for its involvement, however, the EU's role in pollution control has developed unevenly—both chronologically and in terms of intensity—across pollution media.

Somewhat surprisingly, given its transboundary nature, air pollution was not the first type of pollution addressed by the EU. Instead, water and waste pollution were featured in the first Environmental Action Programme in 1973; air pollution was added in 1980. There are different theories regarding this sequencing, some related to the nature and saliency of water and waste pollution as compared to air pollution—the latter often being less visible and more a matter of scientific fact than of personal experience—and others to the related assumption that Member States were fairly successful in controlling air pollution as compared to other forms of pollution.[2]

While the EU now plays a central role in the regulation of air pollution, water pollution, and waste, its role in the regulation of soil pollution and chemical substances remains more limited. For soil pollution, this may be explained by the static and local nature of soil, which provides limited subsidiarity justification for EU involvement. EU involvement with the regulation of chemicals and dangerous substances is more complex: while chemical regulation has been extensive and long-standing—tracing back as far as 1967—the regulatory regimes are primarily linked to the internal market and trade, rather than explicitly focusing on these substances' environmental impacts.[3] At the same time, the way chemicals are regulated is based almost entirely on their potential effects on human and environmental health.

The varied nature of polluting activities, polluting actors, and pollution's impacts is reflected in the wide range of regulatory instruments employed by the EU's pollution control legislation. Traditional command-and-control regulation—through standard setting and permitting—is widespread in all areas of pollution control. At the same time, EU pollution regulation has pioneered some innovative regulatory approaches, such as a collaborative approach between the EU, the Member States, and non-state actors, including industry and environmental NGOs, in setting standards.[4] The EU has also pushed for a streamlined cross-media approach for pollution caused by large industrial installations: these installations should be able to apply for a single permit that covers all their polluting activities, combining requirements on air, water, and waste.[5] Though not always entirely successful, these approaches reflect the EU's legal commitment to integration of environmental objectives into all of the more specific pollution control regulations and directives.

The EU has a vast legislative framework on pollution control. Most pollution regulations and directives are highly technical and require extensive and costly implementation measures from the Member States. Generally, Member States have significant discretion in how they structure the implementation of EU policies. This distribution of authority allows Member States to implement pollution control regimes in light of variation in local conditions. The frequent use of directives in environmental law reflects the pragmatic need to interface with "on-the-ground" environmental conditions and the legal prerequisite for the EU to act "proportionally" (that is, to not adopt more prescriptive laws than are required).[6] At the same time, the discretion that Member States have in implementation also leads to frequent compliance gaps, which arise where Member States faultily implement the relevant directives, fail to enforce them on private actors under their control, or fail entirely to comply.[7]

TREATY ON THE FUNCTIONING OF THE EUROPEAN UNION,
ARTICLE 11: THE INTEGRATION PRINCIPLE

"Environmental protection requirements must be integrated into the definition and implementation of the Union policies and activities, in particular with a view to promoting sustainable development."

The effectiveness of EU environmental law is generally dependent on enforcement. In the EU, public enforcement of environmental law takes place at two levels. First, the European Commission ensures that Member States implement EU environmental law, and that they put in place relevant processes and institutions to secure compliance of private actors affected by the national laws that implement EU environmental law. Second, the Member States themselves tend to be in control of directly enforcing the compliance of private actors at the national level[8]—though their enforcement is subject to the compliance gaps mentioned above.

Although Member States' noncompliance with EU pollution control requirements remains relatively common, enforcement actions by the Commission to force Member States' compliance are relatively rare. This can be partially explained by capacity constraints within the Commission. It also suggests that public enforcement actions may not be considered the most effective way of ensuring compliance by the Member States in these areas, and that the Commission frequently opts for alternative ways to ensure compliance, such as technical support in implementation.

The relative dearth of public enforcement actions in pollution control increases the importance of the potential role of private enforcement. EU law empowers private actors to bring lawsuits against Member States for faulty or lacking implementation *and* against other private parties. The former is referred to as vertical private enforcement (against Member States) and the latter as horizontal private enforcement (against other private actors).

A final feature of EU pollution control regulation is its relationship to, and often basis in, international law. In relation to transboundary pollution, many international and bilateral treaties already existed between Member States before the creation of the EU. Some EU legislation, especially in the area of water and air pollution, explicitly builds on these preexisting bilateral and multilateral agreements between Member States. Other EU legislation implements international treaties with non-EU countries to which the Member States and/or the EU are a party.

DISCUSSION QUESTIONS

1. Should pollution control be in the hands of one actor? Who is better placed to set pollution standards: the EU or the Member States? Does the answer to this question vary by the type of pollution?

2. Should individuals or other non-governmental actors have more say in pollution standards? If so, how? Should their influence be direct (for example, through participation in standard setting) or indirect (through voting and/or market power)?

LEGAL SNAPSHOTS:
POLLUTION CONTROL IN THE EU

The next sections provide a series of "snapshots" explaining how the EU regulates five types of pollution: air pollution, water pollution, soil pollution, chemical substances, and waste.

Other types of pollution exist, including light pollution, noise pollution, and aesthetic pollution. The latter are highly local in impact, and while they may be indirectly subject to EU regulation—for instance, through their inclusion in impact assessments for large infrastructure projects, as prescribed by EU law—their regulation tends to be in the hands of national, if not local, governments. They will be mentioned when relevant to the other (transboundary) types of pollution discussed in our snapshots.

AIR POLLUTION
DEFINITION

Air pollution is the contamination of air by materials or substances that are present at higher-than-normal concentrations, which may have adverse effects on humans or on nonhuman organisms.[9]

DISTINCTIVE CHALLENGES OF REGULATING
AIR POLLUTION

One of the primary challenges of air pollution comes from its high stakes: it is by far the deadliest type of pollution in the EU, as it is in most of the world. Studies suggest that air pollution is responsible for approximately six hundred thousand premature deaths per year in Europe.[10] Pollution levels and types vary significantly across the EU. Generally speaking, air pollution is worst in areas that are heavily populated and/or where industry is concentrated, and in Member States that industrialized later and are still adopting cleaner technologies. Particularly in urban areas, traffic is one of the main causes, responsible for up to 75 percent of air pollution in some areas. Geographic features can also affect air quality. For example, cities surrounded by mountains may experience higher levels of air pollution even when air pollution controls are stringent, simply because pollution that is emitted may be "trapped" over the city.

Air pollution is typically characterized by high mobility—many forms of air pollution drift with the wind—and by difficulties in detection, given that most air pollutants are not detectable to an untrained observer. As a result, the behaviors that cause air pollution may not be easily connected to their consequences and therefore may be (politically) harder to regulate. They can also be harder to control by individuals, who must rely primarily on government action to regulate air quality.

Different air pollutants can have a wide range of effects on the human and nonhuman environment, and these effects may demand different regulatory responses. In the case of some pollutants, only prolonged exposure at high levels has a noticeable effect. Other pollutants create immediate and highly harmful consequences, which may require a more immediate regulatory response. Furthermore, while some pollutants (called "primary pollutants" in the EU) are emitted directly into the atmosphere, other pollutants ("secondary pollutants" in the EU) are formed in the atmosphere through reactions between precursor pollutants. This means that even if a substance is not harmful on its own, its reaction with another (possibly naturally occurring) substance can create harmful effects.

Finally, regulatory challenges often vary with the source of the pollution. Some air pollution sources, like power plants or chemical plants, are stationary and concentrated. Regulating these sources often requires management of significant quantities of pollutants and may also implicate the challenging informational burdens of attempting to regulate mixtures. On the bright side, the stationary nature of such sources means that polluting behaviors are relatively easy to identify, regulate, and measure. Nonstationary sources, like cars or lawnmowers, may lead to greater diffusion of pollution. Finally, highly hazardous air pollutants, which can be expected to cause cancer, birth defects, or even sudden death, implicate many of the same challenges as general regulation of chemical substances.[11]

KEY EU LEGAL APPROACHES TO AIR POLLUTION

This snapshot discusses the key directives and regulations that form the backbone of the EU's legal approaches to air pollution. EU air pollution control spans numerous activities across various sectors, some of which are touched on only briefly in this overview. The online air pollution resources provided by the Commission offer accessible and comprehensive coverage of particular control measures.[12]

Legislative Strategy

There are three main pillars to the EU's clean air strategy:[13]

1. *Ambient air quality standards.* These have been set for ground-level ozone, particulate matter, nitrogen oxides, dangerous heavy metals, and a number of other pollutants.

2. *National emission ceilings.* These have been established for the most important transboundary air pollutants: sulfur oxides, nitrogen oxides, ammonia, volatile organic compounds, and particulate matter.

3. *Emission standards for key sources of pollution.* These include mobile sources such as vehicle and ship emissions, as well as stationary sources related to energy and industry.

This snapshot will discuss three fundamental EU legislative instruments related to these goals: the Air Quality Framework Directive, the National Emission Ceilings Directive, and the Industrial Emissions Directive.[14] All three instruments address a range of pollutants (see spotlight 6), and all three tend to have some relationship to international treaties on air pollution to which the EU and its Member States are a party. There are also important differences between the three directives and regulations: they regulate different sources and activities, and they use different types of regulatory standards in their regulation of behavior.

While EU legislation on air pollution is quite comprehensive, the implementation of air pollution control regimes is left almost entirely to the Member States. In addition to bringing occasional enforcement actions against noncompliant Member States, the EU also exercises "soft power" by providing substantial financial support to Member States' air pollution control programs (1.8 billion euros between 2014 and 2020).

One key regulatory instrument for emissions is excluded here, namely the EU Emissions Trading Scheme, which regulates most of the EU's greenhouse gas emissions (as discussed in detail in chapter 8, in light of the link between greenhouse gas emissions and climate change).

Air Quality Framework Directive

The 2008 Air Quality Framework Directive (AQFD)[15] sets air quality standards regarding several key pollutants: sulfur dioxide, nitrogen dioxide, other nitrogen oxides, particulate matter, benzene, carbon monoxide, and ozone. It does so through quality standard setting. This approach is meant to respect the key EU principles of subsidiarity and proportionality by regulating only the absolute essentials at the EU level, leaving the Member States ample discretion in how the environmental aims are achieved.

Under the AQFD, the first step is for Member States to establish zones where air quality assessment takes place. Allowing Member States to define these distinct zones means that maximum consideration can be given to the fact that different areas have different air pollution challenges, in terms of both type and degree of pollution.[16] This also allows for the development of regulatory strategies that take local conditions into account and that may therefore be more effective.

In each of the designated air zones, baseline measurements are taken to establish the levels of targeted air pollution that exist prior to regula-

SPOTLIGHT 6. KEY AIR POLLUTANTS
REGULATED UNDER EU LAW

In the European Union, the most harmful pollutants to human health are particulate matter (PM), nitrogen dioxide (NO_2), and ground-level ozone (O_3). The most harmful air pollutants for ecosystems are ozone (O_3), ammonia (NH_3), and nitrogen oxides (NO_x). EU legislation also covers sulfur dioxide (SO_2), carbon monoxide (CO), benzene (C_6H_6), and toxic metals such as arsenic (As), cadmium (Cd), lead (Pb), and nickel (Ni). The occurrence of the latter category of pollutants in the air is relatively low in the EU, but their presence can contribute to the deposition of toxic metals in soils, sediments, and organisms.

PARTICULATE MATTER

PM includes all solid or liquid particulates emitted into the air by virtually any activity that burns materials or generates dust. This includes natural sources such as volcanoes or water mist. Within the EU, long-term exposure to PM leads to 391,000 premature deaths a year. PM is classified as either PM_{10} ($\leq$10 micrometers in diameter) or $PM_{2.5}$ ($\leq$2.5 micrometers in diameter).

NITROGEN DIOXIDE

Emission of NO_2 by vehicle exhausts and industrial boilers (or other processes that burn fuel at high temperatures) can lead to the creation of atmospheric ozone, thereby contributing to effects such as acid rain and eutrophication of coastal waters. Within the EU, exposure to NO_2 leads to 76,000 premature deaths a year.

GROUND-LEVEL OZONE

Ground-level ozone is emitted mainly by industrial and energy facilities, vehicle exhausts, gasoline vapor, and chemical solvents. Exposure causes health problems such as asthma and leads to the eutrophication and acidification of ecosystems. Within the EU, exposure to O_3 leads to 16,400 premature deaths a year.

tory intervention. For each pollutant, the AQFD identifies a *lower assessment threshold* and an *upper assessment threshold*. Depending on whether baseline measurements fall above, below, or between these two thresholds, Member States are obliged to take more or fewer ongoing measurements in a particular assessment zone.[17] In brief, the higher the initial assessment, the more prescriptive and detailed ongoing assessment is required (for details, see figure 4).

The actual air quality of a specific zone is regulated through the AQFD benchmarks (table 5), which, confusingly, can also be referred to as "thresholds," as well as "values" and "levels." While all the benchmarks shown in table 5 are important, the consequences of breaching limit and target values are most acute: Member States must establish an air quality plan for the relevant zone (Article 23 AQFD). The Directive does not impose any requirements on the substance of such a plan, apart from setting a minimum data requirement.[18] If a Member State is in danger of exceeding the alert threshold for nitrogen dioxide, benzene, and PM10, the requirements on the required short-term air quality plan are slightly more prescriptive (see table 5).[19]

This structure is generally understood to afford very large discretion to Member States in dealing with air pollution. But that discretion, while

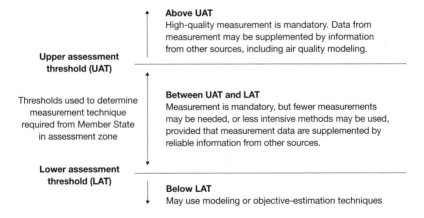

Figure 4. AQFD Assessment Thresholds.

TABLE 5

AQFD Quality Thresholds, Levels, and Values

Benchmark	Use	Consequence	Source
Critical level	Pollution level that presents risks to some environmental receptors, but not to humans	Pollution should stay below this level but no particular action is required by member state	Article 2 and Article 14 AQFD
Alert threshold	Pollution level that presents a risk to human health or environment, even if brief exposure	Public information duty and possible adoption of short-term air quality plan by member state	Article 2, Article 18 and Article 24 AQFD
Limit value	Maximum value for a given pollutant	Member State must establish air quality plan	Article 23 AQFD
Target value	Like limit value but scientific uncertainty or political disagreement prevents setting of limit value	Member State must establish air quality plan	Article 23 AQFD

wide, is not open-ended. The Court of Justice has read limits to this discretion into the Directive, and has reviewed adopted measures for "effectiveness" and "adequacy."[20] As a result, while Member States may structure air quality plans in many different ways, the resulting plan must satisfy judicially enforced standards of effectiveness and adequacy.

Despite the support the CJEU has provided to EU-level enforcement of the AQFD, enforcement actions of the Commission continue to lag behind the observed cases of AQFD infringement by Member States. Private enforcement has proven particularly important in this area. The CJEU has interpreted both the AQFD and the National Emission Ceilings Directive (see below) as being capable of having direct effect, which means that private actors can bring claims based on the provisions of these directives. Specifically, this means that private citizens can force Member States to act on their obligations to draw up air quality plans.

National Emission Ceilings Directive

The National Emission Ceilings Directive (NECD) is another legislative means through which the EU addresses five of the most important air pollutants: nitrogen oxides, non-methane volatile organic compounds, sulfur dioxide, ammonia, and fine particulate matter.[21] National emission ceilings are standards that apply to pollutants that create harmful environmental impacts such as acidification, eutrophication, and ground-level ozone pollution.

The first NECD was adopted in 2001, as a means to implement the 1999 Gothenburg Protocol[22] to the Convention on Long-Range Transboundary Air Pollution,[23] to which both the EU and its Member States are signatories. Although the NECD was intended in part to satisfy international legal obligations, the national emission ceilings set by the NECD were more ambitious than those set by the Gothenburg Protocol and the Montreal Protocol (see spotlight 7). In addition, the NECD requires Member States to prepare annual emission inventories and projections.[24] Importantly, and comparably to the AQFD, the NECD did not prescribe the methods through which Member States would have to achieve their emission standards.[25]

A revised NECD was adopted in 2016, with even more stringent national emission ceilings established for 2030, at levels in line with international recommendations from the World Health Organization.[26] The approach of the 2016 NECD is much the same as its predecessor in terms of the balance between EU emission standards and Member State discretion as to how to achieve these standards. Member States also continue to have to report their emissions,[27] including a broader range of pollutants than those affected by the national emission ceilings.[28] This means that the reporting obligations overlap with, and are supportive to, those under the AQFD. An important change is the require-

SPOTLIGHT 7. THE OZONE-DEPLETING
SUBSTANCES REGULATION

Ozone-depleting substances are substances that destroy the Earth's protective ozone layer. The EU's approach to these substances is largely driven by international law, and particularly by the 1985 Vienna Convention for the Protection of the Ozone Layer and the 1987 Montreal Protocol on Substances That Deplete the Ozone Layer. Since the 1990s, the EU has adopted a number of regulations that implement the Vienna and Montreal goals. The current version of the Ozone-Depleting Substances Regulation (Regulation 1005/2009 on substances that deplete the ozone layer) includes a detailed list of substances that are to be phased out and eventually banned. This means that by 2020, the only ozone-depleting substances that will be allowed on the EU market are those that are used as feedstock, those present in installations created before 1997, those used in lab research or as part of controlled destruction, and those that are inevitable byproducts of certain industrial processes.

The Montreal Protocol is widely considered one of the most successful environmental treaties of all time, with universal ratification and a very high compliance rate. The success of the Montreal Protocol has led to extensive scholarly research into the factors that created this atypically effective instrument of international law. Many consider the flexibility of the protocol and US support for it as key factors. The fact that it was possible to create affordable alternatives to ozone-depleting substances is also thought to have played a large role in its success. The EU's regulation of ozone-depleting substances has been similarly successful, no doubt aided by the strong preexisting international regime.

ment on Member States to create "national air pollution control pro-grammes" by April 1, 2019. The latter, which must detail how compliance with the 2020 and 2030 emission standards will be achieved, will be evaluated by the Commission and made available to the public.

Based on the reported and projected emissions as supplied by Member States in 2017 and 2018,[29] twenty Member States do not consider themselves on track to meeting their 2020 reduction commitments for one or several pollutants. Moreover, all Member States will fail to meet one or more of their 2030 commitments.

Industrial Emissions Directive

The AQFD and the NECD adopt a cross-sectoral approach, focusing on the effect of polluting activities rather than regulating specific actors, actions, or industries. By contrast, the Industrial Emissions Directive (IED) targets distinct actors: heavy industrial polluters.[30]

The IED requires that authorities based in Member States ensure that any regulated facilities respect the environmental standards and prescriptions of the Directive, and that all their activities related to air and water pollution, soil treatment, and waste generation are regulated by a single permit,[31] typically referred to as *integrated pollution prevention and control* (IPPC) permits. So, while the IED is discussed here as a mechanism for air pollution control, its approach in fact covers several media, including water and soil.

This integrated approach—initially developed in Directive 2008/1/EC, concerning IPPC—is often lauded as one of the EU's most inno-vative pollution control instruments. By addressing cross-media pollu-tion, the IED reduces incentives for industry to transform pollution from one medium to another (for example, by incinerating solid waste), because regardless of final medium, the emission must be permitted. The integrated permit process has also proven popular with industry, as it reduces the complexity and cost associated with applying and maintaining multiple permits for multiple forms of pollution.

IPPC permits contain emission limit values, environmental quality standards (which restrict the amounts of pollution that can be measured in air, water, or soil), and, at times, technological and specification standards. The emission limit values are set according to a "best available techniques" (BAT) standard.[32] While every Member State can design its own IPPC process and develop its own permitting institutions, the resulting permit must "achieve a high level [of] protection of the environment taken as a whole,"[33] and the applicant must be able to apply for the permit within a single process, even if several authorities are involved.[34]

The use of "best available technology" standards like BAT is relatively common in environmental law. Determining best available techniques is notoriously difficult, however, as opinions on what is "best" and what is "available" vary, especially depending on how one views the role of costs. Traditionally, account is taken of what technique is economically feasible, or feasible without entailing excessive costs (such as might drive an industry bankrupt).[35] Even this relatively simplified approach, however, requires determination of which techniques are required by the standard.

The EU's method of determining best available techniques is an innovative one, based on an ambitious collaborative process that

---

BEST AVAILABLE TECHNIQUES

The phrase "best available techniques" (BAT) refers to a standard used by policymakers and regulators that requires selection of design, technology, and operating procedures *(techniques)* that are the most effective and up-to-date in terms of preventing or minimizing adverse environmental impacts, that are generally considered accessible and affordable for installations that are representative of the sector *(available)*, and that are capable of delivering a high level of environmental protection *(best)*.

involves experts from Member States, industry, and environmental organizations, coordinated by the European IPPC Bureau at the European Commission's Joint Research Centre in Seville, Spain.[36] This "Seville process" results in "BAT reference documents,"[37] which are consequently adopted by the Commission as implementing decisions. These then form the basis for permit conditions.

There are several strengths to the collaborative Seville process, such as the involvement of various actors. However, there are also important weaknesses: the resulting documents are a mixture of technical and political considerations, which can make it difficult to trace the reasons for any particular BAT designation, and which create special pressures on the accessibility and transparency of the process. To address concerns about environmental interests being protected, the involvement of environmental groups is formally protected by the IED. Yet critics still warn that there are practical reasons—such as language, information, and access to resources—why these groups may be less effective than industry at advocating the techniques they consider the "best." Relatedly, privacy laws restrict information about who is present at meetings, making it harder for citizens to gain insight into—and oversight of—the process. As a result, while the collaborative learning facilitated by the Seville process may generate significant value, and while it provides an innovative approach to addressing the generally challenging question of which industrial techniques are "best," implementation of the approach has proven to be complicated in practice.

TAKEAWAYS

✓ Air pollution poses distinctive regulatory challenges for many reasons, including its high stakes, high mobility, difficulties of detection, and the variety of types and sources of air pollutants. Much of EU air pollution control is directly linked to international treaties on the subject. The presence of these international obligations and regimes typically reinforces EU legislation in this area.

✓ The EU has an extensive air pollution agenda, focused on ambient air quality standards, national emission ceilings, and emission standards for key industrial sources of pollution. Member States have very substantial discretion in implementing most air pollution standards, and Member State compliance continues to be a concern.

✓ The Air Quality Framework Directive (AQFD) regulates key pollutants through quality standards. Member States can determine how to achieve the standards, while the EU sets the acceptable pollution levels and timelines for pollution abatement.

✓ The National Emission Ceilings Directive (NECD) implements the 1999 Gothenburg Protocol to the Convention on Long-Range Transboundary Air Pollution. It sets emission standards for Member States but does not prescribe methods of achieving these standards.

✓ The Industrial Emissions Directive (IED) relies on "best available techniques" (BAT) benchmarks. The process of setting these benchmarks is collaborative and involves public and private actors.

DISCUSSION QUESTIONS

1. How would you determine how much air pollution is safe?
2. What method of standard setting do you think is most effective: the one used by the AQFD, the NECD, or the IED? Or would a different method be better?
3. Do you think more environmental regulation should adopt the collaborative approach for setting best available techniques under the IED? Why (not)?

WATER POLLUTION

DEFINITION

Water pollution is the contamination of water by materials that are out of place or that are present at higher-than-normal concentrations, which may have adverse effects on humans or on nonhuman organisms.

DISTINCTIVE CHALLENGES OF REGULATING WATER POLLUTION

The first key challenge in the management of water pollution is the diversity of uses for water. It is a resource for drinking, for agriculture, and for industry. It is used to cool power plants. It is a habitat and a medium for transport. It can be used for recreation and for exploiting other resources, such as fish. Substances and conditions that constitute pollution for one type of use may be desirable or even a precondition for another.

A second key challenge comes from the wide variety of behaviors that can create water pollution. Some of these behaviors are concentrated (as with industrial emissions from a pipe into a river) and some are quite diffuse (as with littering, applying fertilizer, or washing cars). At the same time, water can become polluted from characteristics or events in the nonhuman environment—for example, contamination from naturally high levels of soil arsenic in central France. This means that regulatory regimes that are intended to address water pollution must find ways to address many types of human behavior, while simultaneously managing complex natural processes.

A third challenge comes from two specific hydrogeological and chemical properties of water. First, water (and therefore the pollution it carries) is at least somewhat mobile. This creates geographic distance, sometimes vast, between the source of water pollution and its impacts. Second, when water is moving, it tends to channel itself into recurring pathways that are generally unidirectional. This means, in many cases, that pollution relationships are similarly unidirectional: upriver actors can pollute the water for downriver actors, but downriver actors have no reciprocal opportunity to pollute. This can create bargaining problems and distributional issues between polluter and pollutee, especially where downriver pollution accumulates from multiple upriver emissions. These challenges are particularly pronounced with respect to the Maas, Rhine, and Schelde River basins, which flow through several Member States, near major population centers, and are used by heavily polluting industries.

Finally, there are distinctive distributional challenges related to pollution of drinking water. Clean drinking water is a fundamental need that is often provided as a public service in developed countries. Most people in the EU have access to good-quality drinking water, though in some Member States the quality of drinking water in rural areas lags behind that in cities. In rural Hungary and Romania, for example, and on the Greek islands, drinking water often fails to meet minimal safety standards. Although high-quality drinking water can also be obtained through private markets, including through filtering and bottling, the costs associated with purchasing water can create distributional and equity concerns. Moreover, bottled water creates a large environmental impact itself. In regions where filtered and bottled water are costly yet necessary, questions of the appropriate quality standards for drinking water and what the conditions for access and use should be are particularly salient.

KEY EU LEGAL APPROACHES TO WATER POLLUTION

Water is the most comprehensively regulated natural resource in EU environmental regulation. Water pollution has been on the EU's environmental agenda since the 1970s, even before the existence of an EU environmental competence. This can be explained by the transboundary nature of many of the EU's water-based resources and by the similar transboundary nature of the pollution affecting them. In fact, for

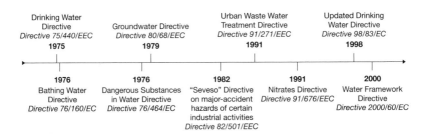

Figure 5. Time Line of EU Water Legislation.

many Member States, recognizing EU authority in water pollution contexts presented a valuable opportunity to simplify the complex network of bilateral and multilateral treaties that traditionally existed for the regulation of this environmentally and economically important resource.

International law continues to be an important influence on EU water law, but the EU has also developed its own approach, which covers small, as well as transboundary, bodies of water while simultaneously relying on "macro-regional strategies"[38] that cover areas across Member States. Another important feature of the EU approach is the way in which it regularly revises and changes its water law, incorporating experiences and scientific information from different sources, including civil society. The 1975 Drinking Water Directive was the first significant piece of EU legislation on water; it has been substantially amended and expanded over the years and incorporated into the EU's more general water policy, embodied in the Water Framework Directive. Both of these regimes are discussed in more detail below.

Water quality is a key concern for EU citizens, many of whom have supported EU action on this issue for a long time. In 2012, an average of 68 percent of citizens in twenty-five EU countries, and up to 94 percent in some countries, labeled water quality a "serious concern."[39] The main perceived threats are chemical pollution (84 percent), mainly from agriculture, and climate change (55 percent). Historically, citizen support has also been an important bottom-up driver for EU water policy, as reflected in the current legislation, which mandates citizen participation in many processes and particularly in planning processes.[40]

In addition to the legislative strategies discussed below, there are several other important pieces of water-related environmental legislation, such as the 2008 Marine Strategy Framework Directive.[41] Because our main focus is on water pollution, not all of these instruments are directly relevant here. However, it is good to note their existence, especially given the EU's integrated approach to water, which combines environmental, ecological, and human and plant health objectives.

Water Framework Directive

By the 1990s, this patchwork approach to water quality led to a broad call for the revision of EU water law, coming from the Member States, the European Commission, the European Parliament, and the Council of Ministers. Yet despite the shared understanding that change was needed to make EU water law less fragmented and more effective, intense disagreement on the shape of these changes between the Council, Commission, and Parliament delayed the adoption of the Water Framework Directive (WFD) by almost twelve years. The WFD was finally adopted in 2000.

It would be hard to overstate the importance of the WFD for modern water management in the EU, and for EU environmental law more generally. It incorporates several pioneering regulatory approaches, which have been both lauded and criticized.[42] In part because it absorbs many preexisting water regulation directives, the WFD is complicated and somewhat lengthy: its consolidated version amounts to ninety-three pages.[43] Some important water regulations also continue to exist alongside the WFD (including the Drinking Water Directive, discussed below). Moreover, the WFD must be read together with two other "daughter" directives: the 2006 Groundwater Directive (adopted on the basis of Article 17 WFD)[44] and the 2008 and 2013 Priority Substances Directive.[45]

SCOPE

The WFD sets out a framework for the "protection of inland surface waters, transitional waters, coastal waters and groundwater" (Article 1). In doing so, it relies on ecosystem-based objectives and planning processes that take river basins as their organizational units (Articles 3 and 5). This is of central importance because it means that preexisting legal borders are not decisive; even if a river basin crosses national borders, the organizational unit must reflect the water body's ecosystem.[46] Water quality standards in the EU are set differently depending on whether the water is categorized as "surface water" or "groundwater" (for details, see spotlight 8).

OBJECTIVES

The WFD is not solely a water pollution regime; rather, to address the complexity of competing water uses and the interactive effects of water quality on ecosystems, it adopts five broad environmental objectives: addressing pollution, promoting sustainable water use, protecting the aquatic environment, protecting groundwater, and contributing to the mitigation of floods and droughts. These environmental objectives are in addition to the Member States' obligation to prepare river basin management plans that include a program of measures (Articles 4 and 11).[47]

Importantly, Article 4 of the WFD distinguishes between different types of water (groundwater, surface water, protected areas), which each receive different types and standards of protection. The different standards of water quality are complex, interrelated, and partly reliant on other directives (see spotlight 8).

Article 9 of the WFD incorporates the "polluter pays" principle into EU water law. It provides that all social and environmental costs should be taken into account when pricing water, and that this principle must be included in the Member States' river basin management plans.

SPOTLIGHT 8. WATER QUALITY STANDARDS IN THE WATER FRAMEWORK DIRECTIVE (WFD)

For all bodies of water, the non-deterioration provision applies (Article 4 WFD). This is a legal obligation on the Member States to "implement the necessary measures to prevent deterioration of [the body of water's] status."

SURFACE WATER

For surface water, good chemical and ecological status must be achieved (Article 2 WFD). Achieving good chemical status requires complying with water quality standards established for chemical substances at the EU level (these can be found in the thirty-three standards in Annex II of the 2008 Priority Substances Directive *combined with* the twelve standards under the 2013 Priority Substances Directive). The process to determine good ecological status is set out in Annex V of the WFD. Member States must go through a number of steps to show that they have achieved this standard (involving the use and condition of the body of water). Good ecological status is often intuitively linked to the "naturalness" of the water, but any such "natural" status of the water is very difficult to determine scientifically and historically.

GROUNDWATER

For groundwater, Article 2 of the WFD sets a quantitative requirement and a requirement of good chemical status (both defined in Annex V). The combination of a quantitative and qualitative standard is particularly important for groundwater, as its quality is strongly affected by unsustainable reductions in quantity. These requirements must be read together with the measures of the 2006 Groundwater Directive (specifically Article 3 and Part B of Annex II), which sets out a minimum list of pollutants that must be controlled.

Notably, for groundwater the standard of good ecological status does *not* apply, as it does to surface water. Member States are, however, required under the Groundwater Directive to prevent any "significant upward trend in concentration of pollutants."

SPOTLIGHT 9. BATHING WATER

The EU has been responsible for the regulation of bathing water since 1976 (Bathing Water Directive 76/160/EC). The adoption of the Water Framework Directive (WFD) necessitated the updating of the Bathing Water Directive (Directive 2006/7/EEC). The WFD has changed the management of bathing water insofar as there is now an overarching requirement of improvement, a greater emphasis on public information, and an annual reporting requirement. The updated Bathing Water Directive also incorporates the non-deterioration clause set out in the WFD. Most significantly, the 2006 Bathing Water Directive obliges Member States to classify bathing water as either poor, sufficient, good, or excellent (Article 5). If bathing water is classified as poor for five consecutive years, a permanent bathing ban may have to be imposed. The changes to the Bathing Water Directive thus far appear to be successful: in 2015, 84 percent of bathing water sites were classified as "excellent"; in 2017, this was 85 percent. Those rated "poor" amount to 1.4 percent, a number that has not changed in the past five years.*

* European Environment Agency Report, European Bathing Water Quality in 2015, No. 9/2016, p. 4; European Environment Agency Report, European Bathing Water Quality in 2017, No. 2/2018, p. 5.

CONCENTRATED AND DIFFUSE SOURCES

OF POLLUTION

Although concentrated and diffuse sources of pollution are often regulated differently in water pollution regimes around the world, the EU does not distinguish between them for the purposes of the WFD. Instead, Article 10 of the WFD simply stipulates that Member States must adopt a combined approach for concentrated and diffuse sources of pollution, leaving further decisions about the management of pollution sources to the discretion of the Member States within their river basin management plans.

Drinking Water Directive

The EU has regulated drinking water since 1975, when it issued its first major piece of water quality legislation: the Drinking Water Directive (DWD). There have been several updates to the original DWD, the latest in 2015.[48] The core purpose of the Directive has remained consistent, however: to protect the quality of water that is intended for human consumption. Over the years, quality standards have gone up, reflecting increased scientific understanding of the effects of the consumption of chemicals and other pollutants on human health, as well as continued accomplishments in increasing the quality of European drinking water.

Under the DWD, the standard applied to "drinking water"—all water coming from taps, tankers, bottles, or containers and all water used in the food-processing industry[49]—is that the water must be "wholesome and clean."[50] The interpretation of this standard by the Directive is threefold: first, it requires Member States to ensure that water is "free from any micro-organisms and parasites and from any substances which, in numbers or concentrations, constitute a potential danger to human health."[51] Second, the water must meet the minimum requirements set out in Annex I of the DWD.[52] These minimum requirements list forty-eight microbiological, chemical, and indicator parameters, all of which are considered to have significant effects on water quality. To set the stringency of drinking water standards, the EU relies primarily on the WHO's guidelines for drinking water[53] and on the Commission's scientific advisory committee.[54] Third, and finally, Member States have to ensure that deterioration of drinking water is prevented and/or stopped.[55]

SPOTLIGHT 10. RIGHT2WATER AND
EUROPEAN CITIZENS' INITIATIVES

European public concern for water quality is high, a phenomenon evidenced by the success of the European Citizens' Initiative called Right2Water.

European citizens' initiatives are a democratic innovation of the EU that allows citizens to suggest concrete legal changes in any area where the European Commission has the power to propose legislation (including the environment, as well as agriculture, energy, transport, and trade). Launching an initiative requires seven EU citizens, of voting age, from seven different Member States. Once an initiative gathers a million signatures, with minimum thresholds reached in at least seven countries, the European Commission must decide whether to take action or not.

The Right2Water Initiative, which garnered 1.68 million votes and met minimum thresholds in thirteen Member States, far exceeded the minimum standards needed to force legislative consideration. In response, the Commission was required to include a guarantee in its legislative agenda measures that all EU citizens would continue to have free access to water and sanitation, and to exclude water resources from internal market rules.

In implementing Right2Water, the EU cannot act outside its established competences. As a result, the greatest impact of the Right2Water initiative is likely to be heightened monitoring of Member States' implementation of drinking water standards.

As in most areas, Member States are allowed to implement these standards through the measures they consider most appropriate. However, the achievement of these standards is mandatory, apart from some limited grounds for (temporary) derogation (which apply in unusual circumstances when the Member States are temporarily allowed to deviate from the DWD's requirements).[56] The fact that a Member State may have taken "all practicable steps to secure compliance" is an insufficient defense in cases of noncompliance.[57] Central to the compliance process is the requirement of regular reporting.[58] If a report shows that drinking water does not comply with standards, the Member State must act: first, through immediate investigation into the cause, and then, if there is a danger to human health, by taking remedial action as soon as possible.[59]

As in other areas of environmental law, some problems with implementation remain. That said, the quality of drinking water in the EU is generally high, so much so that the majority of people in the EU take continuous access to clean drinking water for granted.[60] Nevertheless, increasing droughts and scarcity are raising public awareness of water as a resource. This concern undergirded the first-ever successful European Citizens' Initiative, Right2Water, which was signed by 1.68 million EU citizens.

TAKEAWAYS

✓ Key challenges to water pollution control include the diversity of uses for water, the variety of behaviors that can create water pollution (including both concentrated and diffuse uses), the fact that moving water tends to form unidirectional channels, and, finally, the distributional challenges, particularly those related to drinking water control.

✓ The Water Framework Directive (WFD) is the main legislative device for water policy in the EU. It sets standards for different types of water bodies and forces Member States to adopt river basin management plans to achieve these water quality standards. The WFD also regulates bathing water.

✓ The Drinking Water Directive (DWD) sets standards for all drinking water in the EU based on a "wholesome and clean" water requirement. It is implemented by the Member States, which must report regularly on the quality of drinking water.

DISCUSSION QUESTIONS

1. Does it make sense to force Member States to regulate concentrated and diffuse sources of water pollution through a combined approach?

2. Do you agree with the EU's decision to regulate the quality of drinking water when it comes out of the "tap," rather than at the source? What are the benefits of such an approach?

3. Is it a good idea for water pollution to be so significantly controlled at the EU level? Are there reasons why it might make sense to have (more) control of water quality at the local or Member State level?

SOIL POLLUTION

DEFINITION

Soil pollution is the contamination of soils by materials that are out of place or that are present at higher-than-normal concentrations, which may have adverse effects on humans or on nonhuman organisms.

DISTINCTIVE CHALLENGES OF REGULATING SOIL POLLUTION

Soil pollution can accumulate from a variety of sources, including industrial and agricultural land uses. Common activities causing soil pollution include mining, activities of heavy industry, corrosion of underground storage tanks, intensive farming, and leaching of solid or liquid wastes. The most common chemicals involved are petroleum hydrocarbons, pesticides, heavy metals, and solvents. Importantly, while many soil pollutants originate with human behavior, it is also possible to have higher-than-normal concentrations of pollutants, such as arsenic, which occur naturally in some soils.

Soil formation is an extremely slow process, which makes soil essentially a nonrenewable resource. Soil can function as a habitat and provides many essential ecosystems. The geographic distribution of soil pollution varies by type—linked, for example, to industrial activity, mining, agriculture, or urbanization. Apart from soil pollution in the traditional sense, there are also other activities that can damage soil and its ability to provide essential environmental functions. An example of this is soil sealing, where ground is covered with impermeable materials.

Because soil pollution becomes embedded in the affected soil, it can be expensive to remediate, requiring either removal or treatment of contaminated soil. In case of removal, the contaminated soil still has to be managed. Soil pollution also has a complex and interactive relationship with other media of pollution. It can cause air and water pollution—for example, where toxic chemicals in soil leach into groundwater or where soil (naturally) contributes to air pollution by releasing volatile compounds through the decomposition of organic materials. At the same time, soil pollution can be caused by other forms of pollution—for example, where acid rain acidifies the soil or where agricultural runoff leads to high levels of nitrogen in the soil.

A final complicating factor is that certain concentrations of potentially damaging material can be beneficial for some soil uses. High-nitrogen additives, for example, can be highly beneficial to farmers as fertilizer or, more generally, as "soil improvers." Yet when water runoff over high-nitrogen soils accumulates, it creates serious water quality problems, leading to algal growth and fish kills. The tradeoffs between the positive uses and harmful effects of these types of additives pose special challenges in setting soil pollution policy.

KEY EU LEGAL APPROACHES TO SOIL POLLUTION

The EU does not currently have a comprehensive or coherent soil pollution policy, and past attempts to develop such a policy have failed. As a result, soil pollution, and the more broadly defined *soil protection* as used by the EU, is covered indirectly through various related EU policies such as water and air pollution, agriculture, chemicals, and waste. For example, sites with soil contaminated by hazardous waste are managed—to the extent they are managed by the EU at all—through waste regulation. Moreover, only a few Member States have legislation specifically targeting soil protection. At the same time, soil pollution is a growing problem in the EU. The most recent report on this issue—published in 2016 and covering the EU Member States and several other countries in the European Economic Area—shows that the costs related to soil pollution, broadly defined, for the thirty-nine surveyed countries amounted to 4.2 billion euros.[61] Moreover, failure to have a coherent EU policy on soil is increasingly considered an obstacle to achieving EU biodiversity and climate change goals.

In 2006, the Commission published its "Thematic Strategy for Soil Protection."[62] The strategy is built around four pillars:

1. framework legislation with protection and sustainable use of soil as its principal aim;
2. integration of soil protection in the formulation and implementation of national and Community policies;
3. closing the current recognised knowledge gap in certain areas of soil protection through research supported by Community and national research programmes;
4. increasing public awareness of the need to protect soil.[63]

The "Strategy" statement was accompanied by a proposed Soil Framework Directive[64] and an impact assessment of the different regulatory options considered by the EU.[65]

In 2010, however, a minority of Member State representatives in the EU's Environmental Council blocked further progress on the Soil Framework Directive. Though mostly treated as an environmental issue, this resistance could be explained by the fact that soil protection is closely linked to issues of land use and spatial planning, and thus to questions of local development and economies. In the EU, those activities fall squarely

SPOTLIGHT 11. THE DOOMED SOIL
FRAMEWORK DIRECTIVE

The proposed Soil Framework Directive would have set common criteria by which areas at risk of erosion, organic matter decline, salinization, compaction, and landslides would be identified, as well as areas at risk of contamination.

The inclusion of this relatively wide range of soil-related problems can be explained by the EU's focus on soil management and protection, as compared to a narrower focus on soil pollution. Apart from setting these "common criteria," the Soil Framework Directive would have left all other key decisions to the Member States, including risk acceptability, level of ambitions regarding targets to be achieved, and choice of regulatory instruments.*

Though relatively modest in its initial proposal, the Soil Framework Directive would have created an opportunity for starting a shared frame of reference for soil protection across the EU—something that was (and now remains) missing from EU policy.

* For details, see European Commission, "Communication from the Commission: Thematic Strategy for Soil Protection" COM (2006) 231 final.

within Member State sovereignty, and any environmental issue that may touch on matters of land use or spatial planning is therefore subject to the special legislative procedure, giving more powers to the Council of Ministers than to the European Parliament (see spotlight 11).

After the failure of the proposed directive on soil protection, the Commission published a policy report that showed the progress on the implementation of its Thematic Strategy for Soil Protection in 2012.[66] Despite the report showing a continuing and growing need for soil protection, the proposal for the Soil Framework Directive was eventually withdrawn by the Commission in 2014. Soil protection was nevertheless

TABLE 6

Soil-Related EU Legislation

Legislative measure	Elements Linked to Soil Protection
Sewage Sludge Directive (86/278/EEC)	Soil protection from sewage sludge used on agricultural land
Water Framework Directive (2000/60/EC)	Measures aimed at obtaining good ecological status in all water bodies
Nitrates Directive (91/676/EEC)	Implementation of good agricultural practices in vulnerable areas
Industrial Emissions Directive (2010/75/EU)	Cross-media approach that includes soil
Sustainable Use of Pesticides Directive (2009/128/EC)	Risk assessments need to include soil issues
Common Agricultural Policy	Compulsory cross-compliance scheme considers soil issues

included as a priority issue in the seventh Environmental Action Programme, which ambitiously includes the aim of a sustainable land management strategy within the EU by 2020.[67]

In the absence of an EU-wide soil protection strategy, there are several other legislative instruments that do touch on soil pollution, most of which have been discussed in the preceding snapshots. Table 6 lists the most important ones and their links to soil protection. Apart from these, LIFE (the EU's financial instrument for the environment) also funds projects related to soil. Key examples include projects addressing soil erosion, soil sealing, carbon capture, and contaminated land.

One area of soil pollution control that is notably missing from EU soil-related legislation is local soil contamination, such as that resulting from industrial contamination. Soil contamination is widespread; according to a report by the European Environment Agency, there are at least 2.5 million potentially contaminated sites in the EU.[68] Of those

SPOTLIGHT 12. SOIL SEALING

Soil sealing is an example of a type of soil degradation that is not caused by pollution, but rather by other human activities. Soil sealing takes place when the ground is covered with impermeable material, such as concrete for infrastructure and buildings. It is most common in urban areas and areas that are subject to urbanization. The EU, like most other areas in the world, has undergone rapid urbanization since the 1950s, leading to an increase in urban area of 78 percent. This development has not been slowing down; between 2006 and 2012, there was an increase of 6,360 km^2 (comparable to sixty times the area of Paris) in the EU's sealed area.

There is no coordinated EU effort to reduce soil sealing. However, the EU has mapped Member State policies on this topic and has developed a set of best practices that combines current efforts and expert guidance on how to best address this problem. The Commission communication* on this topic is not a legislative or binding measure; it is a form of soft law that is supposed to assist Member States in addressing this specific issue. Developing a shared approach to best practices is especially valuable in this area because soil sealing tends to be irreversible, leading to biodiversity loss, increased risk of flooding, and water scarcity. The Commission's Guidelines are an example of an EU strategy in the absence of legislative competence.

* European Commission, "Commission Staff Working Document: Guidelines on best practice to limit, mitigate or compensate soil sealing" SWD (2012) 101 final/2.

identified, only 15 percent have been remediated.[69] Because there is no EU-wide strategy on the regulation of these sites, the definition and treatment of contaminated sites differ widely between Member States. The management of these sites costs an estimated 6.5 billion euros per year.[70] While the majority of these costs are borne by companies, an average of 42 percent of the total expenditure comes from public budgets.[71] Moreover, this amount does not take account of the indirect costs of soil contamination, only the remediation of land directly affected.

TAKEAWAYS

✓ Soil pollution policy is complicated by the fact that soil pollution accumulates from a variety of sources (including both human and naturally occurring sources), by the high costs of remediation, and by its complex and interactive relationship with other forms of pollution.

✓ There is no single authority or legal instrument tasked with managing soil pollution in the EU. An attempt to create an EU-wide directive on soil protection failed.

✓ Soil pollution is addressed indirectly through EU policies on waste, water and air pollution, and chemicals. However, none of these measures are specifically designed for soil protection, which raises questions regarding their effectiveness.

✓ The EU lacks any EU-wide strategy or regulation of contaminated sites. As a result, the definition and treatment of contaminated sites differ widely between Member States.

DISCUSSION QUESTIONS

1. When can soil pollution be considered a transboundary environmental problem? On what basis can the EU claim competence to regulate soil-related problems that are not transboundary?

2. What benefits or drawbacks might come from an EU-wide strategy addressing contaminated sites? What benefits or drawbacks flow from addressing contaminated sites differently in different Member States?

CHEMICAL SUBSTANCES
DEFINITION

Chemicals are compounds or substances that have been purified or prepared (in particular, artificially) and that are suspected of causing a risk of harm to humans or the environment. Because these substances offer some benefits—as with pesticides, adhesives, or solvents—they are often created purposefully, although they can also be generated as a waste byproduct of other processes.

DISTINCTIVE CHALLENGES OF REGULATING CHEMICAL SUBSTANCES

Purposefully generated chemicals implicate different regulatory requirements than substances created as waste or as unintended byproducts. Regulations must strike a balance between the positive expected uses of these chemicals and their possible negative environmental impacts. As a consequence, management of chemicals often involves complex and fact-specific considerations, such as the need to formulate a method to identify and compare the benefits of use and the risks of exposure. This prioritization is complicated further when substances are new and when information about their likely impacts is scarce or uncertain.

As with waste products, the regulation of chemicals requires an understanding of complex and often interactive processes. Different chemicals can combine to create increased (or decreased) harm. Moreover, chemicals can be accumulative and highly persistent, which can both delay and compound their observable harmful effects over time. Although chemicals are generally classified and regulated by reference to their toxicity for humans, they have important impacts on the non-human environment.

Chemical regulation implicates heightened stakes for regulators and can generate emergency conditions—for example, when there are sudden releases of toxins such as chemical spills and similar accidents. At the same time, the economic necessity of chemicals in virtually every industrial process and product makes their regulation an economic, as well as environmental and health, concern.

KEY EU LEGAL APPROACHES TO CHEMICAL SUBSTANCE REGULATION

The EU has regulated trade in chemicals since the 1960s, on the basis of its central role in the European economy. Directive 67/548/EEC ("on the approximation of laws, regulations and administrative provisions regarding the classification, packaging and labelling of dangerous substances") aimed to ensure the free movement of chemical substances within the internal market.[72] Although the regulatory regime was initially focused on economic concerns, health and environmental considerations have gradually been integrated into chemical regulation. This process accelerated with the codification of the environmental principles of precaution and prevention and of a high level of health and environmental protection in the EU treaties. That said, even today, most EU chemical regulations continue to be adopted on the basis of Article 114 of the Treaty on the Functioning of the European Union (on the EU's internal market competence). As a result, some regulatory provisions are geared more toward accommodating trade than ensuring environmental safety (for example, the short testing window required for ecotoxicological studies).

By far the most important pieces of legislation on chemicals are Regulation (EC) 1907/2006 "concerning the Registration, Evaluation, Authorisation and Restriction of Chemicals," known as the REACH Regulation;[73] and Regulation (EC) 1272/2008 "on the Classification, Labelling and Packaging of Substances and Mixtures," known as the CLP Regulation.[74] Alongside these regulations, there are many other directives and regulations that control specific substances or products, which leads to significant regulatory complexity in this area.

REACH Regulation

Throughout the twentieth century, chemicals were regulated by a myriad of EU regulations and directives. In the early 2000s, the REACH Regulation was adopted with a view toward streamlining the regulation of chemicals. The consolidated REACH Regulation extends over 500 pages and is considered one of the most technically complex pieces of EU legislation. It is also one of the most widely studied of the EU's environmental laws. One reason for this is that parties who want to import chemicals into the EU have to follow the REACH requirements.[75] Another reason is that the REACH Regulation is widely viewed as a model for how chemical regulation can be structured to regulate new and existing substances, while placing the burden of information-gathering on manufacturers and importers rather than regulators.

Central to the REACH strategy is the registration of chemicals (Articles 5–24 REACH), which is mandatory for all manufacturers, importers, and some downstream users of chemical substances in quantities of at least one metric ton per year. Without registration, substances may not be traded (Article 5). Before a chemical can be registered, manufacturers and importers are required to gather information on the impacts the substance has on human health and the environment, and to file that information with the European Chemicals Agency (ECHA) in Helsinki. To date, tens of thousands of chemicals have been registered.

Interestingly, to help address the costs borne by industry in the registration process, the REACH Regulation provides for private-party information exchange forums (called substance information exchange forums), where parties can collaborate in fulfilling the registration requirements. Although this innovation has proven popular with industry, it has raised questions regarding transparency, data quality, and potential collusion between regulated actors.[76]

Registration forms the basis for evaluation under the REACH Regulation (Articles 40–54). Evaluations are undertaken by Member State authorities and then sent to ECHA. ECHA determines what further action is taken, which can include placing a substance on the "substances of very high concern" list (Annex XIV of REACH), adopting restrictions on the marketing and/or use of the substance, or authorizing its use. In coming to these decisions, ECHA first does risk assessment—a scientific evaluation of the potential adverse effects, based on the data provided by industry. Most decisions are made on the basis of risk assessment, though if information is controversial or initially limited, such assessments can take place over many years. The risk assessment of the flame retardant decaBDE, for example, took ten years to complete, during which 234 studies were reviewed.[77] If, during the risk assessment, regulators conclude that the risk is unclear and that it is unlikely that further information will improve the situation, then they apply the precautionary principle and prohibit the substance from being introduced into commerce. Parties have the right to appeal such determinations through the ECHA Board of Appeal.[78]

The REACH Regulation further manages the risks associated with chemical use by requiring manufacturers and importers to provide downstream users with safety data sheets (Article 31). These are mandatory for all chemicals listed in the CLP Regulation, showing one of the ways in which these two regulations interact.

CLP Regulation

Disclosure regimes focus on informing people about the risks of dangerous substances, as a means of regulating these risks. In the EU, the most important chemical disclosure regime is the CLP Regulation, which came into force in 2009 and is based on the 1967 Directive on Dangerous Substances.[79] The 1967 Directive was explicitly aimed at protecting public health, especially that of workers exposed to dangerous substances and chemicals.

The CLP Regulation serves three basic functions. First, it provides for classification of substances into a variety of different types based on the risks they pose (for example, carcinogenicity or reproductive toxicity). Typically it requires suppliers to categorize the substances they supply, in a process called "self-classification."[80] Second, suppliers must then label categorized substances (or mixtures including those substances) in packaging, before they may place a product on the market. Finally, classifications are maintained in a database, the Classification and Labelling Inventory, which provides basic classification and labeling information on registered substances.

The CLP Regulation's influence—specifically through its classification of substances and chemicals—is very far-reaching. Classification affects the regulation of these chemicals under the REACH Regulation (see above), but also under many other pieces of legislation, including the IED, the WFD, the Cosmetics Regulation,[81] and the Seveso II Directive on major-accident hazards.[82]

Other Dangerous Substances

Additional legislative instruments apply to specific types of chemicals. For example, biocides and pesticides are regulated by the 2012 Biocidal Products Regulation and the 2009 Regulation on Plant Protection Products[83] and are exempt from the REACH Regulation.[84] Other substances that are regulated under the Cosmetics Regulation, the Ozone-Depleting Substances Regulation, or the EU pharmaceutical rules are subject to these regulations, but they are potentially also subject to REACH and CLP requirements.

TAKEAWAYS

✓ Chemical regulation presents distinctive challenges because it requires a balancing act between beneficial economic uses and potentially negative health and environmental impacts.
✓ The REACH Regulation is the EU's umbrella legislation for chemicals. It is focused on assessing chemicals' health and

environmental risks and, famously, puts the burden of proof on manufacturers and importers to show that a substance does not pose a risk to human or environmental health. Compliance with REACH is a precondition to operating within the EU chemicals market, increasing the global impact of the regime.

✓ The CLP Regulation sets out classification rules for chemicals and dangerous substances. These classifications affect a substance's treatment under many other pieces of legislation, making it an important example of environmental cross-governance.

✓ Dangerous substances are often also regulated by product- or industry-specific rules in addition to the REACH and CLP Regulations.

DISCUSSION QUESTIONS

1. How should society weigh the usefulness of chemicals against their toxicity? What should be done when the toxicity of a chemical is unknown—is it better to err on the side of limiting the use of useful but potentially dangerous substances, or to allow useful substances to be used unless it is clear they are also unreasonably harmful?

2. Does the adoption of a precautionary approach, which bans chemicals unless they have been proven safe, make sense for the regulation of chemicals, or should the burden be on the regulator to prove that a substance is harmful before it can be banned or restricted?

WASTE MANAGEMENT
DEFINITION

Waste is a material or substance that is discarded as no longer useful, often as the result of an otherwise valuable activity. Waste is often classified as solid waste (nonhazardous waste in solid, as opposed to liquid or gaseous, form), hazardous waste (waste with properties that make it dangerous to human health or the environment), or radioactive waste (waste from nuclear reactions, including spent nuclear fuel). So-called wastewater— water that has been used in a home, business, or industrial application and is then discarded—is typically regulated as a form of water pollution.

DISTINCTIVE CHALLENGES OF WASTE MANAGEMENT

Particular types of waste can implicate specific challenges, depending on the behaviors that create the waste and the risks posed by waste transport, storage, and disposal. Moreover, waste management implicates substantial interactions with other forms of pollution control, in that poorly managed waste can lead to water pollution or soil pollution, incineration of waste can cause air pollution, and the production of toxic substances can create waste.

Municipal solid waste—trash or garbage—consists of everyday items that are used and then discarded, including product packaging, food scraps, and paper products. Because generation of trash is extraordinarily diffuse, a significant aspect of trash management involves transportation activities designed to concentrate the waste for recycling and disposal.

Hazardous waste, by contrast, is often the result of concentrated industrial processes, which offers opportunities for direct regulation at the industrial plants. This is easier than the regulation of diffuse consumer activity, such as the disposal of batteries or paint cans. The hazards of the underlying material, however, create special risks in its transportation, storage, and disposal, and many hazardous wastes present long-term risks to humans and ecosystems if handled inappropriately.

Like hazardous waste, the generation of nuclear waste tends to be highly concentrated. The special hazards of nuclear waste heighten issues surrounding transportation, storage, and disposal. In addition, nuclear waste implicates distinctive challenges because of long time horizons: nuclear waste takes many hundreds of thousands of years to decay, and there is significant uncertainty in predicting long-term effects and likelihood of leakage.

Waste disposal tends to concentrate an undesirable environmental impact in one location. As a result, waste disposal implicates local protectionism—sometimes referred to as the "Not in my backyard," or NIMBY, phenomenon. This can also create distributional challenges in determining where—and next to whom—waste services are sited. Demographically, undesirable land, which can be used as landfill, tends to be located near poorer communities and communities of people who face housing or other social discrimination and, thus, have limited choices in where they can live. Roma communities, for example, are particularly likely to be impacted by locally undesirable land uses such as landfills.[85]

Finally, unlike many other forms of pollution, the management of waste gives rise to economic opportunity in the form of a significant industry. In the EU, over 1.1 million people are employed by the waste management industry.[86]

KEY EU LEGAL APPROACHES TO WASTE MANAGEMENT

The EU produces over 2.5 billion metric tons of waste a year. Per capita, Europeans produce about six metric tons of waste a year; about half a metric ton of that is household waste.[87] Construction and mining are responsible for almost two-thirds of the waste produced (60 percent). Municipal waste, at 10 percent, is a relatively small proportion of overall waste produced, although managing municipal waste in Europe—as elsewhere—poses special challenges. About 36 percent of waste is recycled EU-wide, though recycling rates vary substantially by Member State and have been increasing in most regions in recent years. As a result, the safe management, recycling, and disposal of solid and hazardous waste forms a large industry in all EU Member States.[88]

Waste management has a long history in EU environmental law, tracing back to the first Environmental Action Programme and the 1975

directives on waste oils and waste.[89] In 2008, the Waste Framework
Directive (WaFD) was adopted in an effort to simplify the complex
legislation in this area.[90] Its aim, in keeping with the older directives it
replaced,[91] is to protect the environment and human health from
adverse impacts of waste generation and management and to improve
the efficiency of resource use. The WaFD covers several types of waste,
but it needs to be read together with specific directives and regulations
on landfills, hazardous waste, and radioactive waste, as discussed below.

The most important feature of the WaFD is its introduction of the
so-called EU Waste Hierarchy (Article 4 WaFD), which sets out the
most preferable solutions to waste management. Waste prevention is
considered the best option and should be prioritized where possible.
This is followed, in decreasing order of preference, by preparing for
reuse, recycling, other recovery, and, ultimately, disposal. Member
States are directed to create waste prevention programs, alongside
waste management programs, that incorporate this hierarchy, although
the actual choice of how to achieve the WaFD's goals can be determined by the Member States on the basis of environmental fit.[92] The
WaFD also defined several key concepts of EU waste law, such as the
definition of "waste" itself, as well as concepts such as "recovery" and
"disposal," which are particularly important for the management of
waste.

In 2015, the Commission published a communication on "Closing the
Loop—An EU Action Plan for the Circular Economy."[93] The aim of
the plan was to treat waste as a resource and to turn the EU into a "circular economy"—an economy that seeks to keep resources in use as
long as possible by reusing, recovering, and regenerating products and
materials at the end of their service life. While the proposed policies
extend significantly beyond waste management, waste management
would play a key role in transitioning to a circular economy.

As a result of this communication, a new revised legislative framework on waste came into force in July 2018. In this framework, the
(amended) WaFD continues to be the central legislative instrument.[94]

SPOTLIGHT 13. DEFINING "WASTE"

The legal definition of *waste* used in EU waste management legislation has developed over time and has proven controversial. This is mostly due to the potential economic value of waste and the related importance of ownership, as well as the need to legally allocate management and disposal risks. The details of this definition continue to develop through case law, but the main features are as follows:

Waste is defined as "any substance or object the holder discards or intends to discard or is required to discard" (Article 3 WaFD). The "holder" does not have to have legal ownership, only physical control of the object.

Byproducts of production processes are *not* waste if further use of the substance or object is certain, if it can be used directly without further processing, if it is produced as an integral part of a production process, and if its further use is lawful (Article 5 WaFD).

End of Waste is an EU concept recognizing that waste can also be transformed into a different product. This happens if the product has been successfully recycled or recovered (Article 6 WaFD).

Intrinsic Commercial Value is a property of waste, according to a Court of Justice ruling.* This means that internal market rules apply to the movement of waste (as a "good" within the market).

* Case C-129/96 *Inter-Environnement Wallonie ASBL v. Région wallone* ECLI:EU:C:1997:628.

An interesting addition to the EU's legislative waste strategy has been the Single-Use Plastics Directive, which addresses the ten single-use plastic products (such as straws and plastic cutlery) and fishing gear most often found on Europe's beaches and seas (see spotlight 14).

As is common for most areas of EU pollution control legislation, there are issues with Member States' implementation of the WaFD. Waste is one of the sectors with the highest number of infringement cases (in which Member States are challenged by the Commission for under-compliance or noncompliance), and illegal landfills remain a

---

SPOTLIGHT 14. SINGLE-USE PLASTICS

In the EU, ten single-use plastic products and certain fishing gear are responsible for 70 percent of marine litter, resulting in high environmental costs (projected at 22 billion euros by 2030) and consumer costs (6.5 billion euros).

In 2019, the EU adopted a directive to regulate such plastics, known as the Single-Use Plastics Directive.* The Directive bans plastic-stemmed cotton buds (or swabs), cutlery, plates, straws, drink stirrers, and sticks for balloons. It also forces Member States to reduce the use of plastic food containers and drinks cups and to ensure collection of 90 percent of single-use plastic drink bottles by 2025. Producers must assist in covering the costs of waste management and cleanup. Moreover, labeling requirements will be imposed on plastic products to raise awareness of the negative impact of single-use plastics and fishing gear. Fishing gear, which accounts for 27 percent of all beach litter, will be regulated chiefly through producer responsibility schemes, such as responsibility for waste collection and awareness-raising activities.

* Directive (EU) 2019/904 of the European Parliament and of the Council of 5 June 2019 on the reduction of the impact of certain plastic products on the environment, OJ L 155, 12.6.2019, pp. 1–19.

serious problem in several Member States. This is particularly problematic because many Member States have yet to successfully follow the EU Waste Hierarchy, with many still relying heavily on landfills to dispose of their waste. In order to strengthen the EU's recycling goals, the WaFD was amended in 2018 to incorporate more ambitious Member State requirements on reuse and recycling. Specifically, Article 11 now sets a minimum goal of 55 percent recycling for municipal waste by 2025, to be increased to 60 percent and 65 percent in 2030 and 2035, respectively.[95] Moreover, there is a binding target to reduce landfilling to a maximum of 10 percent of municipal waste by 2035.

Solid Waste

The majority of solid waste created in the EU comes from mining and quarrying (25 percent), followed by manufacturing (10.3 percent).[96] Some solid waste that poses special dangers is regulated as hazardous waste (as discussed below). Household waste represents 8.5 percent of the EU's total waste creation, totaling 242 million metric tons in 2016. This is an average of 486 kilograms per EU inhabitant, or 1.3 kilograms per day (by comparison, the global average is 0.75 kg/day, and the US average is 2 kg/day).[97] Behind this average, however, is substantial variation across Member States, ranging from 272 kilograms per year (0.75 kg/day) per capita in Romania to 781 kilograms per year (2.1 kg/day) per capita in Denmark. These differences can be explained by differences in economic wealth and consumption, but also by differences in municipal waste management. Member States also vary significantly in the proportion of their waste industry that is private versus public, with most having some share of each.[98] Although household and municipal waste is a relatively small percentage of the waste produced, the management of municipal waste remains politically sensitive within the EU, partially due to the visibility and daily impact of any mismanagement. Solid waste, including municipal waste, is regulated mainly

TABLE 7

EU Law on Solid Waste

Laws	Solid Waste Focus
Directive 2008/98/EC	Waste Framework Directive
Directive 1999/31/EC	On the landfill of waste
Regulation (EC) 2150/2002	On waste statistics
Regulation (EC) 1013/2006	On shipments of waste
Directive 94/62/EC	On packaging and packaging waste
Directive 2000/53/EC	On end-of-life vehicles
Directive 2005/64/EC	On type-approval of motor vehicles with regard to their reusability, recyclability, and recoverability
Directive 2006/66/EC	On batteries and accumulators and waste batteries and accumulators
Directive 2012/19/EU	On waste electrical and electronic equipment
Directive (EU) 2015/720	On the consumption of lightweight plastic carrier bags
Directive 2006/21/EC	On the management of waste from extractive industries

through the WaFD, though the latter is supplemented by a number of specific laws on landfills, waste statistics, waste shipment, and packaging, as well as specific provisions regarding certain consumer items.

Landfills used to be the main method of municipal waste disposal. However, between 1995 and 2017, the share of municipal waste that was landfilled fell by 59 percent (from 145 million to 58 million metric tons). This means that only 23 percent of municipal waste is now sent to landfills. Waste incineration is a relatively new, but growing, form of waste management in the EU, having increased by III percent since 1995, accounting for 68 million metric tons in 2017. While incineration reduces the amount of space needed for landfills and the risk of soil pollution and water pollution from landfilled waste, it increases air pollution. Incineration is regulated under the IED rather than any of the waste directives.[99] Recycling and composting account for the largest share of municipal waste management (47 percent).

Hazardous Waste

Hazardous waste has been regulated by the EU through separate directives since the 1970s (see table 8). These provisions were largely incorporated into the WaFD, which defines hazardous waste as "waste which displays one or more of the hazardous properties listed in Annex III" (Article 3).[100] Member States can, however, consider waste that is not in Annex III as hazardous, if they can support their assessment with scientific evidence.[101] Similarly, they can treat waste listed as hazardous as *nonhazardous* if scientific evidence supports such a change.

More generally, the WaFD obliged Member States to "take the necessary action to ensure that the production, collection and transportation of hazardous waste, as well as its storage and treatment" fulfill the criteria of the Directive.[102] This includes the ability to trace such waste throughout the disposal process.[103] The disposal of hazardous waste is strictly regulated, both within the EU and outside it. The Basel Convention, implemented through Regulation 1013/2006 (on shipments of waste), regulates the shipment of hazardous waste from developed to developing countries. The Regulation bans both the export of hazardous waste to "developing countries" (defined as all countries that are not members of the Organisation for Economic Co-operation and Development) and the export of nonhazardous waste for disposal. At the time of this writing, slightly more than half of hazardous waste in the EU is landfilled.

TABLE 8

EU Law on Hazardous Waste

Law	Hazardous Waste Focus ☠
Decision 93/98/EEC	On the conclusion, on behalf of the Community, of the Convention on the control of transboundary movement of hazardous wastes and their disposal (Basel Convention)
Decision 97/640/EC	On the approval, on behalf of the Community, of amendment to the Convention on the control of transboundary movement of hazardous wastes and their disposal (Basel Convention)
Regulation (EC) 1013/2006	On shipments of waste
Regulation (EC) 1272/2008	On classification, labelling and packaging of substances and mixtures (CLP Regulation)
Directive 2001/65/ECU	On the restriction of use of certain hazardous substances in electrical and electronic equipment

Radioactive Waste

European Member States were some of the first adopters of radioactive energy generation, and the EU's 130 nuclear reactors generate around 30 percent of the EU's electricity. This necessitates the management of significant quantities of radioactive waste within the EU, most of it from both past and ongoing electricity generation. As of 2013, there were 3.13 million cubic meters of radioactive waste and spent nuclear fuel; 70 percent of this has been disposed of, while 30 percent remains in temporary storage, awaiting appropriate disposal facilities.[104]

Nuclear reactors are (or were) located in sixteen Member States; some of the other Member States have no nuclear program at all (including no research programs).[105] Virtually all (99.7 percent) of the radioactive waste in the EU is located in the sixteen Member States that have (or had) nuclear power plants. The distribution among

SPOTLIGHT 15. EURATOM

The Euratom Treaty was signed together with the founding treaties of the European Union (then the European Economic Community) in 1957. It established the European Atomic Energy Community
(Euratom), which, although separate from the EU, is governed by the
EU institutions and has the same Member States.

Euratom ensures the safe use of civilian nuclear activities, specifically for power generation, research, and medical use. While
nuclear power is regulated by the Member States, there is a "Community framework" for the safety of nuclear installations in the EU
(Directive 2014/87/Euratom). Euratom also plays an important role
in the coordination of nuclear research through its Research and
Training Programme.

these countries is quite uneven: France is the largest user and producer
of nuclear energy and is home to 44 percent of the EU's nuclear waste.
It is closely followed by the United Kingdom (38 percent), with Germany a distant third (7 percent). Other than electricity generation, the
remaining sources of radioactive waste are the uses of radioactive
materials for medical, research, industrial, and agricultural purposes.

The storage and management of radioactive waste in the EU takes
place in a decentralized manner and, historically, has been left almost
entirely to the Member States. In 2011, a directive was adopted for the
creation of a community framework that would coordinate the safe
management of spent fuel and radioactive waste. Under this directive,
Member States are obliged to provide for national arrangements that
provide a high level of safety, which includes the creation of national
programs for the management of radioactive waste (see table 9). These
plans must be reported to the Commission.[106] The effectiveness of
presented plans varied widely, with some Member States suggesting

TABLE 9

EU Law on Radioactive Waste

Law	Radioactive Waste Focus
Regulation (Euratom) 1493/93	On shipments of radioactive substances between Member States
Directive 2006/117/Euratom	On the supervision and control of shipments of radioactive waste and spent fuel
Directive 2011/70/Euratom	Establishing a Community Framework for the responsible and safe management of spent fuel and radioactive waste

repository types that had been explicitly rejected by other Member States as ineffective (see table 9).

As of yet, there is no open and operational repository for spent nuclear fuel in the EU, and the first such repository is not predicted to be operational until 2022–30,[107] by which time France, Finland, and Sweden may have established deep geological facilities appropriate for long-term disposal. In the absence of current disposal options, however, there is a continual increase in the amount of spent nuclear fuel and other intermediate- and high-level radioactive waste in temporary storage facilities.

Another problematic issue surrounding radioactive waste is its transport—typically referred to as "shipment." Member States are generally expected to manage spent fuel within their own territory. Even so, radioactive material is transported within the EU every day—though, admittedly, most of this is low-level material. Directive 2006/117/Euratom establishes a system of prior authorization for any shipment that departs from, goes through, or ends in the EU. Moreover, shipments to Africa, Caribbean or Pacific countries, Antarctica, or any country that may not have the resources to manage this type of waste are prohibited. Guidelines for shipment are constantly updated in line with best practices and international standards.[108]

TAKEAWAYS

✓ Regulation of waste requires involvement with the waste
management industry and is complicated by the fact that
concentration of waste tends to create undesirable land uses,
which then interact with other forms of pollution. In addition,
municipal solid waste presents challenges from the diffusion
of its creation; control of hazardous waste is complicated
by the hazards of the underlying material; and nuclear
waste has to be managed over extraordinarily long time
horizons.

✓ The Waste Framework Directive (WaFD) sets out the
general waste strategy of the EU, including its Waste
Hierarchy, which sets out the preferred methods of waste
prevention.

✓ Solid waste is mostly regulated through the WaFD, along with
specific directives on landfill and consumer goods. About a third
of total waste in the EU is recycled, though this includes the
majority of municipal waste. In recent years, there has also been
an increase in waste incineration.

✓ Hazardous waste is regulated primarily through the WaFD. The
export of hazardous waste to non-EU countries is banned, in
line with the international Basel Convention.

✓ The decision to use nuclear power, and the authority to develop
plans to address resulting spent nuclear fuel, is in the hands of
the Member States. The management and shipment of
radioactive waste is coordinated through Euratom.

DISCUSSION QUESTIONS

1. How centralized should waste management policies be? Does
the answer depend on the type of waste being managed—solid
waste, hazardous waste, or nuclear waste?

2. Waste management sites, such as landfills, are locally undesirable, even though they serve a valuable social function. How and where should they be sited?

3. Is it a good idea to ban single-use plastics? If so, why have more countries not (yet) done so? If not, is there a better way to address the introduction of single-use plastics into the waste stream?

4. How well does the EU address the distinctive challenges posed by waste management?

POLLUTION CONTROL: SUMMARY

The EU approach to pollution control varies according to the type of pollution addressed. In general, however, EU pollution control law is characterized by goal setting at the European level, often in line with international obligations, combined with particularly onerous implementation and enforcement obligations for the Member States.

KEY TERMS

AIR POLLUTION Higher-than-normal concentrations of materials, including chemicals, that are out of place in air.

DOSE-RESPONSE Relationship between the amount of a substance an organism is exposed to and the harm and response the exposure causes.

EXPOSURE REDUCTION Amending behaviors so that there is less exposure to pollution and, thus (hopefully), less harm.

SOIL POLLUTION Higher-than-normal concentrations of materials, including chemicals, that are out of place in soil.

WATER POLLUTION Higher-than-normal concentrations of materials, including chemicals, that are out of place in water, including drinking water.

DISCUSSION QUESTIONS

1. Which type of pollution is most important (or are they all equally important)? Why do we care about pollutants at all?

2. How can regulators know when they have created a successful pollution control regime?

3. Should regulators seek to eliminate all pollution? If not, how should they determine how much pollution is tolerable?

NOTES

1. European Environment Agency, "Costs of Air Pollution from European Industrial Facilities, 2008–2012: An Updated Assessment," EEA technical report no. 20/2014.

2. See also Suzanne Kingston et al., *European Environmental Law* (Cambridge University Press 2017), at 298.

3. See also chapter 1 spotlight.

4. Detailed in this chapter's snapshot on "Air Pollution."

5. For details, see the section "Industrial Emissions Directive" in this chapter.

6. Article 5(3) Treaty European Union. The relationship between competences, subsidiarity, and proportionality is discussed in detail in chapter 2.

7. Recent infringement cases and outcomes are available at http://ec.europa.eu/environment/legal/law/press_en.htm.

8. Who is responsible for this at the subnational level, and how, varies from Member State to Member State.

9. Greenhouse gas emissions are a type of air pollution that contributes to climate disruption. They are addressed in more detail in chapter 8.

10. World Health Organization, see www.euro.who.int/en/health-topics/environment-and-health/air-quality/news/news/2014/03/almost-600-000-deaths-due-to-air-pollution-in-europe-new-who-global-report. For the most recent EU study, see www.eea.europa.eu/publications/air-quality-in-europe-2018.

11. See the snapshot on "Chemical Substances" in this chapter.

12. The European Commission provides a rich source of information on all the EU's air-related programs at http://ec.europa.eu/environment/air/index_en.htm.

13. Full documentation is available at http://ec.europa.eu/environment/air/clean_air/index.htm. This version was adopted in 2013.

14. In addition to the three key legislative instruments discussed in this section, there are many air pollution control laws that govern specific sectors, activities, or actors. Important examples include the following: Regulation (EC) No. 715/2007 on type approval of motor vehicles with respect to emissions from light passenger and commercial vehicles and on the access to vehicle repair and maintenance information; Directive 97/68/EC on the approximation of the laws of the Member States relating to measures against the emission of gaseous and particulate pollutants from internal combustion engines to be installed in non-road mobile machinery; Directive 2004/42/CE on the limitation of emissions of volatile organic compounds due to the use of organic

solvents in certain paints and varnishes and vehicle refinishing products; Directive 2012/33/EU on the sulphur content of marine fuels; and Regulation (EU) 2016/1628 on requirements relating to gaseous and particulate pollutant emission limits and type-approval for internal combustion engines for non-road mobile machinery.

15. Directive 2008/50/EC on ambient air quality and cleaner air for Europe, OJ 2008 L 152/1.

16. Article 4 AQFD.

17. This process is detailed in the Commission's "Guidance on Assessment under the EU Air Quality Directives," http://ec.europa.eu/environment/air /pdf/guidanceunderairquality.pdf, at 9.

18. See also Annex XV AQFD.

19. Article 24 AQFD.

20. Case C-237/07 *Janacek* ECLI: EU:C:2008:447, para 46.

21. Directive 2001/81/EC on national emissions ceilings for certain atmospheric pollutants, OJ 2001 L 309/22.

22. Protocol to Abate Acidification, Eutrophication, and Ground-level Ozone, Gothenburg (Sweden), 30 November 1999, in force 15 May 2005, 1593 UNTS 287; available at www.unece.org/env/ltrap/multi_html.

23. Geneva (Switzerland), 13 November 1079, in force 16 March 1983, 1302 UNTS 217; available at www.unece.org/env/lrtap_h1.html.

24. Article 7 NECD.

25. See Joined Cases C-165/09 and C-167/09 *Stichting Natuur en Milieu and Others* ECLI:EU:C:2011:348.

26. Directive (EU) 2016/2284 of the European Parliament and of the Council of 14 December 2016 on the reduction of national emissions of certain atmospheric pollutants, amending Directive 2003/35/EC and repealing Directive 2001/81/EC.

27. These data are compiled and checked by the European Environment Agency and the European Topic Centre on Air Pollution and Climate Change Mitigation; see https://acm.eionet.europa.eu/.

28. The pollutants are specified in Annex I of the NECD and include the five main air pollutants—nitrogen oxides (NO_x), non-methane volatile organic compounds (NMVOCs), sulfur dioxide (SO_2), ammonia (NH_3), and particulate matter ≤2.5 micrometers in diameter ($PM_{2.5}$)—as well as carbon monoxide (CO), particulate matter ≤10 micrometers in diameter (PM_{10}), and, if available, black carbon (BC) and total suspended particulate matter (TSP); the heavy metals cadmium (Cd), lead (Pb), and mercury (Hg) and, if available, the additional heavy metals arsenic (As), chromium (Cr), copper (Cu), nickel

(Ni), selenium (Se), and zinc (Zn); and persistent organic pollutants (POPs), including selected polycyclic aromatic hydrocarbons (PAHs), dioxins and furans, polychlorinated biphenyls (PCBs), and hexachlorobenzene (HCB).

29. Report available at www.eea.europa.eu/publications/nec-directive-reporting-status-2018.

30. Directive 2010/75/EU on industrial emissions, OJ 2010 L 334/17.

31. Article 4(1) IED.

32. The definition given in the box "Best Available Techniques" is based on Kingston et al., *European Environmental Law,* at 325.

33. Article 1 IED.

34. Article 5(2) IED.

35. For the role of cost-benefit analysis in BAT, see David Pearce, "Cost Benefit Analysis and Environmental Policy" (1998) 14(4) *Oxford Review of Economic Policy* 84–100.

36. See http://eippcb.jrc.ec.europa.eu/index.html.

37. Available at http://eippcb.jrc.ec.europa.eu/reference/.

38. Kingston et al., *European Environmental Law,* at 341.

39. See "Flash Eurobarometer 344: Attitudes of Europeans towards Water-Related Issues," March 2012, http://ec.europa.eu/commfrontoffice/publicopinion/flash/fl_344_sum_en.pdf.

40. See, for example, Article 14 WFD.

41. Directive 2013/39/EU.

42. See, e.g., Giorgos Kallis and David Butler, "The EU Water Framework Directive: Measures and Implications" (2001) 3 *Water Policy* 125–142.

43. Available at https://eur-lex.europa.eu/legal-content/EN/TXT/PDF/?uri=CELEX:02000L0060–20141120&from=EN.

44. Directive 2006/118/EC.

45. Directive 2012/39/EU.

46. Many Member States already had a national system similar to this in place.

47. These plans and the implementation of the WFD more generally are subject to routine assessment. Reports can be accessed at http://ec.europa.eu/environment/water/water-framework/impl_reports.htm.

48. Directive 98/83/EC on the quality of water intended for human consumption OJ L 330/32. A consolidated version of the Directive can be found at https://eur-lex.europa.eu/legal-content/EN/TXT/PDF/?uri=CELEX:01998L0083–20151027&from=EN.

49. See Articles 2 and 3 DWD.

50. Article 1(2) DWD.

51. Article 4(1)(a) DWD.

52. Article 4(1)(b) DWD.

53. Information available at www.who.int/topics/drinking_water/en/.

54. Information on the Scientific Committee on Health and Environmental Risk is available at https://ec.europa.eu/health/scientific_committees/environmental_risks_en.

55. Article 4(2) DWD. This is the same standard as in the non-deterioration provision of Article 4 WFD, discussed in this chapter.

56. See Annex I DWD.

57. Case C-337/89 *Commission v. United Kingdom* ECLI:EU:C:1992:456, paras 24–25.

58. Articles 7 and 13, Annex II, and Annex III DWD. The Commission provides synthesis reports every cycle, which citizens can use to be informed about the quality of drinking water across the EU, available at http://ec.europa.eu/environment/water/water-drink/reporting_en.html.

59. Article 8 DWD.

60. European Environment Agency, "Europe's Environment: The Fourth Assessment" (2007) 96.

61. European Commission Joint Research Centre, "Status of Local Soil Contamination in Europe" (2016), available at https://ec.europa.eu/jrc/en/publication/status-local-soil-contamination-europe-revision-indicator-progress-management-contaminated-sites.

62. European Commission, "Communication from the Commission to the Council, the European Parliament, the European Economic and Social Committee and the Committee of the Regions: Thematic Strategy for Soil Protection" COM (2006) 231 final.

63. Ibid., at 6.

64. Proposal for a Directive of the European Parliament and of the Council establishing a framework for the protection of soil and amending Directive 2004/35/EC, COM (2006) 232 final.

65. European Commission, "Commission Staff Working Document: Thematic Strategy for Soil Protection—Summary of the impact assessment" COM (2006) 231 final.

66. European Commission, "The implementation of the Soil Thematic Strategy and ongoing activities" COM (2012) 46 final.

67. Full text available at https://eur-lex.europa.eu/legal-content/EN/TXT/PDF/?uri=CELEX:32013D1386&from=EN.

68. Membership in the European Environment Agency extends beyond the EU's twenty-seven Member States.

69. See recent data by the European Environment Agency, available at www.eea.europa.eu/data-and-maps/indicators/progress-in-management-of-contaminated-sites-3/assessment.

70. See www.eea.europa.eu/highlights/soil-contamination-widespread-in-europe.

71. Ibid.

72. OJ 1967 L 196/1.

73. OJ 2006 L 396.

74. OJ 2008 L 353/1.

75. For details, see Anu Bradford, "The Brussels Effect" (2012) 107 *Northwestern University Law Review* 1.

76. See also Commission Implementing Regulation (EU) 2016/9 on joint submission of data and data-sharing in accordance with Regulation (EC) No. 1907/2006, OJ 2016 L3/41.

77. See http://ec.europa.eu/environment/chemicals/reach/pdf/publications/final_report_pp.pdf.

78. For recent appeals and decisions, see https://echa.europa.eu/regulations/appeals.

79. Council Directive 67/548/EEC of 27 June 1967 on the approximation of laws, regulations and administrative provisions relating to the classification, packaging and labelling of dangerous substances, OJ 196/1.

80. Some seven thousand chemicals are subject to harmonized categorization under Annex VI CLP.

81. Regulation (EC) No. 1223/2009 on cosmetic products OJ 2009 L 342/59.

82. Directive 2012/18/EU on the control of major-accident hazards involving dangerous substances, OJ 2012 L 197/1.

83. Regulation (EU) No. 528/2012, OJ 2012 L 167/1 and Regulation (EC) No. 1107/2009, OJ 2009 L 309/1.

84. Article 16 REACH.

85. Krista Harper et al., "Environmental Justice and Roma Communities in Central and Eastern Europe" (2009) 19 *Environmental Policy and Governance* 251.

86. For a discussion of the waste management industry in the EU, see European Public Service Union, "Waste Management in Europe," www.epsu.org/sites/default/files/article/files/Waste%20Management%20in%20Europe.%20Good%20Jobs%20in%20the%20Circular%20Economy%20for%20web.pdf.

87. See DG Environment, http://ec.europa.eu/environment/waste/index.htm, for updated figures on EU waste production and policies; and Eurostat: Waste, https://ec.europa.eu/eurostat/web/environment/waste, for statistics on waste production and recycling.

88. See ibid., at 19–21 (listing employment in waste management by Member State).

89. Directive 75/439/EEC and Directive 75/442/EEC, respectively.

90. Directive 2008/98/EC on waste.

91. Specifically, the 2007 WaFD and the Directive on Waste Oils OJ 1975 L 194/23 and Directive 91/689/EEC on Hazardous Waste, OJ 1991 L 377.

92. Article 29 WaFD.

93. European Commission, "Communication from the Commission: Closing the loop—An EU action plan for the Circular Economy" COM (2015) 614 final.

94. For the most recent amendments to Directive 2008/98/EC, see Directive 2018/851. Full set of amendments under the 2018 review available at https://eur-lex.europa.eu/legal-content/EN/TXT/PDF/?uri=OJ:L:2018:150:FULL&from=EN.

95. Article 11(2)(c)(d)(e), consolidated Directive 2008/98/EC (WaFD).

96. 2016 EU Waste Statistics, available at https://ec.europa.eu/eurostat/statistics-explained/index.php/Waste_statistics#Total_waste_generation.

97. For an overview of waste production around the world, see World Bank, "What a Waste 2.0: A Global Snapshot of Solid Waste Management to 2050," https://openknowledge.worldbank.org/handle/10986/30317.

98. European Public Service Union, "Waste Management in Europe," www.epsu.org/sites/default/files/article/files/Waste%20Management%20in%20Europe.%20Good%20Jobs%20in%20the%20Circular%20Economy%20for%20web.pdf.

99. See this chapter's section on "Air Pollution."

100. The classifications in Annex III must be read together with the definitions of hazardous properties in Regulation 1272/2008 and Regulation 440/2008 of 30 May 2008 laying down test methods pursuant to Regulation (EC) No 1907/2006 of the European Parliament and of the Council on the Registration, Evaluation, Authorisation and Restriction of Chemicals (REACH). REACH is discussed in detail in this chapter's snapshot on "Chemicals and Dangerous Substances."

101. Article 7 WaFD.

102. Specified in Article 13 WaFD.

103. Articles 35 and 36 WaFD.

104. See "Report from the Commission the Council and the European Parliament on progress of implementation of Council Directive 2011/70/EURATOM and an inventory of radioactive waste and spent fuel present in the Community's territory and the future prospects," https://eur-lex.europa.eu/legal-content/EN/TXT/PDF/?uri=CELEX:52017SC0161&from=EN.

105. A full overview of activities is given in European Commission, "Commission Staff Working Document: Inventory of radioactive waste and spent fuel present in the Community's territory and the future prospects" SWD (2017) 161 final.

106. Article 13(1) and 14(1) Directive 2011/70/Euratom.

107. See the report cited in note 104.

108. The report of the most recent meeting (2011) of the Standing Working Group can be found at https://ec.europa.eu/energy/sites/ener/files/documents /49th_meeting_dec_2011.pdf.

CHAPTER SEVEN

Ecosystem Management

This chapter sets out the essentials of the EU legal approach to ecosystem management. It begins by defining the general problems presented by ecosystem management. It then describes the fundamentals of the European approach to these problems, before providing snapshots of the strategies on which the EU relies for four important types of ecosystem management: (1) protecting and promoting general biodiversity; (2) protecting and restoring particular wildlife; (3) protecting special types of ecosystems, particularly habitats; and (4) protecting and managing particular spaces, specifically those used for agriculture.

ECOSYSTEM MANAGEMENT AS AN ENVIRONMENTAL PROBLEM

Ecological systems, or *ecosystems*, are geographic areas where living entities (plants, animals, and other organisms) and nonliving entities (water, air, and soil) interact in mutually interdependent ways. Ecosystem management seeks to preserve, sustain, and secure whole ecosystems and the qualities of ecosystems that are deemed valuable.

Since humans evolved, human activities have affected ecosystems. When performed deliberately, however, ecosystem management requires policymakers to trade off competing social, cultural, and environmental values, as when they must balance the destruction of a biodiverse wetland against the social benefits of development. In managing the ecosystems under their control, policymakers may choose to allow, prevent, or mitigate ecosystem degradation, which occurs whenever valued aspects of an ecosystem are harmed. Policymakers may also attempt to repair past degradation through ecosystem restoration, or to purposefully change existing ecosystems to secure more of whatever is valued.

To accurately predict the impacts of policy choices on ecosystems, policymakers depend on information about how living and nonliving entities relate to and depend on one another, through time as well as over space. As discussed in chapter 1, the impacts of human action on the nonhuman environment are typically diffuse and complex, implicating a series of natural and scientific processes that can be difficult to detect, predict, and understand. Where ecological systems are involved, these impacts may be particularly interactive, such that a small change in input may create substantial environmental consequences both within that ecosystem and within related ecosystems. Management of these impacts is made all the more complicated by scientific research suggesting both that many ecosystems exhibit some level of resilience to disruption and that there may also be nonlinear "tipping points" where even small changes may destroy entire ecosystems. To prevent unintentional and irreversible consequences, ecosystem management systems must incorporate some method for collecting and processing information about the nonhuman environment, and about the likely impacts of human (in)action. In many cases, however, that information is likely to be incomplete, and impacts may remain uncertain or change rapidly.

Even where ecosystem managers can call upon high-quality scientific information, they still face substantial policy challenges. These include defining the geographic and temporal spaces that should be protected; coordinating ecosystem management with other environmental policies; and, most controversially, determining which qualities of ecosystems are valuable enough to justify policy intervention.

One set of important policy decisions is related to the appropriate scope of ecosystem management. How far into the future should ecosystems be protected, and when ecosystems are being restored, to what point in time should they be restored? While many countries have adopted rhetoric about maintaining "sustainable ecosystems," commentators increasingly warn that the term *sustainability* can be misleading in obscuring value-laden decisions about the time frame of concern, the benefits and costs that matter, and the relative priority of economic, social, and environmental benefits and costs over time.[1] Attempts to manage ecosystems are further complicated by the fact that plants, animals, and other organisms may develop biological and environmental interdependencies with adjacent ecosystems, or even with plants, animals, and organisms that are geographically distant. The difficulty of defining ecosystems geographically leads to substantial tension in determining what level of government (local, Member State, EU, international) is best suited to manage any particular ecosystem.

The regulatory complexity of ecosystem management is not limited to managing multiple levels of government. The interaction between ecosystem management and other environmental regimes—including legal mechanisms for managing the sources of potential harm to ecosystems, such as pollution policy or natural resource use—adds another layer of complexity. For example, schemes for managing aquatic ecosystems must often account for risks of acid rain, a potentially devastating source of aquatic ecosystem degradation, which increases the acidity of rivers, lakes, and aquatic environments and leads to toxic leaching of soil-based aluminum. Acid rain risk, however, is primarily driven by emissions of sulfur dioxide and nitrogen oxide, gases that are typically regulated through air pollution regimes.

Finally, goal setting for ecosystem management is inherently controversial because different peoples and groups hold clashing views about which qualities of an ecosystem should be promoted, to what extent, and why. One of the key ways to quantify the value of ecosystems is to focus on which benefits they provide to humans. These "ecosystem services"[2] range from providing food and water, to regulating climate and flood risk, to providing cultural and recreational opportunities.[3] While the identification of ecosystem services can be helpful for policymakers, it also raises the important (and controversial) question of whether ecosystems are valuable solely because of their "services"— that is, for how they harm or benefit humans—or whether ecosystems should also be managed to protect nonhuman plants, animals, or organisms for their own sake, regardless of their benefit to humans.

Legal systems have developed different answers to the question of when—if ever—the law ought to protect nonhuman interests. In most jurisdictions, environmental law remains focused—sometimes exclusively—on shaping the environment for the benefit of humans. Yet there is a growing number of exceptions to this general rule. In New Zealand, for example, the Whanganui River ecosystem has been recognized as a legal entity with the same rights, duties, and liabilities as any legal person. Similarly, the Ganga and Yamuna River systems in India were granted legal personality by the Indian High Court in 2017.[4] The EU has not gone as far as creating legal personality for nonhuman environmental entities, and it is unclear whether the CJEU would have the jurisdiction to do so. Nevertheless, the protection of nonhuman interests is a salient feature of EU environmental law. For example, animal welfare is an EU value that is enshrined in Article 13 of the Treaty on the Functioning of the European Union, and legislation has existed on the protection of animals used for scientific purposes since 1986.[5]

KEY CHARACTERISTICS OF EU ECOSYSTEM MANAGEMENT

The EU is historically rich in biodiversity and wildlife, some of which are unique in the world, and it comprises a wide range of ecosystems, ranging from the arid eastern steppes to the boreal forests, and from the Arctic to the coastal Mediterranean. Since the start of the twentieth century, the pressure placed on these ecosystems by human habitation and consumption has led to the rapid decline of species and habitats throughout Europe. The EU has played a central role in slowing—in some cases even reversing—that decline. Yet significant tensions remain between the EU and many Member States with respect to implementation of EU law and programs in this area.

Because ecosystems are tied to geographic space, land-use and property-law regimes play an important role in ecosystem management. Within the EU, decision making connected to land use and property law continues to be the prerogative of the Member States,[6] each of which has different domestic delegation arrangements with local and municipal governments. The political and legal reality of land use is a complicating factor in an already environmentally complex regulatory problem: the natural and ecological borders of ecosystems seldom overlap with legal jurisdictions (within and between Member States), which creates a patchwork system of regulation and can lead to community action problems where a larger ecosystem is spread across multiple jurisdictions.

Growing awareness of the transnational interdependence of ecosystems, and the resulting need for coordinated nature and biodiversity protection, has created space for EU involvement in ecosystem management. The earliest example of this is the Birds Directive, first adopted in 1979[7] (even before the EU had acquired environmental policy competence), which continues to be one of the pillars of the EU's ecosystem management policy. It has been joined by the Habitats Directive, the Natura 2000 network, and a collection of other directives and regulations, many of which implement the international treaties to which the EU and its Member States are parties. The implementation of these directives and regulations is placed in the hands of the Member States, and the tension between having to allow for variations in environmental conditions and ensuring high environmental quality has created significant challenges to their effectiveness.

Apart from conservation efforts, EU ecosystem management includes specific regulation of some ecosystems, including agricultural land and

TABLE 10

Important EU Laws Related to Ecosystem Management

Law	Year Enacted	Target
Birds Directive	1979 (last amended 2009)	Protects all 500 wild bird species naturally occurring in the EU
Habitats Directive	1992	Protects endangered and threatened organisms, ecosystems, and ecosystem components
CITES Regulation	1996	Regulates the trade of wild flora and fauna by implementing the CITES treaty
Marine Strategy Framework Directive	2008	Establishes a framework for community action in marine environmental policy
Invasive Alien Species Regulation	2015	Prevents and manages the spread of invasive alien species
Timber Regulation	2013	Regulates timber markets in order to reduce illegal logging
Zoos Directive	1999	Regulates the keeping of wild animals and biodiversity conservation in zoos
Trade in Seal Products Regulation	2009	Bans trade in seal products, with the exception of Inuit or other indigenous communities

fisheries. The economic importance of these ecosystems plays a particularly explicit role in their management. In both these areas, the EU has extensive competence—with respect to fisheries, the EU's competence is exclusive—and its policies are often environmentally and economically controversial. Much of the controversy has centered on the question of whether the EU is sufficiently attentive to the environmental impacts of managing and promoting agricultural and/or marine ecosystems. For example, the EU's Common Agricultural Policy used to be agnostic to environmental impacts.[8] Only the more recent versions of it include some analysis of the environmental impacts of agricultural policy.

The EU's approach to ecosystem management is characterized by a complicated division of competence between the EU and its Member States; implementation by Member States, on which the effectiveness of EU policies depends; and continued tension between the economic and environmental value of ecosystems.

DISCUSSION QUESTIONS

1. Who benefits from good ecosystem management, and who suffers from poor ecosystem management?

2. How should policymakers balance the economic value of ecosystems with their environmental value?

3. How can policymakers or the public know that an ecosystem is being managed poorly? What about when a system is being managed well?

LEGAL SNAPSHOTS:
ECOSYSTEM MANAGEMENT IN THE EU

The next sections provide a series of "snapshots" explaining how the EU engages in four important types of ecosystem management: (1) protecting and promoting general biodiversity; (2) protecting and restoring particular wildlife; (3) protecting special types of ecosystems, particularly habitats; and (4) protecting and managing particular areas, such as those used for agriculture.

BIODIVERSITY

DEFINITION

Biological diversity, or *biodiversity*, represents the variety of life in a habitat or ecosystem. This may refer to diversity within species, between species, and/or among ecosystems.

DISTINCTIVE CHALLENGES OF MANAGING
BIODIVERSITY

Science has described about 1.5 million species of life on Earth, though scientists estimate that the true number could be closer to ten million. Diverse species, and interactions between those species, have developed over millennia in response to vastly varying environmental, natural, and human-led processes. Biodiversity is a measure of the number and variety of these forms of life.

It is intrinsically challenging to understand the health and resilience of every variety of life in even a single habitat or ecosystem; understanding the best policies for promoting biodiversity across habitats and ecosystems is even more complex. This means that, for biodiversity policy, informational burdens loom large. Often, however, there is limited information about the long-term and systemic impacts of changing or eliminating specific forms of life.

Even where policymakers have significant information about the variety of life in an ecosystem, they still face tough policy choices about when and how much to prioritize biodiversity over competing values. One particularly common tension comes from trade-offs between biodiversity and development: much of the time, developing land for economic purposes destroys at least a portion (and sometimes all) of the variety of life on that land.

Trade-offs like these often require policymakers to determine whether, how, and why they value biodiversity. Is biodiversity good only for the ways that it benefits humans through ecosystem services—for example, by offering the potential for lifesaving new medical treatments or (indirectly) by sustaining other life-forms within the relevant ecosystem? Is it also valuable for separate moral or ethical reasons—for example, because humans have an obligation to protect nonhuman populations or to sustain the Earth as they found it? Policymakers' answers to these difficult questions can inform whether they adopt general biodiversity policies, which seek to promote and protect the variety of life regardless of the type of life or its apparent value to humans, or whether they adopt more specific policies tailored toward preserving specific ecosystems or particular forms of life.

KEY EU LEGAL APPROACHES TO BIODIVERSITY

The EU is a signatory of the Convention on Biological Diversity, an international treaty that entered into force in 1992,[9] aimed at ensuring the development of national biodiversity plans and the international sharing of the benefits that arise from genetic resources.

The EU Biodiversity Strategy

The EU adopted its first European-level biodiversity strategy in 1998. This strategy is the umbrella under which specific EU legislation regarding ecosystems, species, and habitats has been adopted. Although it remains central to EU-level ecosystem management, the strategy has

---

SPOTLIGHT 16. CONVENTION ON BIOLOGICAL DIVERSITY

The Convention on Biological Diversity, sometimes called the "Biodiversity Convention," is a multilateral agreement designed to develop strategies for the conservation and sustainable use of biological diversity. It refers to "the intrinsic value of biological diversity" and "the ecological genetic, social, economic, scientific, educational, cultural, recreational and aesthetic values of biological diversity and its components."

The Convention has been ratified by 196 parties, including the European Union and 192 of the 193 UN states. It requires signatories to prepare a national biodiversity strategy and creates a set of incentives for conservation and sustainable use, including a funding mechanism for developing countries that commit to critical biodiversity conservation projects.

Two protocols have been adopted under the Convention: the Cartagena Protocol on Biosafety (adopted in 2000) and the Nagoya Protocol on Access to Genetic Resources and the Fair and Equitable Sharing of Benefits Arising from Their Utilization to the Convention on Biological Diversity (adopted in 2010). The Nagoya Protocol is often considered particularly important for achieving equitable sharing of global natural resources. However, it has proven problematic to ensure a comprehensive application of the protocol, and many state parties include only certain types of species in their national implementing legislation.

---

been widely viewed as less effective than was hoped and has gone through several reviews and restatements since its inception.[10] The most recent reiteration came in 2010, when six specific targets were adopted.[11]

One of the foundations of the strategy is a formal recognition that biodiversity and other ecosystem services have intrinsic as well as economic value. To better quantify ecosystems' economic value, the EU cofounded the global TEEB (The Economics of Ecosystems and Biodiversity) initiative.[12] As with many other initiatives pursued under the six biodiversity targets, TEEB is a collaboration with European and non-European partners and builds on the network set up under the Convention on Biological Diversity. In addition to pursuing formal international collaborations, the EU's biodiversity strategy explicitly incorporates and seeks to address global biodiversity (see table 11, target 6).

A second core principle underlying the strategy is the "no net loss" principle, which dictates that when negative impacts on biodiversity cannot be avoided, then, at the very least, equivalent gains must be achieved elsewhere in order to avoid a net loss in biodiversity. This principle has led to compensation schemes, particularly under the Birds and Habitats Directives, but has not yet been operationalized with respect to unprotected species and habitats.

Finally, the EU has set up several finance schemes, such as the Natural Capital Financing Facility, for helping Member States achieve biodiversity goals.[13] Biodiversity goals have also been incorporated into the EU budget, which means that all structural funds run by the EU—a key means for the EU to steer regional development—must take account of biodiversity impacts when allocating funds (see table 11).

Achievement of the EU's biodiversity goals continues to be hampered by many Member States' underperformance. Some have suggested that tougher enforcement is needed by the EU, whereas others blame the structure of the program itself for the lack of successful implementation. This ongoing controversy has led all legislation under the EU's biodiversity program to be reviewed under REFIT, the European Commission's Regulatory Fitness and Performance Programme, aimed at making EU law simpler and less costly.

Zoo Policy and Invasive Species

Apart from the EU's overarching principles and goals, as articulated in its biodiversity strategy, there are two specific EU regulations directly

TABLE II

EU Biodiversity Targets for 2020

Target	Goal
Target 1	**Protect species and habitats** – By 2020, requires "secure" status for 100% more habitats and 50% more species
Target 2	**Maintain and restore ecosystems** – By 2020, requires restoring at least 15% of degraded ecosystems, and an increase in green infrastructure
Target 3	**Achieve more sustainable agriculture and forestry** – By 2020, requires measurable improvement of species affected by agriculture and forestry
Target 4	**Make fishing more sustainable and seas healthier** – By 2015, fishing is required to be sustainable; by 2020, fish stocks and European seas are required to be healthy
Target 5	**Combat invasive species** – By 2020, invasive species must be identified and priority species controlled or eradicated
Target 6	**Help stop the loss of global biodiversity** – By 2020, the EU must step up contributions to avert global biodiversity loss

related to biodiversity loss: the Zoos Directive and the Invasive Alien Species Regulation.[14]

The Zoos Directive regulates the keeping of wild animals in zoos and sets up a legal framework that is aimed to ensure biodiversity conservation in zoos. Member States have to implement the Directive through the adoption of a licensing and inspection system.[15]

The Invasive Alien Species Regulation addresses animals and plants that are not native to the environment where they are found and that cause harm to their new environment. These species cause damage to the EU's economy, costing billions of euros every year, and pose a serious threat to many native plants and animals.[16] Because many invasive species are widely dispersed, the EU partly relies on citizens to monitor invasive species through contributions to the European Alien

Species Information Network.[17] Generally, the EU's competence in this realm rests on the presumption that the transnational nature of many of these species makes an EU-wide approach more effective than a national approach.

TAKEAWAYS

✓ Regulation of biodiversity is challenging both scientifically and politically. From a scientific perspective, it is challenging to identify and understand the long-term and systemic impacts of changing or eliminating specific forms of life. From a political perspective, it can be challenging to know how much to prioritize biodiversity over competing values, like promoting development or supporting agriculture.

✓ The EU is a signatory to the Convention on Biological Diversity and has adopted its own biodiversity strategy, which interacts with, and builds on, that Convention.

✓ The measures under the EU's biodiversity strategy depend heavily on Member States' implementation and enforcement. Both have caused problems in this area, leading to review of the strategy and several revisions since the initial adoption in 1998.

✓ In addition to its general biodiversity strategy are two EU-specific initiatives—the Zoos Directive and the Invasive Alien Species Regulation—related to particular aspects of biodiversity.

DISCUSSION QUESTIONS

1. Should, and could, biodiversity be monetized?
2. Can there ever be sufficient biodiversity? How might such a standard be set?
3. Who benefits from biodiversity?

WILDLIFE

DEFINITION

Wildlife are undomesticated animals that live in their natural habitats.

DISTINCTIVE CHALLENGES OF WILDLIFE REGULATION

The most salient use of wildlife law is the protection of endangered species: forms of life whose continued existence is imperiled. Other policies seek to protect species that have cultural or social value, or permit the purposeful hunting or killing of other forms of wildlife.

As with other forms of ecosystem management, a fundamental challenge of wildlife law is the informational burden of determining how human behaviors are likely to affect the variety of forms of wildlife that the law might target. The burdens of identifying and understanding particular forms of life can be particularly great when those organisms are rare or endangered, since by definition these organisms are fewer in number and thus often difficult to detect.

Another critical policy determination in wildlife law is the decision of which types of life to protect, and how much. The decision of which forms of life are valuable, either to humans or intrinsically, is morally and ethically complex and is generally informed by social and cultural values. As a result, different jurisdictions often come to very different outcomes in determining which forms of life deserve the most protection, and the level of protection those forms of life deserve. For example, many more legal protections exist for animals than for plants. Because animals are mobile, however, wildlife schemes to protect animals must account for the fact that animals cross property and national boundaries, complicating questions of property rights, jurisdiction, and interstate cooperation. Such concerns are heightened for particularly mobile life-forms such as migratory birds.

Wildlife law can also pertain to the indirect protection of species through the regulation on trade in these animals and their products.

This is most often done for species whose endangerment and hunting have high social salience, such as seals or whales. However, the hunting of these animals and the use of their products also tends to have high cultural value, particularly for indigenous peoples. Moreover, the latter groups are often not the cause of any endangerment, which creates direct tension between preservation and indigenous traditions.

KEY EU LEGAL APPROACHES TO WILDLIFE MANAGEMENT

EU legislation protects European wildlife both directly and indirectly. The EU does not have any specific, recognized competence to address wildlife protection; rather, legislation on wildlife is derived from the EU's environmental competence and its competence on the internal market.

While the EU plays a crucial role in the protection of wildlife for certain highly mobile species, such as birds,[18] many activities involving wildlife are reflections of long-standing national cultural practices, which means that Member States retain decision-making power with respect to many forms of wildlife. Hunting is a prime example of such an activity. The EU has regulated some forms of hunting or hunting practices, often as a result of international agreements on trade in endangered or otherwise valued species. For the majority of hunting practices, however, the EU has to rely on voluntary agreements and cooperation with national actors, such as the European Charter on Hunting and Biodiversity.[19]

Even in areas where Member States retain competence, however, the EU often plays an indirect, supporting role in wildlife policy. An example of this is the 2018 EU Pollinators Initiative, which creates a pan-European network aimed at gathering information on pollinator decline and addressing its causes.[20] There are also EU-wide prohibitions on trade in animals and animal products. These regulations are based partly on EU initiatives, such as the ban on leghold traps in hunting,[21] and partly on international obligations, such as those under the Convention on International Trade in Endangered Species of Wild Fauna and Flora (CITES).

The most important direct EU protection of wildlife is provided by the Birds Directive (on the conservation of wild birds), the oldest piece of EU environmental legislation and a cornerstone of the EU's ecosystem management policy. Another key piece of EU wildlife policy is the regulation that implements CITES. Both are discussed below.

Birds Directive

The Birds Directive was adopted in response to customary hunting in Southern Europe and North Africa, which was thought to be a threat to migratory bird populations. It is widely viewed as having been highly effective at protecting those populations and remains a cornerstone of EU wildlife protection policy.

The protection offered by the Birds Directive[22] is aimed at restoring wild bird populations "at a level which corresponds specifically to ecological and scientific requirements, while taking account of economic and recreational requirements."[23] The Directive imposes responsibilities on Member States in order to achieve this aim, which vary in stringency according to the level of endangerment of the bird species or their habitat.

The habitats and diversity of all wild bird species, which are listed in Annex 5 of the Directive, must be "maintained or re-established." Of the species protected, 194 species (listed in Annex 1) are considered particularly threatened. For these birds, the Member States are required to designate Special Protection Areas (SPAs), which represent an important link between the Birds Directive and the Habitats Directive (see our next snapshot), the two pillars of the EU's biodiversity agenda. The Habitats Directive relies on a similar designation strategy for conservation sites; together with the SPAs and marine conservation sites, these sites combine to form the Natura 2000 network (see spotlight 17).

SPOTLIGHT 17. NATURA 2000 NETWORK

The Birds Directive and the Habitats Directive rely on the "designation strategy": identifying specific areas for nature conservation as the foundation for all other conservation actions. Sites designated under these directives combine to form the Natura 2000 network. The Natura 2000 viewer (http://natura2000.eea.europa.eu) shows all the sites and maintains information about each of them.

COVERAGE

In 2019, the Natura 2000 network included 27,863 sites across the Member States, covering 1,336,151 km^2 in combined land and marine areas (17.9 percent of European land area). The national coverage of the Natura 2000 sites within the Member States ranges from 9 percent to 38 percent, with a higher proportion of protected habitat types and species being located in the Mediterranean, Continental, and Alpine Regions as compared to the Atlantic Region. Natural and seminatural habitats and species such as large carnivores are more common in the Central and Eastern European Member States.

DESIGNATION OF SITES

Under the Birds Directive, EU Member States have to identify those sites that are "most suitable territories" to protect migratory bird species and species listed in Annex 1 of the Directive. The Habitats Directive instructs Member States to designate sites that are natural habitats (Annex I) or habitats of specific species (Annex II). Designation of sites under both directives is done purely on the basis of scientific criteria. This results in three types of sites, all of which impose different conservation obligations:

SPA—Special Protection Area under the Birds Directive
SCI—Site of Community Importance under the Habitats
    Directive
SAC—Special Area of Conservation under the Habitats Directive

---

MARINE SITES

The European Commission considers the Natura 2000 network mostly "complete" on land, insofar as few additional land sites are expected to be designated. However, designation of marine areas has been much slower, largely due to limited availability of necessary scientific information. The adoption of the 2008 Marine Framework Directive is supposed to assist in improving this situation. Designation of Marine Protected Areas has proven more legally complex than designation of sites under the Birds and Habitats Directives, as there are a number of different legislative instruments with different definitions of these areas. For example, the Habitats Directive lists nine marine habitat types and sixteen marine species that require marine site designation, and the Birds Directive lists sixty bird species whose conservation requires marine site protection.

Member States have special obligations to protect SPAs. While Member States should "strive to" avoid pollution and deterioration of all wild bird habitats, there is a requirement to take "appropriate measures" to avoid pollution in SPAs. Once an area has been designated an SPA, the Habitats Directive becomes applicable to the area,[24] overruling some of the obligations that were previously listed in the Birds Directive. The resulting system of protection is arguably stronger than under the Birds Directive, though fairly comparable. These measures include the mandatory creation of special conservation regimes, and any development projects in these areas become much more complicated, if not impossible.

Given the additional obligations they impose on Member States, it is perhaps not surprising that the designation of SPAs has been subject to intense debate before the CJEU. Generally, Article 2 of the Birds Directive states that the Member States can "take account of economic and recreational requirements" in meeting their legal obligations; in one important case, Member States sought to use this provision to argue that

SPA designations should be subject to economic and recreational requirements. However, the Court held that the protection awarded to SPAs is greater than that given other areas, and therefore the more general considerations of Article 2 do not apply to these special areas.[25] This means that the Member States' margin of discretion in designating SPAs is limited to scientific, ornithological criteria and that it excludes economic and recreational interests.[26] Moreover, once an area has been designated an SPA, any changes to it can be justified only rarely, where exceptional general (social or economic) interests are found to outweigh the general ecological interest represented by the Directive.[27]

Apart from habitat-based protection, the Birds Directive also regulates hunting, which is prohibited for all species except those in Annex 2, and even then, only in prescribed ways: outside of breeding, rearing, and return migration season,[28] and only through certain methods.[29] Related practices that could negatively affect populations, such as disturbances to nests and breeding grounds,[30] are also banned. Similarly, any trade in live or dead wild birds is prohibited.[31]

CITES Regulation

The CITES Regulation is the key piece of legislation used to implement the EU's international obligations under CITES, which provides a number of protections to wildlife through limiting trade of animal and plant products. CITES entered into force in 1975, and the EU has been responsible for its implementation since 1984. The EU's role with respect to CITES is based on its competence on the internal market and CITES's trade focus, not—as might be expected—its environmental competence. The EU itself did not become a signatory of CITES until 2015, because the Convention only allowed for state parties until 2013.

CITES aims to protect wildlife by regulating, and often prohibiting, the trade in wild flora and fauna. It does so by setting up a permitting scheme that differentiates between three categories of species, which are listed in the CITES Appendices.[32] The listing of species in Appen-

TABLE 12

CITES Appendices

Appendix	Species	Protection
Appendix I	Species threatened with extinction *1,003 species and 42 subspecies*	Trade is authorized only in exceptional circumstances
Appendix II	Species that are not yet threatened with extinction but may become so *34,596 species and 12 subspecies*	Trade is strictly regulated
Appendix III	Species that are subject to regulation within the jurisdiction of a party and for which the cooperation of other parties is needed to prevent or restrict their exploitation *202 species, 14 subspecies, 1 variety*	Regulation depends on party

dices I and II (threatened with extinction or soon-to-be-threatened) requires a two-thirds majority by the parties to CITES. The parties are free to add native species to Appendix III on their own initiative.

The EU's CITES Regulation follows the CITES categorization but adopts stricter protection for several species in Appendices II and III. It has also adopted *reservations* regarding a few species, which means that for those species, the CITES protection does not apply. The EU has, for example, expressed reservations regarding three subspecies of foxes and four taxa of mink, which had been placed on Appendix III by India. For the species on these lists, the Regulation puts in place procedures and documentation requirements, which extend to any movement of live specimens. It also dictates minimum sanctions that Member States must impose for infringements. Even though the Regulation is directly applicable, implementation of national law has been adopted by each Member State, because many of the issues stipulated in the Regulation remain under their sovereignty.[33]

The CITES Regulation also creates a number of authorities at the EU level, such as the Committee on Trade in Wild Fauna and Flora, the Scientific Review Group, and the Enforcement Group. Though not administrative agencies as traditionally understood, these authorities are still an interesting example of EU-level institution building. The authorities are made up by Member State representatives but are convened and chaired by the European Commission. In addition, each Member State has at least one CITES authority that is responsible for issuing permits and certificates (see table 12).[34]

In 2016, the EU increased its efforts regarding the issue of wildlife trafficking, which it considers a key threat to certain endangered species, through a joint action plan that combines the powers of the Commission, the European External Action Service, Europol (the European Police Office), Eurojust (an EU agency that enables judicial cooperation), and the Member States.[35]

TAKEAWAYS

✓ EU competence to regulate wildlife is limited; its competence is strongest with respect to migratory species and/or species protected by international law.

✓ The most important EU legislation on wildlife is the Birds Directive. A key power under this Directive is the designation of Special Protection Areas (SPAs).

✓ Another important part of EU wildlife protection is related to implementation of the international treaty known as CITES.

✓ Wildlife protection and management often interacts with, and relies on, long-established cultural practices that are very country specific, making it harder for the EU to regulate.

DISCUSSION QUESTIONS

1. Is it more important to protect rare species, whose continued existence is endangered, or common species? Which is more likely to have significant ecosystem impacts: protecting rare or

common species? Which type of species is more likely to be culturally important?

2. How stringently should protected species be protected? Is it wise to protect those species and their habitats regardless of the cost of the protection? If not, how much cost is too much?

3. How important is it to respect and maintain cultural practices surrounding wildlife, like hunting?

MANAGEMENT OF SPECIAL ECOSYSTEMS: HABITATS

The EU is home to several "special" ecosystems that are rare (within the EU or globally) and/or exhibit unique features that allow them to sustain life-forms that cannot survive elsewhere. The management of each of these systems poses particular challenges. The main way in which the EU protects these special environments is through habitat management.

DEFINITION

A habitat is a type of natural environment, characterized by a unique mix of physical and biological features, where specific species live. In order to be a suitable habitat for a specific species, a habitat must enable it to find food, shelter, and mates for reproduction.

DISTINCTIVE CHALLENGES OF THIS TYPE OF ECOSYSTEM MANAGEMENT

Each animal or plant species depends on at least one habitat with favorable conditions for its survival. Some species, and some habitats, are more robust or flexible than others. Humans have been very successful at surviving in most conditions by adapting their habitats to their own needs. Sadly, many species cope less well with habitat loss and degradation, something that has become increasingly common because of the environmental pressures of human activity. Forestry, agriculture, tourism, and human settlement all contribute to habitat endangerment, which is the main cause of modern species collapse and a direct threat to biodiversity.

Managing habitats involves vexing challenges for regulators. Scientists continue to identify previously unknown species, and knowledge of global species and what they require to survive remains highly incomplete. Moreover, the interaction between habitats and the species that live in them are often symbiotic: species are often crucial for the habitat's survival, just as the habitats ensure species survival. Habitats are also often home to numerous species and are connected to surrounding habitats in important ways, making it even harder to identify all the consequences of habitat degradation. Even without human interference, habitats change over time, responding to climatic changes and/or the natural incursions of a new species. Most habitat, and many species, can withstand gradual changes. However, sudden shocks, such as accelerated climate change or the arrival of an invasive species, can endanger the continued existence of the habitat.

Finally, the regulation of habitats poses special political challenges because habitats are geographic spaces that exist independent of national and international borders. As a result, to regulate habitats successfully, many regulatory actors have to be involved, and effective reversal of habitat degradation and loss has proven extremely difficult. That said, most countries have adopted some form of habitat protection, often linked to the protection of one or more endangered species that depend on the habitat.

KEY EU LEGAL APPROACHES TO HABITAT MANAGEMENT

Alongside the Birds Directive, the 1992 Habitats Directive forms the second pillar of the EU's nature law program. The Habitats Directive adopts a designation strategy similar to that of the Birds Directive, insofar as it relies on the designation of certain areas as a threshold for protection.[36]

SPOTLIGHT 18. ENVIRONMENTAL IMPACT ASSESSMENTS

Since 1985, public and private actors active in the EU are obliged to conduct environmental impact assessments (EIAs) for certain cat-egories of plans.* The developer of the project must provide a com-petent authority—typically at the national level—with information on the environmental impact of the project. This is then evaluated by environmental authorities and affected parties, after which the competent authority reaches a decision, taking into consideration these consultations. This decision is made public and may be challenged before the courts.

Since 2001, most public plans and programs—to be distinguished from the individual projects subject to EIAs—are subject to strategic environmental assessments (SEAs).**

Apart from applying—in part—to different types of activities and actors, the requirements of EIAs and SEAs are fairly similar. A key difference is that under an SEA all reasonable alternatives must be assessed, whereas for an EIA these alternatives are under the discretion of the developer. In addition, Member States must monitor significant environmental effects of the approved plans in order to identify unforeseen adverse effects and undertake appropriate remedial action, as well as ensure that the reports are of sufficient quality.

* Directive 2014/52/EU on the assessment of the effects of certain public and private projects on the environment, OJ L 124/1.
** Directive 2001/42/EC on the assessment of the effects of certain plans and programmes on the environment, OJ L 197/30.

This is a two-step process: first, Member States conduct a comprehensive assessment of all habitat types and species in their territory to produce a list of proposed Sites of Community Importance (SCIs); the list is then reviewed by the Commission and the European Environment Agency, which determine the final list of SCIs to be adopted. After their designation as SCIs, these sites need to be designated as Special Areas of Conservation (SACs) as soon as possible (within a maximum of six years). Both SCIs and SPAs are included in the Natura 2000 network.

EU habitat regulation covers only a subset of the EU's species and habitats: those that are considered to be especially endangered, vulnerable, rare, or important. Alongside the Natura 2000 sites, Member States continue to be able to designate areas as national parks or other protected areas, subject only to national law, as long as these areas are not deemed to be of European importance.

As with other protected areas, the designation process for identifying SCIs and SACs under the Habitats Directive has been complicated and controversial. Member States and the Commission have clashed both on the criteria that should be used for designation and their respective weighting. In the end, the Court of Justice's interpretation of the Habitats Directive has determined that environmental protection should be the paramount consideration for designating an SCI/SAC, even if economic, social, and cultural considerations may also play a role.[37]

Once an area is designated an SCI, Member States incur obligations regarding its protection and conservation, and economic activities in these areas are restrained. These obligations are expanded once the area changes status and becomes an SAC. The most important provisions can be found in Article 6 of the Habitats Directive; among these provisions, paragraphs 6(2)–(4) apply to both SCIs and SACs; Article 6(1) applies only to SACs.[38] Article 6(1) of the Habitats Directive provides that Member States must establish "necessary conservation measures" for the "appropriate management" of these areas. While clearly important, the responsibilities set out in the remainder of Article 6 are considerable and applicable to both SCIs and SACs.

Article 6(2) stipulates that "appropriate steps" must be taken to avoid deterioration of the habitat or disturbance of its resident species. The Member States retain great discretion as to their interpretation of these responsibilities, although a rich body of case law has developed as to acceptable parameters of protective strategies under Article 6(2).[39]

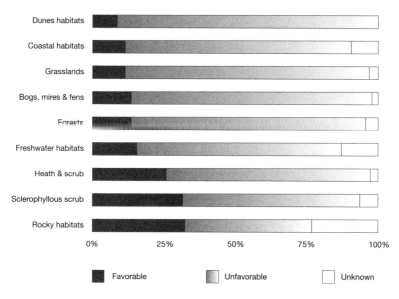

Figure 6. Conservation Trends by Habitat Type.

By far the most important provision of the Habitats Directive is Article 6(3), which imposes two obligations on the Member States: first, the implications of any plan or project likely to have a significant effect on the site, either individually or in combination with other plans or projects, must receive an appropriate assessment "in view of the site's conservation objectives." Second, where the assessment is negative, permission for the development should be refused, unless compensation for the environmental losses can be guaranteed and/or there is an overriding public interest. The Court's interpretation of each of these elements—including "any plan or project," "significant effect," and "appropriate assessment"—has been extremely strict, so as to prevent any erosion of the Directive's goals by the Member States. That said, national courts remain empowered to interpret many other relevant issues, such as the standard of "no reasonable scientific doubt" applicable to negative environmental impacts, which reduces the effect of the Court of Justice's rulings.

Despite the Habitats Directive's protection, the most recent status report on habitat protection by the European Commission shows that only 16 percent of protected habitats have a "favorable conservation status." The overwhelming majority of habitats have an unfavorable status, with 47 percent of the assessments being "inadequate" and 30 percent being "bad."[40] Perhaps even more worryingly, 30 percent of habitats are still deteriorating, while only 4 percent show any improvements so far.[41]

TAKEAWAYS

✓ The Habitats Directive is a key part of the EU's Natura 2000 nature conservation program, focused on the designation and management of Special Areas of Conservation.

✓ Habitat Special Areas of Protection, together with Marine Protected Areas and the Special Protection Areas of the Birds Directive, combine into the Natura 2000 network. This is the largest coordinated network of protected areas in the world.

✓ Despite the relative success in designating habitats as protected, effective protection has proven difficult. Only 4 percent of habitats have been found to be "improving," while 36 percent continue to deteriorate.

DISCUSSION QUESTIONS

1. Which types of ecosystems deserve special protections? Do the EU's criteria of "endangered, vulnerable, rare or important" areas make sense? Should individuals' different reasons for valuing an ecosystem matter to how that ecosystem is protected?

2. Why do you think habitats continue to deteriorate, even after being designated a Special Protection Area, a Marine Protected Area, or a Special Area of Conservation?

AGRICULTURE

DEFINITION

Agriculture is the cultivation of land and rearing of animals to provide food, fiber, and other products for human consumption. Agriculture purposefully prioritizes the interests of selected species—including agricultural crops, livestock, and tree crops—over other species, such as weeds and pests. Agricultural land use often infringes on, or entirely replaces, other land uses, such as habitats for wild animal and plant species. However, agricultural ecosystems can also provide habitats or sources of food for such animals. Agriculture operates as a powerful industry and serves a central role in maintaining food security.

DISTINCTIVE CHALLENGES OF REGULATING AGRICULTURE

It is hard to overstate the role of agriculture in shaping human civilization. The domestication of animals and the farming of land allowed people to create enduring settlements and to live together in bigger groups, forming the early beginnings of cities and towns over eleven thousand years ago. Since then, the scale of agriculture, and of human settlements, has increased a thousandfold—giving rise to industrial agriculture based on large-scale monoculture (relying on the rearing of only one crop, such as corn or wheat), which now dominates world agricultural output in terms of volume. At the same time, billions of people continue to depend on subsistence agriculture, providing barely enough for their own needs.

Globally, agriculture is the dominant type of land use, occupying 40 percent of available land mass.[42] Agriculture provides key ecosystem services—by providing food, fiber, and other products—and, in turn, relies on and affects many other ecosystem services. It can assist in the regulation of soil and water quality, sequester carbon, support biodiversity, and provide cultural services. However, agriculture can also be the source of numerous ecosystem disservices, including loss of wildlife habitat, nutrient runoff, sedimentation of waterways, greenhouse gas emissions, and pesticide poisoning of humans and nontarget species. Regulating these trade-offs is difficult for policymakers and may be increasingly difficult as food security is threatened by climate change and growing populations. Finally, agriculture's reliance on other ecosystem services, notably fresh water, imposes heavy burdens on connected ecosystems.

The market-driven demand for agricultural products can come in direct conflict with environmentally sustainable supply levels. Moreover, globalization has made this demand global, while production is still local. In some cases, this can mean that domestic regulation is informed by foreign preferences that do not take account of local environmental conditions. Importantly, while agricultural productivity can vary significantly year to year as a result of weather and other conditions, the demand for food remains relatively stable. As a result, many countries have chosen to heavily subsidize food production, in the hope that doing so creates a kind of margin of safety through overproduction to ensure that there is always sufficient food. In many cases, however, these subsidies introduce market distortions that lead to overcultivation of one or a few crops. This multitude of pressures on agriculture and the ecosystems it relies on makes food regulation difficult and often ineffective.

Because of the relationship between humans and the land on which they live, agricultural practices often reflect cultural traditions, making it difficult and potentially controversial to change established practices. In the absence of agriculture, many rural areas would lose their main or only source of income. Furthermore, some people and groups attach value to the agricultural way of life, which—in Europe in particular—is often seen as a counterbalance to an increasingly urbanized society and is sometimes held to have traditional cultural value.

Finally, agricultural policy faces the puzzling question of which species to cultivate. This includes selection of specific species—such as wheat—as well as trade-offs between animal and plant cultivation. In addition, agricultural policymakers face the question of what to do with genetically modified organisms (GMOs)—organisms that have been genetically engineered to have some agriculturally desirable trait. Knowledge on the impact of GMOs on agricultural (and surrounding) ecosystems, and on humans through consumption, is still developing. As a result, different countries have adopted different regimes to deal with GMOs. Some, like the EU, have banned their use almost entirely, while others, like the United States, permit and even encourage broad use of GMOs.

KEY EU LEGAL APPROACHES TO AGRICULTURE

The EU's Common Agricultural Policy (CAP) was launched in 1962, long before any European environmental competence existed. Rather than an environmental measure, the CAP was an economic device, based on the important place of agriculture in the economy of founding Member States (particularly France) and the EU's internal market. The CAP remains the most central instrument in agricultural regulation, although some related EU laws (such as the Timber Regulation) have been adopted since.[43] Over twenty-two million people are directly employed by EU agriculture (and another twenty million in related services), and the EU is a net exporter of agricultural food products.

The CAP's current aims are set out in Article 39 of the Treaty on the Functioning of the European Union.[44] Notably, none of the CAP's six aims refers to environmental goals. As a result, any positive environmental impact of the CAP is ancillary, even accidental; in particular, many claim that the CAP has reduced biodiversity by supporting the industrialization of agriculture.

The CAP is also economically controversial. Many Member States resent the heavy subsidization of farming in other Member States, especially France and Spain, and believe that agriculture in the EU is no longer economically or environmentally sustainable. Proponents consider the CAP essential in ensuring food security in the EU, maintaining the way of life of rural communities, and closing the income gap between rural and urban workers.[45]

TABLE 13

Aims and Financing of the Common Agricultural Policy

Pillar	Purpose	Financing (based on 2018 budget)
Income support	Direct payments to farmers to support environmentally friendly farming and their role in taking care of countryside	41.74 billion euros European Agricultural Fund
Rural development measures	To ensure development of rural areas, mainly through national and regional programs	14.37 billion euros European Agricultural Fund for Rural Development
Market measures	Allows EU to intervene in difficult market situations, e.g., sudden price drops due to oversupply	2.7 billion euros European Agricultural Fund

The CAP's goals are achieved through income support,[46] market measures,[47] and rural development measures.[48] All of these measures are administered and paid for by the EU from the European budget.[49] The CAP's funding is perhaps its most contentious aspect: the total funding for 2018 amounted to 58.82 billion euros—almost one third of the EU's entire budget, which is funded by Member States' contributions.

Importantly, the substance and budget for each cycle of the CAP are proposed by the Agricultural Commissioner and then voted on by the Council of (Agricultural) Ministers—made up by national ministers. The European Parliament plays only a consulting role in this process, signaling the high level of Member State control in setting agricultural policy. Payments under the CAP are administered by the Member States, which can decide to assign payments to individual farmers or to regional authorities. Farmers who receive payment under the CAP must adhere to environmental and agricultural standards, and to restrictions on the types of produce they are allowed to farm.

The current CAP runs until 2020. The Commission's proposals for CAP renewal explicitly incorporate environmental and climate goals and show the interaction between agricultural land and other ecosystems more clearly. Regardless of the final form of the new CAP, the following goals must be included: protection of wetlands and peatlands, improved water quality through reduced levels of ammonia and nitrous oxide, and mandatory crop rotation.[50]

TAKEAWAYS

✓ Agriculture is a substantial industry in the EU, which is a net agricultural food exporter.

✓ The main regulatory instrument for agriculture is the Common Agricultural Policy (CAP), which historically has been addressed as a primarily economic policy, without explicit environmental goals.

✓ The subsidization of agriculture in European Member States is controversial, politically and environmentally.

✓ A new CAP will be adopted in 2020. In this revision, more attention is likely to be paid to environmental issues such as water quality, protection of wetlands, and mandatory crop rotation.

DISCUSSION QUESTIONS

1. Do you think that the protection of rural life, specifically through the continued subsidization of otherwise unsustainable agriculture, is a valid basis for the existence of the CAP?

2. Who should decide which species to cultivate—individual farmers, Member States, or the EU? On what basis should agricultural subsidies be allocated?

ECOSYSTEM MANAGEMENT: SUMMARY

Ecosystem management in the EU reflects a series of normative choices about which ecosystems, and which qualities of ecosystems, deserve protection. The EU is a party to the Convention on Biological Diversity and has a series of protections in place for particular ecosystems, such as habitats, and strong protection for endangered animal and plant species through its membership in CITES and through EU-based instruments such as the Birds Directive. Generally speaking, EU agricultural law and policy are administered separately from other environmental schemes. From an environmental perspective, the agriculture of the EU is often particularly noted internationally for the prominence of the controversial Common Agricultural Policy and the very limited use of genetically engineered crops.

KEY TERMS

BIODIVERSITY The variety of life in a habitat or ecosystem.

COMPENSATORY MITIGATION Allowing for the degradation of one habitat, such as a wetland, in exchange for improving (or even creating) a different habitat.

CONSERVATION The protection of a natural environment or species.

ECOSYSTEMS Geographic areas where living entities (plants, animals, and other organisms) and nonliving entities (water, air, and soil) interact in mutually interdependent ways.

GENETIC MODIFICATION The manipulation of an organism's genes using biotechnology, typically to augment desirable traits or delete undesirable ones.

HABITAT The natural home of an animal, plant, or other organism.

NONPOINT SOURCE WATER POLLUTION Water pollution that originates from multiple diffuse sources, as from agricultural runoff or drainage through urban streets.

POINT SOURCE WATER POLLUTION Water pollution that originates from a single identifiable source, such as a pipe or ditch.

SUSTAINABILITY The use of natural resources in a way that is economically, socially, and environmentally viable in the long term.

WETLANDS A transitional ecosystem that forms a link between land and water.

WILDLIFE Undomesticated animals that live in their natural habitats.

DISCUSSION QUESTION

1. Do some ecosystems deserve more protection than others? Why or why not?

NOTES

1. See Robert T. Lackey, "Seven Pillars of Ecosystem Management," 40 *Landscape and Urban Planning* 21–30 (1998).

2. This term was first introduced in Study of Critical Environmental Problems (SCEP), *Man's Impact on the Global Environment* (MIT Press 1970).

3. See United Nations, "Ecosystems and Human Well-being: Synthesis (A Report of the Millennium Ecosystem Assessment)," 2005, at www.millennium assessment.org/documents/document.356.aspx.pdf.

4. See *Mohd. Salim v. State of Uttarakhand & others* (20 March 2017), WP (PIL) 126 of 2014 (Uttarakhand High Court, India). Notably, this ruling was a response to the local government's failure to comply with an earlier ruling of the Court to ensure meaningful protection of the Ganga River system through the creation of a management board.

5. The most recent restatement of this Directive is Directive 2010/63/EU of the European Parliament and of the Council of 22 September 2010 on the protection of animals used for scientific purposes.

6. As explicitly recognized in Article 192(2) Treaty on the Functioning of the European Union.

7. Directive 79/409/EEC.

8. Suzanne Kingston et al., *European Environmental Law* (Cambridge University Press 2017), at 88.

9. Full text available at www.cbd.int/convention/text/default.shtml.

10. For a time line of these developments, see http://ec.europa.eu/environment/nature/biodiversity/policy/policy_dev_en.htm#1998.

11. Commission Communication, "Our Life Insurance, Our Natural Capital: An EU Biodiversity Strategy to 2020," available at https://eur-lex.europa.eu/legal-content/EN/TXT/PDF/?uri=CELEX:52011DC0244&from=EN.

12. See www.teebweb.org/.

13. NCFF is part of the LIFE Programme; see http://ec.europa.eu/environment/life/project/Projects/index.cfm?fuseaction=home.getProjects&strandID=2.

14. Regulation 1143/2014.

15. Directive 1999/22/EC.

16. A list of these species is available at http://ec.europa.eu/environment/nature/invasivealien/list/index_en.htm.

17. See https://easin.jrc.ec.europa.eu/.

18. See the Sustainable Hunting Initiative and the agreement on bird hunting under the Birds Directive, http://ec.europa.eu/environment/nature/conservation/wildbirds/hunting/docs/agreement_en.pdf.

19. This agreement was created together with the Council of Europe; see www2.nina.no/lcie_new/pdf/634991504714143702_Hunting_Charter%5B1%5D.pdf.

20. See http://ec.europa.eu/environment/nature/conservation/species/pollinators/index_en.htm.

21. Council Regulation EEC 3254/91, OJ 1991 L 308/1. The Regulation bans both the use of leghold traps as well as the trade in products from animals caught in such a way, imported into the EU.

22. The Birds Directive (now Directive 2009/147/EU on the conservation of wild birds) was first adopted in 1979. Since then, it has gone through several restatements but the structure of the most recent 2009 codification remains much the same as the original blueprint.

23. Article 2 Birds Directive.

24. Specifically the provisions of Articles 6(2), 6(3), and 6(4) of the Habitats Directive replace the provisions in Article 4(4) of the Birds Directive. Article 6(1) does not apply to these areas, but analogous provisions can be found in Articles 3, 4(1), and 4(2) of the Birds Directive.

25. Case C-57/89 *Commission v. Germany* ECLI:EU:C:1991:89. It should be noted that some of these cases were decided before the coming into force of the Habitats Directive and that the interpretation after the Directive may change.

26. See Case C-355/90 *Commission v. Spain (Santoña Marches)* ECLI:EU:C:1993:331.

27. Case C-57/89 *Commission v. Germany* ECLI:EU:C:1991:89, paras 21–22.

28. Article 7 Birds Directive.

29. Member states are specifically required to outlaw all methods listed in Annex 4 Birds Directive.

30. Article 5 Birds Directive.

31. Apart from the twenty-six species listed in Annex 3 Birds Directive.

32. The up-to-date list of species can be found at www.cites.org/eng/disc /species.php

33. An overview of national implementation laws is available at http:// ec.europa.eu/environment/cites/pdf/national_legislation.pdf.

34. A full list is available at http://ec.europa.eu/environment/cites/pdf /list_authorities.pdf.

35. Full text available at https://eur-lex.europa.eu/legal-content/EN /TXT/?uri=COM:2016:87:FIN.

36. Council Directive 92/43/EEC on the conservation of natural habitats and of wild fauna and flora, OJ 1992 L 206/7.

37. Case C-226/08 *Stadt Papenburg* ECLI:EU:C:2010:10.

38. Article 4(5) Habitats Directive.

39. See Kingston et al., *European Environmental Law,* at 435.

40. The status of 7 percent of habitats is listed as "unknown." See "The State of Nature in the EU," Reporting under the EU Habitats and Birds Directives 2007–2012 (2015), http://ec.europa.eu/environment/nature/pdf/state_of_ nature_en.pdf, at 19.

41. Ibid., at 19.

42. FAO data 2009.

43. Regulation 995/2010. More information available at http://ec.europa.eu /environment/forests/timber_regulation.htm.

44. They are as follows: to increase agricultural productivity by promoting technical progress and ensuring the optimum use of the factors of production, in particular labor; to ensure a fair standard of living for farmers; to stabilize markets; to ensure the availability of supplies; and to ensure reasonable prices for consumers.

45. By some measures, agricultural income in the EU remains 40 percent lower than non-agricultural income. See European Commission, "CAP Explained: Direct Payments 2015–2020," https://ec.europa.eu/agriculture /sites/agriculture/files/direct-support/direct-payments/docs/direct-payments- schemes_en.pdf, at 3.

46. Regulation 1307/2013.

47. Regulation 1308/2013.

48. Regulation 1305/2013.

49. Regulation 1306/2013.

50. For more details, see the Commission's information on the future of the CAP, available at https://ec.europa.eu/info/food-farming-fisheries/key-policies/common-agricultural-policy/future-cap_en.

CHAPTER EIGHT

Climate Change

This chapter provides a primer on the EU's legal approach to regulating climate change. It outlines the many regulatory challenges, presents some background about the EU's historical and current emissions, discusses the predicted impacts of climate change on the EU, and describes the fundamentals of the current European approach to managing climate change—an approach that relies heavily on multilateral cooperation and international law.

CLIMATE CHANGE AS AN ENVIRONMENTAL PROBLEM

Climate change is any significant change in weather—in temperature, precipitation, wind, or other effects—that lasts for a significant period. Climate change forces humans to make costly changes in behavior. It can negatively affect—even devastate—species and ecosystems that cannot adapt. While some changes in climate are normal (insofar as they are part of the natural environment), sudden and extreme changes are considered problematic. When changes in climate are sudden and extreme enough to outpace the speed of natural selection and other natural processes, they can lead to mass extinctions and even to complete ecosystem collapse.

Until the Industrial Revolution, periodic changes in climate were mostly caused by natural phenomena, such as solar flares or volcanic activity. Greenhouse gases (GHGs), including carbon dioxide (CO_2), were emitted through natural, nonhuman processes (such as plant matter decay) and absorbed through other natural, nonhuman processes (for instance, through absorption into the oceans). Plants, animals, and ecosystems adapted to gradual changes in climate and, over millennia, developed into the rich, biodiverse mosaic of life that now populates the planet.

Starting in the Industrial Revolution, however, humans began emitting increasing quantities of GHGs—significantly more than can be absorbed by natural processes. Most of these emissions come from burning fossil fuels like coal and oil. When more GHGs are emitted than are absorbed, the remainder ends up in the atmosphere. The current level of GHGs in the atmosphere is causing changes in weather patterns that are so severe and rapid that they will likely have devastating and irreversible consequences for human, animal, and plant life.

Experts generally agree that reversing anthropogenic climate change is no longer possible. To mitigate some of the impacts, actions must be taken to reduce GHG emissions. At the same time, adaptation strategies are needed to deal with some of the unavoidable effects of climate change. Since the global community became aware of climate change in the early 1970s, it has proven extremely difficult to translate the seemingly straightforward solutions into meaningful regulatory action. There are several reasons for this.

First, although the science connecting human emissions of GHGs to climate change is now uncontroversial within the scientific community,[1] it is challenging to tie individual actions that cause climate change to specific impacts. Climate change has a multitude of diffuse causes; every human action (including breathing!) results in the emission of some GHGs, and it would not be possible, or desirable, to regulate each of these activities. Moreover, those who benefit from GHG-emitting activities—such as industrial activity—do not necessarily shoulder the costs of climate change. The effects of climate change are

SPOTLIGHT 19. CLIMATE SCIENCE

Predicting the timing and location of climate change effects is complex, and the science around climate change has been subject to much controversy. The main international body dealing with these questions is the Intergovernmental Panel on Climate Change (IPCC)—an international panel of more than 1,300 scientists and experts. Its reports (freely available on www.ipcc.ch) are the result of rigorous scientific research. Because these reports form the basis for international negotiations on climate change, they are subject to approval and adoption by the countries that are party to the United Nations Framework Convention on Climate Change. While this increases their legitimacy in the eyes of many, this process has also met with criticism on the basis that the published outcomes are subject to political processes.

The EU has supplemented the findings of the IPCC reports with research by the Joint Research Centre—the European Commission's science and knowledge service, which provides independent research to inform EU policymaking—and research by the European Environment Agency. The Joint Research Centre has developed predictions of the likely economic impacts of climate change in the EU through its PESETA II project (https://ec.europa.eu/jrc/en/peseta-ii). PESETA II maps the potential impacts across ten key areas, including agriculture, energy, river floods, droughts, forest fires, transport infrastructure, coasts, tourism, habitat suitability of forest tree species, and human health.

also diffuse: they are spatially diffuse because GHG emissions anywhere in the world add to the total stock of emissions that may result in negative consequences anywhere in the world, and they are temporally diffuse because the effect of current emissions may not be felt until fifty to a hundred years from now. The fact that people can externalize the costs of their current behavior—costs to be borne by future generations and by others living in other parts of the world—makes it difficult to incentivize them to change that behavior.

Second, despite the well-established link between GHG emissions and climate change, the actual pattern of climate change—its severity, time, scale, and scope—is almost overwhelmingly complex. Although there is widespread scientific consensus that the global climate is changing as a result of human activities, there remains significant uncertainty regarding both short- and long-term consequences of those changes, complicated by the interactive qualities of many nonhuman processes and ecosystems. These uncertainties are further exacerbated by the question of how humans will change their mitigation and adaptation behaviors in the coming years.

Third, the ultimate extent of climate change's impact on nonhuman entities and processes is expected to be devastating, which in turn will create high human costs. However, in calculating these nonhuman and human costs, the complexity and uncertainty surrounding climate change can make it difficult for regulators to determine the appropriate stringency of costly mitigation and adaptation efforts.

Combined, these three characteristics of the causes and effects of climate change amount to the most "wicked" regulatory problem facing governments today.[2] While every person contributes to climate change in many small ways, no single person, state, or country can meaningfully mitigate climate change alone. This creates two additional problems: a *collective action problem*, in which effective mitigation of climate change necessitates action by a multitude of individual countries; and a *free-rider problem*, in which each country prefers to have mitigation and adaptation paid for by other countries.

Moreover, past GHG emissions were largely driven by the industrial development of developed countries, whereas future emissions are expected to be largely driven by the industrial development of developing countries. Understandably, developing countries—which are likely to be more severely affected by climate change—are unwilling to limit

SPOTLIGHT 20. KEY CHALLENGES IN
CLIMATE CHANGE POLICY

- Varied impacts across stakeholders, across borders, and
  through time
- Complex science from multiple disciplines with multiple
  sources of uncertainty
- Challenges coordinating multiple actors who have differing
  past and present causal responsibility, different expected
  impacts, and different interests

their chance for socioeconomic development by halting or significantly slowing industrialization. These complicated questions of how to balance the profits of past emissions (by some) with the costs of future climate change (for others), while considering the need for development of future generations, is often thought to make international collaboration on this topic almost impossible (see spotlight 20).

CLIMATE CHANGE IN THE EU: CAUSES, IMPACTS, AND ATTITUDES

Causal Contributions

Historically speaking, the EU's share of atmospheric GHGs is second only to that of the United States. The Industrial Revolution, which began in the United Kingdom and quickly expanded to much of Western Europe, jump-started the modern acceleration of GHG emissions in the EU (and globally).[3]

The historical emissions of individual EU Member States have varied significantly. In a pattern reflected in the rest of the world, EU countries that industrialized early have contributed significantly more than those that industrialized later. For example, Germany and the United Kingdom are projected to be responsible, respectively, for 3.9 percent and 3.4 percent of global temperature increase in 2100 (compared to the EU's total of approximately 17 percent).[4] Notably, only one other EU Member State is listed in the top ten of historical emitters: France, with 2.5 percent. This is not to say that the other EU countries have little or no historical responsibility for emissions. Rather, it highlights that the situation within the EU is a relatively diverse one, in terms of both historical emissions and present-day circumstances. Importantly, many of the Central and Eastern European countries that joined the EU after 2004 had planned economies until EU membership, leaving them with dated and heavily polluting technologies.[5] This created important mitigation possibilities for the EU—as will be discussed below—but is also a cause of socioeconomic differences between the Member States, which creates continuing differences in mitigation and adaptation needs.

Today, the EU continues to be one of the largest emitters of CO_2, even though collective EU emissions have generally been declining since 1990.[6] CO_2 emissions from fuel combustion, for instance, have dropped by as much as 21 percent from their height. This pattern of generally declining emissions distinguishes the EU from economies such as China (now the largest emitter), India, and Brazil, where emission trends are rising.[7]

As of 2015, per capita EU emissions (at 6.4 metric tons per person per year, as measured in 2014) compared relatively positively to other high-emitting economies, such as the United States (16.5 metric tons per person).[8] Here, too, there is variance between Member States, which is mainly caused by a combination of historical differences in industries, technological advances, and population density. To illustrate, two of the highest per capita emitters within the EU are the Netherlands (11.5 metric tons per person in 2016) and Estonia (14.9 metric tons per person in 2016).[9] While both are relatively small countries, their populations and

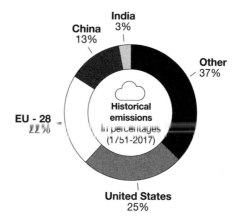

Figure 7. Historical Greenhouse Gas Emissions.

population densities are vastly different: the Netherlands has 17 million people, 488 per square kilometer; while Estonia has 1.3 million people, 30 per square kilometer. Their relative levels of affluence are also very different. Nevertheless, in both countries, the energy sector accounts for 80 percent or more of total emissions.[10] This reflects a general trend across the EU, where energy supply is responsible for the largest individual share (29 percent) of emissions, closely followed by transport and industry.[11] Problematically, although the total amount of EU emissions has shrunk since 1990 as a result of reductions in energy and industrial emissions, other sectors (such as transport and international aviation) have continued to increase their emissions, undercutting overall progress.[12]

Current and Expected Impacts

The EU, like the rest of the world, is already experiencing impacts from climate change. These include reduced water availability, extreme temperatures, floods, droughts, landslides, and accelerated sea-level rise.[13] Current projections estimate that if significant adaptation measures are not adopted, EU household welfare losses will amount to 190 billion

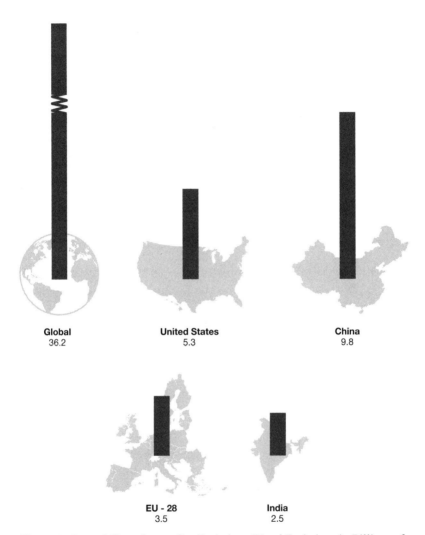

Figure 8. Annual Greenhouse Gas Emissions (Total Emissions in Billions of Metric Tons per Year, 2017).

euros (almost 2 percent of GDP) by 2071.[14] The majority of the damage is expected to be caused by premature mortality (120 billion euros). Other significant areas of damage will be to coasts (42 billion euros) and the agricultural sector (18 billion euros). The distribution of these impacts is uneven across the EU, with the southern regions expected to be far

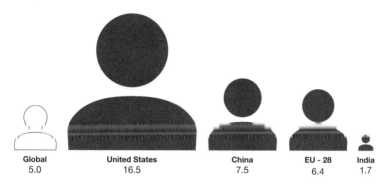

Figure 9. Greenhouse Gas Emissions per Capita (Metric Tons per Person per Year, 2014).

Global 5.0 United States 16.5 China 7.5 EU - 28 6.4 India 1.7

more severely affected.[15] Welfare losses in Northern Europe may be around 0.2 percent of GDP, while in the Central Europe South and Southern Europe regions they are expected to be 3 percent of GDP (accounting for up to 70 percent of overall EU damage; see figure 9).[16]

Public Attitudes toward Climate Change

European citizens generally consider climate change a high-priority political issue and expect action to be taken by political actors at the European level and at the national level. According to a special 2017 Eurobarometer on Climate Change (a survey conducted across all Member States by the EU), 92 percent of EU citizens consider climate change a serious problem.[17] Notably, it is ranked as the third-most-serious global problem, after "poverty, hunger and lack of drinking water" and "international terrorism." This high level of concern for the dangers of climate change is reflected in widespread support for mitigation measures such as renewable energy use, energy efficiency, and the use of public funds to develop clean energies. Most EU citizens believe that these measures will help boost the economy and create new jobs, which strengthens their support.

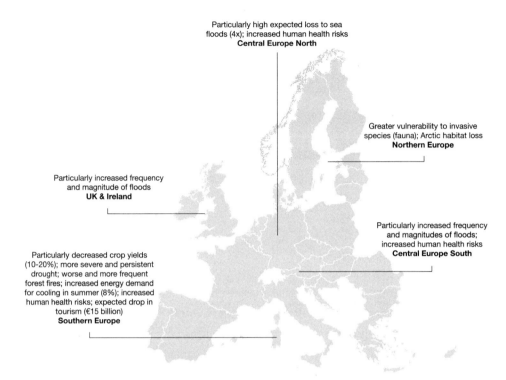

Particularly high expected loss to sea floods (4x); increased human health risks
Central Europe North

Greater vulnerability to invasive species (fauna); Arctic habitat loss
Northern Europe

Particularly increased frequency and magnitude of floods
UK & Ireland

Particularly increased frequency and magnitudes of floods; increased human health risks
Central Europe South

Particularly decreased crop yields (10-20%); more severe and persistent drought; worse and more frequent forest fires; increased energy demand for cooling in summer (8%); increased human health risks; expected drop in tourism (€15 billion)
Southern Europe

Figure 10. Projected Impacts of Climate Change in the EU by the 2080s.

While the survey results indicate that awareness of climate change and support for responses to it are generally high, views vary across Member States, which can affect EU climate policy. First—and perhaps counterintuitively—citizens of the countries least severely affected (based on the impacts described above) consider climate change more problematic than do those that are more vulnerable. Swedish and Danish citizens, for instance, consider climate change the most serious global problem, whereas their Southern and Eastern European counterparts seldom hold this view.[18] Second, attitudes toward climate change appear to vary not only between countries but also over time: in the early 2000s, there was a marked rise of climate skepticism in the

United Kingdom,[19] though membership in the most important climate skepticism group dropped by almost 50 percent between 2011 and 2017.[20] Finally, the rotating presidency of the Council of Ministers—which changes every six months between the Member States to prevent the appearance of bias—can complicate the EU's environmental and climate agenda. For example, in 2018, Bulgaria assumed the presidency and a known climate skeptic, Neno Dimov, was put in charge of the EU's Environmental Council. While the presidency does not confer any special lawmaking powers, the minister from the country holding the presidency does set the agenda for meetings of the Council of Ministers during their tenure. As a result, the Council can either be relatively active and productive during those six-month periods or be brought virtually to a halt. Hence, climate change views in particular Member States—or even the personal views of particular politicians—can play a temporarily outsized role in setting EU climate agendas.

INTERNATIONAL LAW AND CLIMATE CHANGE

Because the causes and effects of climate change are global, uncoordinated domestic approaches to mitigation are widely viewed as unlikely to be successful. For most countries in the world, climate change policy is therefore significantly affected by the terms of international climate change agreements, of which there are many.

By far the most important international climate law is the United Nations Framework Convention on Climate Change (UNFCCC). Signed and ratified in 1992, it sets out the framework within which international climate negotiations take place. The UNFCCC has near-universal membership: 197 countries as of December 2015, including the EU and its Member States. The parties to the Convention meet annually to negotiate additional agreements, or protocols, that work toward the UNFCCC's aim of "stabilizing GHG concentrations in the atmosphere at a level that would prevent dangerous anthropogenic interference with the climate system."[21] The UNFCCC does not set any binding limits on GHG emissions for the parties; rather, it obliges parties to create national inventories, which have helped establish baselines for such binding limits. Thus far, the only climate agreement that has established binding obligations to reduce emissions is the 1997 Kyoto Protocol, which established binding obligations for GHG reductions in developed countries for the period 2008–12.

Negotiating international agreements to address climate change requires coordinating multiple actors that have differing past and present causal responsibility, different expected impacts, and different interests. Even starting on such negotiations can be challenging, which makes a framework for negotiations, such as the one provided by the UNFCCC, particularly valuable. Even with such a framework, questions about the timing and the relative responsibility of developing and developed nations remain perennially thorny. International climate agreements must also find some way to manage the scientific uncertainty involved in modeling climate impacts and predicting the effects of proposed behavioral changes.

As in any area of international law, a significant challenge of using international law to address climate change is the question of enforcement. In the climate change context, this often manifests in disagreements between countries as to whether the targets set in climate agreements should be binding or voluntary. Even for "binding" obligations, of which there are few, it is hard to find effective means of enforcement, as nations remain sovereign in their decision to fulfill these obligations and/or to withdraw from international agreements.

Finally, though nations retain the sovereignty to enter into binding international agreements, the possibility of substantial subnational implementation—of both mitigation and adaptation plans—adds significant complexity. While subnational implementation can generate new and creative approaches to addressing difficult problems, in some cases it can also create a patchwork of policies that are hard to predict and challenging to integrate.

The EU Approach to International Climate Change Law

For most countries in the world, climate change policy is driven largely by the terms of international climate change agreements. The EU's climate change competence—as specified in the EU treaties—is internal as well as external: the EU has the power to set climate change policy for the Member States and to negotiate internationally with third parties in order to combat climate change.[22] As a result, many of the international climate change agreements to which the EU is a party are signed by both the EU and the Member States. Moreover, many agreements allow the EU to be held accountable as a collective, rather than as individual parties.[23] This has a great impact on the enforceability of such agreements because the EU can hold Member States accountable for failing to respect EU commitments, which allows for far stronger penalties than are available in international law. Another crucial consequence of this mix of internal and external competence is the fact that the goals and regulatory instruments of EU climate change policy are closely linked to international climate policy. One key example of this is the EU's heavy reliance on emissions trading, a regulatory tool that is aimed at achieving cost-effective GHG emission mitigation.[24]

The high level of support for EU action on climate change within the EU has made this one of the areas where the perceived legitimacy of EU action is highest. In addition, lack of leadership on climate change in the international arena—especially space left by the United States after it effectively pulled out of the Kyoto Protocol negotiations—has allowed the EU to consider itself a "green leader" on climate change. Overall, the EU's role in international climate change negotiations has been significant and has generally been supported by ambitious internal policies. The EU has invested particularly heavily in pushing for negotiation of international, binding emission reduction goals to replace the Kyoto Protocol—which, as noted above, is the only agreement that includes such binding targets. Such attempts failed until the Paris Agreement was adopted in 2015.

The Paris Agreement was important for several reasons. First, while the UNFCC has long sought to "stabiliz[e] GHG concentrations in the atmosphere at a level that would prevent dangerous anthropogenic interference with the climate system," prior to the Paris Agreement, it was unclear what would constitute dangerous anthropogenic interference. The Paris Agreement clarifies what "dangerous anthropogenic climate change" looks like by stating a clear commitment to limiting global temperature rises to 2°C.[25] Second, the Agreement puts in place legally binding procedural commitments for the parties to create "nationally determined contributions," to prepare national plans to achieve the contributions to mitigation, and to report on them regularly. These commitments are not substantive commitments to a centrally determined level of GHG emission reductions, as was the case with the Kyoto Protocol. Nevertheless, or possibly because of this, only three countries in the world have chosen not to participate in, or to withdraw from, the Paris Agreement: Syria, Nicaragua, and the United States.

Despite high public support for climate mitigation action within the EU, continuing discrepancies between Member States' socioeconomic development and dependency on GHG-intensive industries create ongoing internal tensions. As a result, it is not self-evident that the EU will be able to maintain an ambitious climate regime in all areas.

KEY CHARACTERISTICS OF REGULATING CLIMATE CHANGE IN THE EU

The impacts of climate change, and the activities thought to contribute to climate change, are divided unequally within the EU. This is reflected in diverging positions of Member States regarding climate change mitigation efforts. Nevertheless, EU citizens tend to strongly support EU climate change action.

The EU considers itself, and is widely viewed as, a leader in international attempts to recognize and manage climate change. It has been an

TABLE 14

Important International Climate Change Agreements

Agreement	Year	Ratified by the EU?
United Nations Framework Convention on Climate Change (UNFCCC)	1992	Yes
Kyoto Protocol	1997	Yes
Paris Agreement	2015	Yes
Kigali Amendment to the Montreal Protocol	2016	Yes

important supporter of the UNFCCC, the Kyoto Protocol, and the Paris Agreement. These international commitments have been translated into, but also informed by, internal climate change policy. The importance of international agreements is particularly clear when considering the key regulatory instruments and goals of EU internal climate policy.

Support for climate change mitigation efforts within the EU is traditionally very high, which has facilitated ambitious action by the EU. Given the extensive EU competence in this area, there is relatively little space left for Member State legislation. However, Member States continue to play an important role in implementation, leading to occasional clashes with the EU (see table 14).

DISCUSSION QUESTION

1. Does the EU have a special obligation to respond to climate change, given its historical contribution to the causes of climate change? Should current Europeans be forced to pay for emissions by their parents and grandparents? Similarly, should future Europeans be forced to pay for their parents' and grandparents' failure to mitigate further climate change?

LEGAL SNAPSHOTS:
CLIMATE CHANGE AND THE EU

The next sections provide a series of "snapshots" explaining how the EU manages climate change through mitigation and through adaptation and natural hazard policy.

SPOTLIGHT 21. MEMBER STATE AND LOCAL CLIMATE CHANGE POLICIES

The EU has extensive, almost exclusive competence with respect to climate change policy. At the EU level, the Member States play a vital role through the Council, with EU-wide interests represented primarily through the Parliament and the Commission. As a result, EU policy incorporates and reflects important national interests, as can be seen in the Burden Sharing Agreement related to the Kyoto Protocol and the Effort Sharing Regulation linked to the period 2021–30.

The resulting EU laws and policies—especially on climate change mitigation—leave Member States with some discretion on policy implementation but very little space for additional and/or more ambitious climate policy. More ambitious climate or environmental laws can constitute barriers within the EU's internal market and/or indirect state aid to national industries, both of which are prohibited under EU law (see also spotlight 4, on the internal market and environmental law, in chapter 5).

This situation can lead to political and legal controversy when Member States are pressured to take more ambitious action by constituents (or even by their national courts, as in the Dutch *Urgenda* case—see www.urgenda.nl/en/themas/climate-case). Furthermore, initiatives like the Global Covenant of Mayors for Climate and Energy (www.globalcovenantofmayors.org) set out climate policies tailored to local conditions. As a matter of EU law, these initiatives must comply with and relate to EU law, including EU climate change law. As a matter of EU politics, however, many of these local initiatives are tolerated and even encouraged, as long as they do not undermine EU climate policy or internal market laws.

MITIGATION

DEFINITION

Climate change mitigation seeks to limit the magnitude and rate of long-term climate change. Reducing anthropogenic GHGs is the most important method of mitigation.

DISTINCTIVE CHALLENGES OF CLIMATE CHANGE MITIGATION

In some respects, the mitigation of climate change through the reduction of anthropogenic GHG emissions is a relatively simple task. For mitigation purposes, the location of the emission reductions is irrelevant—even though it might be crucial for the reduction of related environmental impacts, such as air pollution and related health risks—which theoretically opens up the opportunity of reducing emissions wherever in the world it is easiest and cheapest. Such low-hanging fruit can be found specifically in developing economies that rely heavily on pollutive industries that can be made cleaner relatively cheaply by installing newer technologies. Similarly, deforestation—the second-largest source of GHG emissions—is a practice that people might be convinced to forgo if alternative economic opportunities are provided.

Unsurprisingly, the fact that the climate effects of GHG-emitting activities do not occur in the same geographic location also poses significant challenges. It allows people to externalize the effects of their actions, offloading them to others—if one country fails to mitigate, the global consequences will be borne largely by other countries. Similarly, if a country does successfully mitigate, it is likely to reap only a small portion of the total benefits of reduced emissions. The potential to externalize also applies over time, as there is generally a delay between GHG emissions and their impacts on the climate. This temporal element adds to the difficulty of determining how to "price" the mitigation of effects that will emerge in fifty, one hundred, or two hundred years, as compared to the cost of mitigation today.

Another problem is that reductions in GHG emissions in one place are easily offset by increases in another location. This is a central challenge to climate policy in the years to come, because many populous countries are experiencing economic growth that relies heavily on GHG-emitting activities. Even if the main emitters of the past—the EU and the United States—are reducing their emissions, the per capita increase in emissions of countries such as China can easily offset those reductions. This again is a difficult question of politics and fairness, as many developing countries claim a right to economic development such as developed countries have enjoyed in the past. One partial solution to this problem may include "technology transfer" of clean technologies from developed to developing economies, so that the latter can "skip" the most polluting stages.

Apart from limiting GHG emissions by reducing the use of fossil fuels through cleaner technologies or by reducing deforestation, countries can also focus on reducing the need for fossil fuels through use of renewable energy or increased energy efficiency. These initiatives can be undertaken unilaterally and thus are less dependent on international agreements, though their desirability may be limited by potential losses of economic advantage vis-à-vis other countries.

A final category of mitigation possibilities is the "capture" or sequestration of GHG emissions rather than their reduction. This is a relatively new area of climate policy, and the long-term effects of carbon capture and storage are not yet known. The main advantage of such techniques is that they require little or no changes in emission-producing behaviors or technologies, since they rely entirely on taking carbon out of the atmosphere and storing it elsewhere. At the moment, most capture technologies remain prohibitively costly, but that may change in the future.

SPOTLIGHT 22. DISCOUNTING

Policymakers are routinely faced with questions about how many of today's resources to spend on preventing future harms from climate change. Although the costs of mitigation are mostly borne immediately, the benefits may not accrue for decades or even centuries.

Discounting is a method for determining the present value of a benefit or harm that is expected to accrue some time in the future. Typically, the sooner someone receives a benefit, the more valuable it is to them. This is because they get the enjoyment of the benefit for longer and have greater opportunity to invest their resources, and to make those resources grow over time. Conversely, being assured that you will receive a benefit in the distant future holds less value in the present.

Generally, the rate at which money is predicted to gain value (particularly through investment) determines the economic "discount rate." For example, if economists think that money can be invested at a 7 percent rate of return each year, they will choose a 7 percent discount rate to translate future money into its present value.

Calculating the present value of climate change harms—or the benefits of preventing those harms—is complicated by the long time horizons of these harms and benefits, and by the uncertainties in predicting them. High discount rates make even extreme future impacts look small in today's dollars. Very high discount rates can make it seem nonsensical to adopt any kind of mitigation strategy at all.

While discounting of money is not controversial, discounting of environmental impacts—including those caused by climate change—is not widely practiced in the EU. As a result, EU practices for balancing the immediate costs with the future payoffs of mitigation remain relatively qualitative.

KEY EU APPROACHES TO CLIMATE CHANGE
MITIGATION

The EU's current climate change policy is made up of a package of measures set out in a document titled "20 20 by 2020: Europe's Climate Change Opportunity."[26] These measures are focused on achieving three goals: (1) reduction of CO_2 emissions by 20 percent; (2) a shift toward renewable energy, increasing its use by 20 percent; and (3) a 20 percent improvement in energy efficiency.

The creation of this package was so ambitious that it necessitated institutional changes to the European Commission. The Directorate-General for Climate Action (DG CLIMA) was created in 2010 and is the designated lead authority on implementing and directing the climate package. The creation of new Directorates-General is a rare occurrence, so this underscores how important the climate change agenda is to the EU.

Coordinating the climate package within the Commission was extraordinarily complex. Apart from DG CLIMA, numerous other Directorates-General are also involved in climate policy, including the Directorates-General of environment, energy, internal market, transport, agriculture, fisheries, and trade.[27] The package also had to accommodate the diverging positions of Member States, which find themselves at different stages of economic development with varying energy needs.

The 2020 goals were implemented through an ambitious legislative package, which set still more ambitious goals for the period between 2020 and 2030.[28] Specifically, GHG emission reductions must be reduced further—by 40 percent compared to 1990 levels—and the share of renewables must be increased to at least 27 percent of the energy mix. These are binding goals; in addition, the package adopts an indicative goal of improving energy efficiency by at least 27 percent. In addition, for the period ending in 2050, the EU has adopted even more ambitious targets, with a view to establish a decarbonized society and economy, as

TABLE 15

EU Legislation on Climate Change Mitigation

Target	Law
Climate and Energy Package	**The EU Emissions Trading Scheme (EU ETS)** • Directive 2003/87/EC establishing a scheme for greenhouse gas emission allowance trading within the Community • Directive 2004/101/EC establishing a scheme for greenhouse gas emission allowance trading within the Community, in respect of the Kyoto Protocol's project mechanism • Directive 2008/101/EC amending Directive 2003/87/EC so as to include aviation activities • Directive 2009/29/EC amending Directive 2003/87/EC so as to improve and extend the trading scheme **Effort Sharing** • Decision 406/2009/EC on the effort of MS to reduce their GHG emissions to meet the Community's GHG emissions reduction commitments up to 2020 **Renewable Energy** • Directive 2009/28/EC on the promotion of the use of energy from renewable sources **Carbon Capture and Storage** • Directive 2009/30/EC on the geological storage of carbon dioxide
Energy Efficiency	• Directive 2012/27/EU on energy efficiency
GHG Monitoring and Reporting	• Regulation (EU) 525/2013 on a mechanism for monitoring and reporting GHG emissions and for reporting other information at national and Union level relevant for climate change
Transport and Fuels	• Directive 1999/94/EC relating to the availability of consumer information on fuel economy and CO_2 emissions in respect of the marketing of new passenger cars • Directive 2009/30/EC amending Directive 98/70/EC as regards the Specification of petrol, diesel and gas-oil and introducing a mechanism to monitor and reduce GHG emissions
Fluorinated Gases	• Regulation (EC) 842/2006 on certain flourinated GHGs
Forests and Agriculture	• Decision 529/2013/EU on accounting rules on GHG emissions and removals resulting from activities relating to land use, land-use change and forestry and on information concerning actions relating to those activities

laid out in the Commission's "Roadmap for moving to a competitive low carbon economy in 2050."[29]

Three policies play a particularly central role in implementing the EU's climate goals: the Emissions Trading Scheme, renewable energy policy, and energy efficiency policy.

EU ETS

The European Union Emissions Trading Scheme (EU ETS) is one of the most important pieces of legislation adopted as part of the EU's "climate and energy package." The EU's mitigation strategy relies extremely heavily on the EU ETS for achieving its goals. However, the EU ETS's development and performance have not been without difficulty or criticism.

The adoption of the EU ETS is a direct result both of the international climate change negotiations that led up to the Kyoto Protocol *and* of internal EU processes that took place during the same period. In the period preceding Kyoto, the United States had strongly advocated the adoption of (international) emissions trading as a key instrument for emission reduction, based on the success of its Environmental Protection Agency's Acid Rain Program.[30] Simultaneously, the European Commission had tried to achieve internal agreement among the Member States for an EU-wide environmental tax as the main method to achieve the EU's prospective commitments under Kyoto.[31] However, these attempts failed when the Member States vetoed the Commission's proposal. When the United States all but pulled out of the Kyoto negotiations, the EU was keen to fill the resulting power vacuum. The Commission changed its internal strategy and successfully made a strong push in favor of emissions trading within the EU, which allowed it to do the same during the Kyoto negotiations.

The Kyoto Protocol introduced three market-based instruments to facilitate parties' efforts to fulfill their emission limitations: emissions trading, Joint Implementation, and the Clean Development Mechanism.

(Paragraph continues on p. 217)

SPOTLIGHT 23. EMISSIONS TRADING

HOW DOES IT WORK?

Regulated actors, such as power plants, are allocated a set amount of allowances linked to polluting activities, such as the emission of CO_2. These actors are then given the option to reduce their own emissions in order to comply with their emission allowance, or to buy additional allowances from other companies on the market. Periodically, typically every year, regulated actors have to show that their emissions match their allowances.

WHERE IS IT USED?

The first widescale use of an environmental emissions trading program was the US Acid Rain Program, which is widely viewed as extraordinarily successful at cheaply reducing acid rain in the industrialized Northeast of the United States. Today, the EU ETS is by far the largest emissions trading scheme in the world, in terms of both the traded allowances and the geographic scope of activities covered. The second-largest trading scheme is the South Korean ETS, launched in 2015. Other examples include the Regional Greenhouse Gas Initiative in the United States, which covers the states of Connecticut, Delaware, Maine, Maryland, Massachusetts, New Hampshire, New Jersey, New York, Rhode Island, and Vermont; and eight Chinese regional pilot emissions trading schemes, which are meant to combine into a national emissions trading scheme in the near future.

WHAT ARE THE KEY STRENGTHS?

The main selling point of emissions trading is that the decision of how to abate is left to the party involved in the polluting activity. The regulator only sets the absolute "cap" of emissions per industry or country. This allows industry to decide for itself how it can most effectively manage and reduce its emissions. In achieving these reductions, emissions trading can make optimal use of efficiencies: the parties involved in the activities have the most information on the cost of marginal abatement (i.e., the cost of each additional reduction in pollution or emissions) and therefore are well placed to decide whether and how to mitigate. If it is not cost-effective to abate, industry can buy more allowances and/or pay a fine. Technological standards or other types of traditional command-and-control regulation do not allow for this flexibility. Taxes would allow for a lot of flexibility but remove the certainty of a cap. Finally, emissions trading is often expected to increase technological innovation, as companies receive an economic benefit from polluting less.

WHAT ARE THE DOWNSIDES?

The theory behind emissions trading is deceptively straightforward. In a perfect system—where the market for allowances is moderated perfectly and everyone has perfect information about the costs of emissions and abatement and is able to act on those cost considerations—emissions trading is much more cost-effective than most other regulatory instruments. However, perfectly functioning markets seldom exist. Trading schemes continue to rely heavily on government intervention, as someone needs to ensure that the market is functioning properly. Moreover, the threat of fines in case of noncompliance needs to be real and well publicized, or an important incentive for abatement is removed. Finally, in order for emissions trading schemes to stimulate innovation, the price of allowances has to be fairly high, which may mean it is more effective to adopt an additional regulatory instrument that targets innovation.

The EU makes use of all three instruments, through the EU ETS. Since it would be impossible to detail every aspect of the EU ETS in this legal snapshot,[32] our focus will be on the following issues: the (changes in) scope of the EU ETS since its creation in 2005, the method of allocating emission allowances to regulated actors, the respective roles of the EU and the Member States, the relation between the EU ETS and United Nations mechanisms, and likely future changes to the EU ETS.

SCOPE OF THE EU ETS

As of this writing, the EU ETS operates in thirty-one countries: all twenty-seven EU Member States plus the United Kingdom, Iceland, Liechtenstein, and Norway (which have chosen to join the program). It covers approximately 45 percent of all EU GHG emissions.

One important challenge for any environmental trading scheme is the selection of who will be allowed to trade within the scheme. For schemes like the EU ETS, which is intended to govern behavior across many diverse Member States, it was particularly critical to choose the "right" industries to include in the trading scheme (see spotlight 24) and the "right" gases to allow in the trading scheme. As designed, the EU ETS covers eleven thousand heavily energy-using installations. Specifically, it targets CO_2 emissions, nitrous oxide (N_2O) emissions, and perfluorocarbons (PFCs). The scheme allows for trading across these gases by creating a carbon equivalent for N_2O and PFCs.

Crucially, the EU ETS covers only businesses that operate in the EU. This means there are several important "gaps"—for example, so far there are no import restrictions or other costs for products produced outside of the EU that have a high emission profile. This type of measure, also referred to as a "carbon tax" or "border carbon adjustment," has to be designed with care, lest it clash with World Trade Organization laws, which generally prohibit the imposition of tariffs.[33] The EU has not yet attempted to adopt any wide-scale policy on the carbon profile of imports. It has, however, taken other actions to push

---

SPOTLIGHT 24. GASES AND INDUSTRIES
REGULATED BY THE EU ETS

The EU ETS regulates the following gases and the following related industries:

CO_2—power and heat generation; civil aviation; and energy-intensive industries including oil refineries, steelworks, and production of iron, aluminum, other metals, cement, lime, glass, ceramics, pulp, paper, cardboard, acids, and bulk organic chemicals

N_2O—production of nitric, adipic, and glyoxylic acids

PFCs—aluminum production

---

third-party countries to participate in the EU ETS, or at least to be affected by it. The most important example here is the inclusion of civil aviation in the EU ETS. Initially, the EU planned to include all aircrafts landing or departing from a European airport, regardless of the nationality of the airline. This decision met with extremely strong resistance in the international community, including through a statement of the International Civil Aviation Organization[34] and a declaration by twenty-three countries, including the United States, China, Brazil, and India, objecting to the inclusion.[35] As a result, the EU has decided to postpone inclusion of foreign aviation in the EU ETS until 2024, while searching for an international agreement.

METHODS OF ALLOCATION

All trading schemes require some method for allocating allowances among existing and future emitters. In the EU ETS, there are two main ways in which regulated entities can obtain initial allowances: through grandfathering and through auctioning. Grandfathering is much friendlier to the regulated industries, as it provides allowances "for free" based on past emissions. During the initial years of the EU ETS, grandfathering was the central method for allocation and led to greater acceptance of the scheme by industries. It also created several problems, including an incentive for companies to misrepresent their past emissions to receive more free allowances. In turn, this led to very low allowance prices on the market, undermining the ability of the scheme to incentivize emission reductions. Finally, many companies profited on the initial grandfathering policy by charging consumers for the supposed costs of allowances, even when they were not yet paying for those allowances.

Since 2013, auctioning has become the default method of allocation. However, this does not mean that all allowances are auctioned all the time. Many industries that are considered "carbon leakage sensitive" continue to receive free allowances. In total, the Commission estimates that 57 percent of the total amount of allowances will be auctioned during 2013–20, and this percentage looks to remain about the same after 2020.

After the initial allocation, businesses can trade allowances on the market.[36] The price of emission allowances has fluctuated heavily due to the initial over-allocation of allowances to businesses. Because it has been difficult to take allowances off the market in these circumstances, adjusting for this type of "mistake" is difficult until the start of a new trading phase. Thus far, there have been three trading phases of the EU ETS: from 2005 to 2007 (the "learning by doing" phase), from 2008 to 2012 (the "Kyoto Commitment" phase, when the Kyoto reduction goals had to be achieved), and from 2013 to 2020 (known as Phase III).

ROLES OF THE EU AND THE MEMBER STATES

As in most areas of EU environmental law, the EU ETS relies heavily on both the EU and the Member States in its design and implementation. Interestingly, the EU ETS has laid bare many of the potential challenges that can occur when one party (the EU) is responsible for

SPOTLIGHT 25. CARBON LEAKAGE

A key risk of emissions trading is "carbon leakage," which occurs when businesses decide to transfer their production activities to other areas or countries with laxer emission constraints. The result of this could be an increase in total emissions—the exact opposite of what emissions trading looks to accomplish. The absence of a global climate change accord with binding emission reduction targets increases this risk.

the design and goal setting of an instrument while thirty-two other parties (the twenty-seven Member States plus the United Kingdom, Liechtenstein, Norway, Iceland, and, since January 1, 2020, Switzerland) are responsible for its implementation and enforcement.

During the first two trading phases, the Member States were responsible for the distribution of allowances between different industries. There were some guidelines set by the Commission, but the Member States had considerable discretion. This led to over-allocation to some sectors, which lowered the price of allowances and the incentive to comply with the EU ETS. Over time, the Commission tried to remedy these problems, leading to the eventual adoption of a central cap—replacing Member States' ability to distribute allowances among their national industries—in Phase III. The results of this change are not yet clear.

Another issue has been enforcement and oversight of the EU ETS carbon market. While it is conventional to speak about "the" EU ETS market, an EU-wide registry was not put in place until 2012. Before then, all countries participating had individual registries with varying degrees of expertise, funding, and oversight capacity. This decentralized approach complicated enforcement and, thus, facilitated fraudulent activities, including the hacking of several registries, tax fraud schemes, and theft of allowances from national registries between 2008 and 2011.

A key challenge for the development and operation of EU ETS has been accommodating the differences in socioeconomic development of the Member States, while still achieving the EU's shared goals in GHG emission reduction. The EU's climate and energy package is intended to balance these competing concerns. It does so through several mechanisms. First, the Effort Sharing Decision divides the EU's shared GHG goals among the Member States, giving each state a binding national target.[37] Second, within the EU ETS, the "free allocation" of permits to emit assists low-GDP Member States. For example, whereas grandfathering was phased out for power generators in 2013, eight Member States—Bulgaria, Cyprus, Czech Republic, Estonia, Hungary, Lithuania, Poland, and Romania—have been allowed to continue to allocate some free allowances to existing power plants until 2019. This allows those states to develop greener industries over time; indeed, these Member States are required to invest the value of free allowances in modernizing their power sectors.

ROLE OF CREDITS AND INTERNATIONAL OFFSETS

Typically, companies discharge their obligations under the EU ETS by surrendering the correct number of allowances to the European CO_2 Registry by April 30 each year.[38] As an alternative to trading within the EU ETS market or reducing their emissions, companies are also allowed to buy "credits" from projects governed by two market-based instruments created by the Kyoto Protocol: the Clean Development Mechanism (CDM) and Joint Implementation (JI). The projects funded through this credit system can create real value in the host country (typically countries where clean technologies are not yet the default) and often offer a cost-effective alternative to abatement in the EU. For these advantages to materialize, the reductions that take place through these projects have to be "additional"—meaning that they would not have taken place otherwise. Projects in China, which is by far the largest market for CDM projects, have been heavily criticized as not being additional: the concern in such cases is that funding for such projects actually creates perverse incentives for more pollution, which could then be reduced in exchange for credits.[39] To ensure that most reductions take place in the EU, where monitoring is stricter, and where additionality may thus be less of a concern, the EU limits the number of CDM and JI credits that companies can use to satisfy their obligations under the EU ETS.

FUTURE CHANGES TO THE EU ETS

The EU ETS's fourth trading period will start in 2021. The proposed legislation for this phase includes several significant changes to the scheme: the level of reductions will be increased to 43 percent compared to 2005 levels, there will be fewer allocations of free allowances, and two new funds—the Innovation Fund and the Modernisation Fund—will be introduced to stimulate technological innovation and modernization of the power sector. As in the current phase, there will be effort sharing between the Member States, with national reduction burdens ranging from zero to 40 percent (compared to 2005 levels). Each Member State's share will be allocated on the basis of GDP per capita, with lower-GDP Member States bearing a lighter burden.[40]

Another controversial and significant change has been the introduction of the Market Stability Reserve (MSR), which began operating at the start of 2019. It is meant to form a long-term solution to the surplus of allowances that has built up in the EU ETS market due to problems set out above. The basic idea of the MSR is that it should gradually absorb those surplus allowances, which could also help raise the carbon price. In brief, the MSR works as follows. The Commission publishes the total number of allowances every year by May 15. On the basis of this number, allowances may be placed in or released from the reserve. Allowances placed in the MSR will not be auctioned, creating some

additional scarcity in the market. To prevent unpredictable state interference in the market, there are predefined rules on how many allowances can go into the MSR, which means that its implementation leaves
no discretion to the Commission or the Member States. The rule that
allowances can also be released from the reserve is a political compromise to alleviate the concern expressed by some Member States that
carbon costs should not become too high for them or their industries.
However, other Member States wanted to ensure that the goal of carbon scarcity would not be undermined in the long run if too many
allowances were released from the reserve. Therefore, a cancelation
rule was added to the design of the MSR: starting in 2023, allowances
held in the reserve in excess of the auction volume from the previous
year will be permanently invalidated.

Renewable Energy

The second important pillar of the EU's climate change mitigation
strategy is increasing the share of renewable energy in the EU's energy
mix, first to 20 percent (by 2020) and then to 27 percent (by 2030).[41] In
2015, renewable energy generated 15.9 percent of the EU's total energy,
and projections at the time of this writing indicate that the EU is generally on track to meet its 2020 target.[42]

Although the EU is empowered to adopt policy and legislation in
this area, and has set national mandatory targets for Member States to
achieve in increasing renewable energy generation, the EU has faced
political barriers in establishing durable centralized policies for making
and enforcing renewable energy targets. Energy production is a politically sensitive industry in the EU, in part because it was previously
a state monopoly in most Member States. In addition, actions that
impact the energy market often affect other important and controversial issues, including economic growth and production, energy security, local community employment, cultural preferences for fossil

fuel alternatives (such as nuclear energy and shale gas), and economic competitiveness.

In response to changing politics regarding these interactive issues, the EU's renewable energy policy has gone back and forth between being decentralized or centralized. The policy was initially established in a relatively decentralized manner: the 2001 Renewable Electricity Directive called for "national indicative targets" set by the Member States themselves, with the EU taking only a facilitating and coordinating role. Now, under the 2009 Renewable Energy Directive, the policy is centralized: mandatory overall national renewable energy targets for Member States are set and enforced by the EU. The common expectation is that renewable energy policy will be decentralized again after 2020, as outlined in the EU's climate and energy policy framework for goals to be met by 2030. The key change will be that renewable energy targets will be binding at the EU level, rather than the national level,[43] which means that it will be harder for the EU to hold Member States accountable for failing to act on renewable energy targets. Even as it moves toward decentralizing the policy on renewables, however, the EU has taken simultaneous action to increase coordination of energy generation across Member States through its "Energy Union" strategy (see spotlight 26), which it launched in 2015.

Two of the most important features of the 2009 Renewable Energy Directive are (1) national mandatory targets and national action plans and (2) the compatibility of renewable energy measures with the EU's internal market.

NATIONAL TARGETS AND PLANS

The Renewable Energy Directive sets out national mandatory targets for each Member State, ranging from 10 percent to 49 percent use of renewables by 2020.[44] This includes consumption through use of electricity, heating and cooling, and transportation. There is a separate

SPOTLIGHT 26. ENERGY UNION

As part of its climate and energy package, the EU launched the "Energy Union" strategy in 2015. Closely linked to the EU's climate strategy, the Energy Union aims to coordinate energy supply across Member States. The strategy is meant to generate two important benefits: it addresses the heavy reliance of the EU on foreign-sourced oil and gas, and it creates an internal market in energy, which is expected to have benefits for EU consumers in terms of pricing and reliability.

The Energy Union has five interrelated goals:

Security, solidarity, and trust: diversifying Europe's sources of energy and ensuring energy security through solidarity and cooperation between EU countries

A fully integrated internal energy market: enabling the free flow of energy through the EU through adequate infrastructure and without technical or regulatory barriers

Energy efficiency: improved energy efficiency will reduce dependence on energy imports, lower emissions, and drive jobs and growth

Decarbonizing the economy: the EU is committed to a quick ratification of the Paris Agreement and to retaining its leadership in the area of renewable energy

Research, innovation, and competitiveness: supporting breakthroughs in low-carbon and clean-energy technologies by prioritizing research and innovation to drive the energy transition and improve competitiveness*

The European Commission has heavily emphasized the importance of the Energy Union in achieving the EU's energy and climate goals, including promoting it with a social media hashtag (#EnergyUnion).

* See https://ec.europa.eu/energy/en/topics/energy-strategy-and-energy-union.

uniform target for transportation of 10 percent renewable energy (primarily through biofuels) for each Member State.

As is common for a directive, the Renewable Energy Directive leaves broad discretion to the Member States on how to achieve their targets, setting only minimum expectations and harmonizing procedural and accountability expectations for Member State governments.[45] The most notable of these is the obligation to create a national renewable energy action plan, which includes the Member State's implementation strategy and an estimated trajectory toward goal achievement.[46] These trajectories, together with biannual performance reports, are a means of checking on Member States' progress before the "final" accounting is done in 2020.[47]

INTERNAL MARKET TENSIONS

In order to achieve the renewable energy targets set by the EU, virtually all Member States must rely on some form of subsidy for their energy producers. Without these subsidies, the adoption of sufficient renewable energy into the energy mix is unlikely so long as renewable energy technologies remain marginally more expensive than externality-producing, nonrenewable energy technologies.

Although they can be effective at incentivizing renewable energy production, subsidies are a sensitive subject within the EU's internal market, particularly within the energy industry, which continues to have strong monopolistic features. Renewable energy is therefore one of the areas in which the EU must resolve a tension between its environmental goals and its economic aspirations. This tension arises because a foundational tenet of the EU's internal market is that it seeks to avoid discriminating between products of Member States[48] or distorting the internal market by "favoring certain undertakings or the production of certain goods."[49] Generally, the only exceptions to this blanket ban on such market-distorting measures are aid that has "a social character," provided to individual consumers, and/or aid that addresses damage caused by natural disasters.[50]

Energy Efficiency

The final pillar of the EU's approach to climate change is its policy on energy efficiency, which involves reducing energy consumption by using less energy to achieve the same amount of useful output. Because energy efficiency holds output steady while reducing the need for energy generation, many people consider energy efficiency a cheap and easy way to mitigate GHG emissions and, thus, achieve the EU's climate and energy goals. Moreover, energy efficiency creates many additional indirect benefits, such as greater energy security, innovation, and job creation.

In light of these benefits, the EU has adopted a wide range of measures to incentivize energy efficiency across economic sectors,[51] including obligations to make buildings more efficient;[52] mandatory energy efficiency certificates accompanying the sale and rental of buildings; minimum energy efficiency standards and labeling for a variety of products, such as boilers, household appliances, lighting, and televisions; the preparation of national energy efficiency action plans; and the planned rollout of close to two hundred million smart meters for electricity and forty-five million for gas by 2020.

Although these policies have produced improvements in energy efficiency,[53] energy efficiency policies face a series of ongoing challenges in achieving further improvements. Improvements often rely on purchaser knowledge about increasingly efficient products. Also, the costs of some energy efficiency measures can be significant, especially when it comes to the retrofitting of existing housing stock. In these situations it is common to encounter split incentives between landlords and tenants, whereby the party investing in the improvement does not benefit (sufficiently) from the energy savings. There can also be hidden costs, such as disruption to homes or businesses from shifting to more energy-efficient technologies or practices. Finally, early improvements in energy efficiency may be relatively cheap to develop and implement, but subsequent improvements can require increasingly costly technological development and behavioral shifts. These challenges may limit the ability of the EU to continue improving energy efficiency over time.

TAKEAWAYS

✓ The EU has an ambitious climate change strategy, focused heavily on mitigation.

✓ EU climate policy has developed in line with international climate policy, which means that there is an overlap in goals and regulatory instruments.

✓ The EU ETS is a cornerstone of the EU's climate policy. It is focused on reducing GHG emissions in large industries. It does not (yet) include transportation (apart from aviation), agriculture, or buildings.

✓ The EU has an ambitious renewable energy policy. The main challenges to achieving renewable goals are the decentralized nature of their implementation and the potential clashes with the EU's economic goals and internal market rules.

✓ Energy efficiency represents a cost-effective way to obtain emission reductions and greater energy security. EU instruments in this area rely heavily on information requirements.

DISCUSSION QUESTIONS

1. Should countries set their mitigation policies by reference to the harm their emissions cause for the whole world, or just those within their own borders? Why might it be tempting to adopt the domestic-only strategy? Are there tools that countries might use to encourage other countries to address global impacts?

2. Do you think that the EU ETS should act as the cornerstone of the EU's climate change mitigation policy? Why (not)?

3. Are you concerned about Member States assisting renewable energy industries in ways that may distort the internal market? Why (not)?

4. Do you think courts should play a bigger role in the mitigation of climate change? Or do you think their role should be to focus on the effects of climate change?

5. How should policymakers decide what the "right" level of mitigation is? What kind of information should they use in deciding?

ADAPTATION AND NATURAL HAZARDS
DEFINITION

Climate change adaptation involves adjusting to expected or experienced changes to reduce the damage they cause. Adaptation includes the management of natural hazards, or risks from natural phenomena, that may have negative effects on humans or the environment.

DISTINCTIVE CHALLENGES OF ADAPTATION POLICY AND MANAGING NATURAL HAZARDS

One important and fundamental challenge in adaptation policy is determining the extent to which it makes sense to invest in adapting to the impacts of climate change, versus attempting to mitigate the impacts of climate change before they happen. In some cases, where resources are scarce, this requires a trade-off between investment in mitigation and adaptation strategies.

Regardless of any mitigating measures that are undertaken, some degree of climate change has already happened, and there is little doubt that significantly more will occur over the coming decades. These changes will be disruptive to human life. The extent of the disruption will depend on the scale of the changes that take place and the measures that have been taken to prepare for—and adapt to—the impacts.

There are several distinct challenges to creating successful adaptation policy to address climate change. First, the temporal and geographic diffusion of the effects of climate change poses challenges both for international climate law and for national and regional policymakers. Given the long time horizons involved and the geographic differences of likely impacts (even within countries), choices about the appropriate level of preparation for effects of climate change are likely to be domestically as well as internationally fraught. Consider, for example, that Southern Europe is expected to be disproportionately impacted by climate change, in comparison to other EU regions. The southern region also has a relatively low GDP per capita, which complicates adaptation efforts further, since financing may be needed both from the EU and, indirectly, from richer Member States. This dynamic also takes place at the international level, with the global South being impacted disproportionately by climate change and pressure being placed on the North to support adaptation through climate financing.[54]

A second, related challenge is the complexity of the effects of climate change and the moving target this represents for adaptation efforts. Changes in weather patterns—such as rising temperatures or more or less precipitation—are problematic both "directly," in terms of heat waves, droughts, or floods, and "indirectly," through ecosystem degradation. Such degradation can result in the extinction (or flourishing!) of particular animal and plant species, which may be important in its own right, but which can also be dangerous to human health and welfare. For example, the reemergence of malaria—a disease currently restricted to tropical and subtropical areas—in Romania has become a real possibility due to changes in climate.[55]

Third, the nonhuman impacts of climate change—for instance, irreversible damage to ecosystems and/or species—are hard to quantify without human "side effects" (such as the one just mentioned). This makes the trade-off between costly adaptation investments even more difficult, given the great uncertainty about future effects.

Finally, climate change is causing a series of impacts that have not been seen before, at least in recent human history. Many of these impacts are extreme and catastrophic. Natural hazards present an important example of high-magnitude impacts: climate change is increasing the frequency and magnitude of risks from natural phenomena that may have negative effects on humans or the environment, including floods, wildfire, and hurricanes.

Managing the risks of natural hazards highlights the tension between adaptation and mitigation policy: determining the extent to which it makes sense to invest in adapting to the impacts of climate change is extremely challenging, versus attempting to mitigate the impacts of climate change before they happen. The likelihood and impact of some natural hazards (such as hurricanes, wildfires, and droughts) can be greatly reduced through mitigation. Policymakers can therefore also choose to invest in adaptive strategies to make those hazards less damaging when they do arise. When resources—or political will—are scarce, policymakers may have to choose between mitigation and adaptation, although, when less constrained, they may find that a combination of the two is most effective.

KEY EU APPROACHES TO CLIMATE CHANGE ADAPTATION AND NATURAL HAZARDS

Early international climate change negotiations and law focused almost exclusively on climate change mitigation. As it is becoming increasingly clear that mitigation will not prevent meaningful climate change, and as the immediate effects of climate change are being felt in more places, adaptation is becoming a more visible part of international climate law.

Thus far, the most important climate agreement regarding adaptation is the Paris Agreement, which was adopted in 2015. It establishes a global goal "on adaptation of enhancing adaptive capacity, strengthening resilience and reducing vulnerability to climate change, with a view to contributing to sustainable development and ensuring an adequate adaptation response in the context of the temperature goal [global average temperature increase below 2°C]."[56] The Paris Agreement imposes an obligation on parties to submit periodic adaptation communications to the UNFCCC secretariat in order to track nations' progress on adaptation.[57]

The EU has yet to fully implement the adaptation obligations imposed by the Paris Agreement. Given the EU's strong support for the agreement and its claims to climate leadership, however, it seems likely that EU policy will have to change to reflect these new obligations regarding adaptation. That said, meeting these obligations presents a potential problem for the EU: adaptation has historically been viewed as an entirely national issue, and there is currently no recognized competence to legislate on adaptation. Needless to say, the consequences of national adaptation strategies, or the lack thereof, will impact the entire EU and the goals that it seeks to achieve. It is therefore not unlikely that the EU will claim competence in this area in the coming years, especially with a growing international framework on adaptation, partially negotiated by the EU. Nevertheless, this development of an EU competence would be politically sensitive, and the EU will have to tread lightly.

In the absence of a formal, recognized competence for addressing adaptation policy, the EU has developed several initiatives related to adaptation and natural risk management that support the Member States in regulating these areas. Although these efforts have not led to formal pieces of legislation, they have been important for the development of national strategies and are likely to form the basis for future EU adaptation strategy.

Adaptation

The EU's involvement with adaptation started in 2009, with the adoption of a White Paper titled "Adapting to Climate Change: Towards a European Framework for Action."[58] The White Paper set out a number of deliverables for the EU, aimed at supporting the adaptive efforts of the Member States. Several of the deliverables in the White Paper centered on the creation of the Climate-ADAPT platform (http://climate-adapt .eea.europa.eu), the integration of adaptation into key EU policies, and the financial and technical support of the EU for national adaptation strategies and plans of Member States.

As of January 2020, all Member States—apart from Bulgaria, Latvia, and Croatia—have adopted a national adaptation strategy (NAS).[59] The development and adoption of an NAS is voluntary, and their forms and comprehensiveness vary significantly. Many of them were developed with the support of the EU (for instance through capacity building, workshops, and pre-accession assistance in case of the newer Member States).

The uptake of national adaptation plans (NAPs) has been more limited, with those of nine Member States (Italy, Greece, Poland, Bulgaria, Slovakia, Hungary, Croatia, Slovenia, and Ireland) still missing.[60] NAPs are a requirement under the UNFCCC, which means that all Member States will eventually have to develop such a plan in order to fulfill their international obligations.

The development of the Climate-ADAPT platform, launched in 2012, represents one of the main achievements of the EU on adaptation thus far. The platform, set up as a data exchange that can be used to assist policymakers and stakeholders engaged in adaptation planning, is the result of a partnership between the European Commission and the European Environment Agency. Climate-ADAPT is focused on gathering information on expected climate change in Europe, current and future vulnerability of regions and sectors, adaptation planning and strategies, and the development of adaptation planning tools.

The 2013 EU Strategy on Climate Change Adaptation, the successor to the 2009 White Paper, sets out three main objectives. The first is promoting action by Member States—specifically through the adoption of national adaptation strategies, but also through the support of local initiatives such as the Global Covenant of Mayors for Climate and Energy. Second, the strategy seeks climate-proofing action at the EU level—specifically in vulnerable sectors such as agriculture, fisheries, and cohesion policy. Finally, the strategy promotes better-informed decision making by addressing knowledge gaps.[61]

In November 2018, the implementation of the EU Strategy on Climate Change Adaptation was reviewed by the Commission to assess its effectiveness.[62] Although the resulting report gave a positive overall assessment of the EU's progress on the aims of the strategy, it also highlighted the EU's continuing vulnerabilities to climate impacts.[63] The report specifically underlined the importance of integrating adaptation with sustainable development and disaster risk reduction.

Natural Hazards and Disaster Management

The total reported economic losses caused by weather and other climate-related extremes in Europe in 1980–2016 amounted to more than 436 billion euros.[64] Over 70 percent of this damage was caused by only 3 percent of reported events. This shows the devastating potential of extreme natural hazards, the frequency and intensity of which will likely only increase with climate change.

Member States are in control of the risk management of natural hazards and disasters; the EU's involvement is purely one of supportive and coordinating competence. There are nevertheless some important EU initiatives that seek to lower the risk of natural disasters and improve the response to these incidents. The EU assists in this area in two key ways: through supporting risk management aimed at disaster prevention and by offering aid once a disaster has taken place. In relation to risk management, the European Commission has mapped key natural and man-made disaster risks within the EU, which can be found in the Commission's "Overview" working document.[65] The EU advises Member States on risk management and offers research for, and peer review of, national risk management strategies as a way to strengthen resilience and risk management.[66] The EU also provides an important source of funding, for example through structural and investment funds under the EU's cohesion policy. Given the regional variation in risk profiles, in terms of both likelihood and vulnerability, risk management is increasingly linked to the EU's regional development agenda, which promotes social cohesion, solidarity, and shared progress across the EU. At the EU level, the Commission has adopted an action plan that looks to integrate disaster risk reduction into EU policies, including goals the EU has agreed to as part of the UN's 2030 Agenda for Sustainable Development. The explicit link made between disaster risk reduction and climate change adaptation in the Paris Agreement has provided a legal basis for the EU to move forward on this issue.

When humanitarian emergencies or disasters do occur, the Directorate-General for European Civil Protection and Humanitarian Aid Operations assists Member States.[67] Since July 2017, Member States can also rely on a special EU financial fund for reconstruction if they are affected by a natural disaster. The creation of this fund was a response to the earthquakes that struck central Italy in 2016, and it can be used for any natural disaster that occurred after January 1, 2014. Other types of disaster response include the evaluation of national responses (to floods, for example) in order to create best practices.[68]

TAKEAWAYS

✓ The EU does not currently have competence to adopt adaptation legislation. However, it does have supportive competence to assist Member States in the development of their adaptation strategies, and it may claim competence on this issue in the coming years. In the meantime, Member States are largely responsible for their own adaptation efforts.

✓ The main ways in which the EU is currently involved in adaptation efforts include promoting action by Member States, helping inform Member States' decision making about adaptation, and assisting vulnerable sectors by climate-proofing EU policies.

✓ The EU also lacks competence to legislate on natural hazards. However, the EU financially supports Member States and regions that suffer from natural disasters. It also helps Member States collect information about, and plan for, risk management related to natural disasters and hazards.

DISCUSSION QUESTIONS

1. How much should countries focus on adaptation rather than mitigation? Which is worse: a country that lacks a cohesive mitigation plan, or a country that lacks a cohesive adaptation plan? Must planning for either phenomenon be centralized, or might substantial headway be made even with decentralized or ad hoc policies?

2. Should mitigation strategies focus on catastrophes and disasters, like floods or hurricanes, or on pervasive but smaller changes, such as climate shifts that undermine aquatic ecosystems? If a country cares about both kinds of impacts—catastrophic and chronic—does it make sense to plan for both at the same time, or are different strategies needed to manage them?

CLIMATE CHANGE: SUMMARY

The EU is a significant contributor to both historical and current GHG emissions. The EU is a party to all significant international agreements on climate change, including the UN Framework Convention on Climate Change. It considers multilateralism the main solution to climate change and has positioned itself as a leader in international negotiations.

The EU's internal strategy on climate change mitigation—which is closely linked to international agreements and negotiations on climate change—is more ambitious than most other countries' efforts. The current goals for 2020 and 2030 focus on GHG emission reductions, energy efficiency gains, and increased reliance on renewable energy.

The EU plays a limited role in adaptation policy, which continues to be primarily a responsibility of the Member States. However, as the impacts of climate change are becoming increasingly visible, the EU is starting to play a larger role in information gathering and capacity building for its most affected regions.

KEY TERMS

ADAPTATION Adjusting to expected or experienced changes to reduce the damage they cause.

CLIMATE CHANGE Changes in global climate patterns, specifically those occurring since the late twentieth century, that are attributable largely to increased levels of atmospheric carbon dioxide produced by the use of fossil fuels.

COLLECTIVE ACTION PROBLEM A situation in which people are disincentivized to pursue a joint or common goal.

ENERGY EFFICIENCY The process of reducing energy consumption by using less energy to achieve the same amount of useful output.

FREE-RIDER PROBLEM A situation that occurs when those who benefit from resources, public goods, or other actions do not pay for them, resulting in the underprovision of such goods or actions.

GREENHOUSE GAS A gas that contributes to the greenhouse effect.

MITIGATION Attempts to limit the magnitude and rate of long-term climate change, primarily through reducing anthropogenic greenhouse gas emissions.

NATURAL HAZARDS Naturally occurring physical phenomena caused by either rapid- or slow-onset events, such as earthquakes, avalanches, droughts, or floods.

SOCIAL COST OF CARBON A monetized estimate of the expected impact (either globally or domestically) of emitting a set quantity of carbon dioxide.

DISCUSSION QUESTION

1. Should the EU focus more on mitigation or adaptation in the coming decades? Which do you think will be more important globally? Locally?

NOTES

1. A small but persistent group of politicians and scholars continue to question the existence of climate change and/or its anthropogenic causes. While the existence of this group raises interesting questions, we will focus on the mainstream scientific consensus that is reflected in the reports of the Intergovernmental Panel on Climate Change, available at www.ipcc.ch/publications_and_data/publications_and_data_reports.shtml.

2. See, e.g., Horst W.J. Rittel and Melvin M. Webber, "Dilemmas in a General Theory of Planning" (1973) 4 *Policy Sciences* 2, for one of the early definitions of "wicked problems" and their characteristics.

3. It is worth noting the distinction between GHG emissions generally and CO_2 emissions. While CO_2 is the most common GHG, it is not the most potent one—meaning that while it makes up the largest share of GHGs, other gases are relatively more damaging insofar as smaller quantities create larger effects. As the availability of data on these emissions vary, be mindful that some of the statistics presented refer to GHGs generally, and others only to CO_2.

4. See Climate Analytics, "Historical Responsibility for Climate Change—from Countries *[sic]* Emissions to Contribution to Temperature Increase," 2015, http://climateanalytics.org/files/historical_responsibility_report_nov_2015.pdf.

5. For a historical overview of the situation in Poland, a particularly environmentally vocal EU Member State, see Daniel Cole, *Instituting Environmental Protection: From Red to Green in Poland* (Macmillan and St. Martin's Press 1998).

6. See International Energy Agency, "CO_2 Emissions from Fuel Combustion," 2017, www.iea.org/publications/freepublications/publication/CO2Emissions fromFuelCombustionHighlights2017.pdf.

7. Ibid.

8. Countries with higher per person emissions than the United States—such as Qatar (35.73), Bahrain (21.8), United Arab Emirates (19.3), and Saudi Arabia (16.54)—are mostly those whose economies depend heavily on fossil fuel extraction and refinement.

9. See www.eea.europa.eu/themes/climate/trends-and-projections-in-europe/climate-and-energy-country-profiles.

10. Specifically, 80 percent in the Netherlands (and 96 percent of its CO_2 emissions) and 83 percent in Estonia. See "Greenhouse Gas Emissions in the Netherlands 1990–2016: National Inventory Report 2018," www.rivm.nl /bibliotheek/rapporten/2018–0006.pdf; and "Greenhouse Gas Emissions in Estonia 1990–2016: National Inventory Report," www.envir.ee/sites/default /files/nir_est_1990–2016_15.01.18_submission.pdf.

11. Many Member States combine the emissions of energy supply and industry (especially if the industry is particularly energy intensive), which accounts for the higher percentages in the Netherlands and Estonia.

12. See https://ec.europa.eu/eurostat/statistics-explained/pdfscache/1180.pdf.

13. For an overview, see https://ec.europa.eu/clima/policies/adaptation /how_en#tab-0-0.

14. Based on Joint Research Centre, "Climate Impacts in Europe: The JRC PESETA II Project," 2014, http://publications.jrc.ec.europa.eu/repository /bitstream/JRC87011/reqno_jrc87011_final%20report%20ready_final3.pdf.

15. The report divides the EU into five regions: Northern Europe (Sweden, Finland, Estonia, Lithuania, Latvia, and Denmark), UK & Ireland (UK and Ireland), Central Europe North (Belgium, Netherlands, Germany, and Poland), Central Europe South (France, Austria, Czech Republic, Slovakia, Hungary, Slovenia, and Romania), and Southern Europe (Portugal, Spain, Italy, Greece, and Bulgaria).

16. See Joint Research Centre, "Climate Impacts in Europe."

17. And 74 percent of EU citizens consider it a "very serious" problem. The full report is available at https://ec.europa.eu/clima/sites/clima/files/support /docs/report_2017_en.pdf.

18. Ibid.

19. See Hans Labohm, "Climate Scepticism in Europe," (2012) 23 *Energy & Environment* 1311–1317.

20. See www.independent.co.uk/voices/climate-denial-scepticism-global-warming-policy-foundation-trump-a7552026.html.

21. UNFCCC, article 2.

22. See Article 191(1) Treaty on the Functioning of the European Union (TFEU): "Union policy on the environment shall contribute to pursuit of the following objectives: . . . promoting measures at international level to deal with regional or worldwide environmental problems, and in particular combating climate change."

23. See, e.g., the famous "bubble" provision in the Kyoto Protocol, Article 4: "If Parties acting jointly do so in the framework of, and together with, a regional economic integration organization, any alteration in the composition of the organization after adoption of this Protocol shall not affect existing commitments under this Protocol. Any alteration in the composition of the organization shall only apply for the purposes of those commitments under Article 3 that are adopted subsequent to that revision."

24. The EU Emissions Trading Scheme is explained in detail in this chapter's "Mitigation" snapshot.

25. Article 4 Paris Agreement.

26. European Commission, "20 20 by 2020: Europe's Climate Change Opportunity" COM (2008) 30 final.

27. See also Suzanne Kingston et al., *European Environmental Law* (Cambridge University Press 2017), at 273.

28. European Council Conclusions, 20/21 March 2014, EUCO 7.1.14 REV 1 CO EUR 2 CONCL 1, at 7.

29. European Commission, "A Roadmap for moving to a competitive low carbon economy in 2050" COM (2011) 112 final.

30. For more information on the Acid Rain Program, see A. Denny Ellerman et al., *Markets for Clean Air: The US Acid Rain Program* (Cambridge University Press 2000).

31. See, e.g., European Commission, "Communication from the Commission: Environmental Taxes and Charges in the Single Market" COM (97) 9 final (1997).

32. For further reading, see Josephine van Zeben, *The Allocation of Regulatory Competence in the EU ETS* (Cambridge University Press 2014).

33. See Brian Flannery et al., "Framework Proposal for a US Upstream Greenhouse Gas Tax with WTO-Compliant Border Adjustments," Resources for the Future report, March 2018, www.rff.org/files/document/file/RFF-Rpt-Flannery-Mares-Framework-rev.pdf.

34. International Civil Aviation Organization, "Inclusion of International Civil Aviation in the European Union Emissions Trading Scheme (EU ETS) and Its Impact," ICAO working paper C-WP/13790 (30 September 2011), www.greenaironline.com/photos/ICAO_C.194.WP.13790.EN.pdf, at 2 ("The inclusion of international civil aviation in the EU ETS is a unilateral measure and in contravention to the articles of the Chicago Convention and its Preamble...") and at 5–6 ("Representatives of [the signing countries] ... [o]ppose the EU's plan to include all flights by non-EU carriers ... which is inconsistent with applicable international law").

35. Joint Declaration of the Moscow Meeting on Inclusion of International Civil Aviation in the EU-ETS, 22 February 2012, available at www.greenaironline.com/photos/Moscow_Declaration.pdf.

36. In 2015, 6,677 million metric tons of carbon equivalent was traded on the EU ETS market. The combined estimate gathered by the Commission is available in the fact sheet "The EU Emissions Trading System (EU ETS)," https://ec.europa.eu/clima/sites/clima/files/factsheet_ets_en.pdf, at 5.

37. Decision No 406/2009/EC of the European Parliament and of the Council of 23 April 2009 on the effort of Member States to reduce their greenhouse gas emissions to meet the Community's greenhouse gas emission reduction commitments up to 2020.

38. While there is an EU-wide registry, to make an account parties have to go through a national authority. These authorities are listed at https://ec.europa.eu/clima/policies/ets/registry_en#tab-0–3.

39. See, e.g., www.internationalrivers.org/sites/default/files/attached-files/foe_ir_cdm_fact_sheet_final3_10–08.pdf.

40. Regulation (EU) 2018/842 of the European Parliament and of the Council of 30 May 2018 on binding annual greenhouse gas emission reductions by Member States from 2021 to 2030 contributing to climate action to meet commitments under the Paris Agreement and amending Regulation (EU) No 525/2013.

41. This goal will be reviewed in 2020 with the possibility of increasing it to 30 percent.

42. European Commission, "Renewable energy progress report," 15 June 2015, COM (2015) 293 final.

43. European Council Conclusions, 23 and 24 October 2014, EUCO 169/14 CO EUR 13 CONCL 5, at 3.

44. Directive 2009/28/EC on the promotion of the use of energy from renewable sources, Article 3 and Annex I.

45. See ibid., Articles 5 and 13.

46. All national renewable energy action plans are available at http:// ec.europa.eu/energy/node/71.

47. See chapter 2.

48. Article 34 TFEU. For details, see Catherine Barnard, *The Substantive Law of the EU: The Four Freedoms* (Oxford University Press, 6th ed., 2019).

49. Article 107(1) TFEU.

50. Article 107(2) TFEU.

51. See, generally, Directive 2012/27/EU on energy efficiency. See also the political agreement between the Commission, the Parliament, and the Council (14 June 2018), which includes a binding energy efficiency target for the EU for 2030 of 32.5 percent, with a clause allowing for an upward revision by 2023.

52. Directive 2010/21/EU on the energy performance of buildings (2010) OJ L153/13.

53. The 2017 progress report on energy efficiency showed that final energy consumption has fallen since 2005 in all Member States except Lithuania, Malta, and Poland. However, much of this can be attributed to weather conditions and economic slowdown. The success and implementation of energy efficiency measures vary widely between Member States; see https://eur-lex.europa.eu /legal-content/EN/TXT/PDF/?uri=CELEX:52017DC0687&from=EN.

54. This also raises complicated questions of historical emissions and responsibility for climate change effects, which fall outside the scope of this chapter. See Benito Müller et al., "Differentiating (Historic) Responsibilities for Climate Change" (2009) 9 *Climate Policy* 593.

55. Larisa Ivanescu et al., "Climate Change Is Increasing the Risk of the Reemergence of Malaria in Romania" (2016) *Biomed Research International,* www .ncbi.nlm.nih.gov/pmc/articles/PMC5101366/.

56. Article 7 Paris Agreement.

57. While the form of these communications is up to the parties, several interest groups have provided guidance on potential formats and best practices; see, e.g., https://careclimatechange.org/wp-content/uploads/2017/10 /SVAbriefAdpCommunicationFinal.pdf.

58. Commision, "Adapting to climate change: Towards a European framework for action," COM (2009) 147 final.

59. For a full overview of these plans, see https://climate-adapt.eea.europa.eu/countries-regions/countries.

60. Information verified on 12 February 2019 at https://climate-adapt.eea.europa.eu/countries-regions/countries.

61. See European Commission, "Communication: An EU Strategy on adaptation to climate change" COM (2013) 216.

62. For the full impact assessment, see European Commission, "Commission Staff Working Document: Evaluation of the EU Strategy on adaptation to climate change" SWD (2018) 461 final; this accompanies European Commission, "Report from the Commission to the European Parliament and the Council on the implementation of the EU Strategy on adaptation to climate change" COM (2018) 738 final.

63. See COM (2018) 738 final.

64. Ibid., at 1.

65. European Commission, "Commission Staff Working Document: Overview of Natural and Man-made Disaster Risks the European Union May Face" SWD (2017) 176 final, https://ec.europa.eu/echo/sites/echo-site/files/swd_2017_176_overview_of_risks_2.pdf.

66. An important research resource is the Disaster Risk Management Knowledge Centre; visit https://drmkc.jrc.ec.europa.eu/.

67. See SWD (2017) 176 final. The EU also assists countries outside its borders; for a full overview of activities, see https://ec.europa.eu/echo/index_en.

68. See, e.g., the Flood Emergency Management Systems report available at http://ec.europa.eu/environment/integration/research/newsalert/pdf/responding_floods_europe_new_framework_assesses_flood_emergency_management_systems_486na3_en.pdf.

Conclusions

Over the relatively short period of our existence, we humans have changed the Earth's environment in profound ways and we will continue to do so. But with understanding and care, we can choose to act with knowledge about the likely impacts of our behaviors and to regulate those behaviors through law and other means. This book aims to create a starting point for more and deeper conversations between those working in environmental science (in the broadest sense), foreign jurisdictions, and EU environmental law in order to create the best possible answers to the complicated social and ecological questions of how humans should shape their environments.

One of the main goals of this book was to present the distinctive features of the EU approach to environmental law. As you will have seen in the collection of legal snapshots in part II, the actual legal instruments applied to different environmental impacts are varied and numerous. Despite their many differences, they all reflect defining features of the EU legal system: multilevel governance, technocracy, and the use of risk analysis. They also tend to reflect broader normative considerations, such as those imbedded in the precautionary principle. Learning to identify common strands can help in making sense of seemingly dissimilar, or even conflicting, EU approaches to different environmental problems, as well as provide a basis for comparison between EU approaches and those adopted by other countries.

In writing this book, we aimed to provide information in such a way that readers can make their own independent assessments of the EU approach to environmental law. However, this is not to say that the law is normatively neutral. The status quo of EU environmental law should not be taken as a natural phenomenon, but as the result of human decision making. This means that moving forward, humans have the opportunity to change and to improve legal rules, in the EU and around the world.

Acknowledgments

Many people have contributed to this book's eventual shape and form. We will not attempt to mention them all here. We are grateful to work in a part of academia that is characterized by so many supportive, creative, and generous colleagues.

We would specifically like to thank Chris Backes, Anne Bot, Stephanie Davidson, Alfred Heikamp, Joshua Pike, Petra Siebelink, and Edwin Woerdman, as well as members of the Society for Environmental Law and Economics, our students, and our families for their contributions to making this a better book. We would also like to thank the staff of UC Press for their confidence in the project.

Finally, we would like to thank one another for a delightful coauthorship.

Time Line of EU Environmental Law

United Nations Conference on the Conservation and Utilization of Resources
1949

Entry into force treaty establishing the European Coal and Steel Community
1952

Entry into force Treaties of Rome: EEC and Euratom treaties
1958

Adoption First Environmental Action Programme
1973

Paris Declaration of the Heads of State or Government of the EEC Member States, mentioning the environment
1972

United Nations Conference on the Human Environment
1972

Entry into force Merger Treaty (Brussels Treaty)
1967

Drinking Water Directive
1975

Dangerous Substances in Water Directive
1976

Seveso disaster causing 10 to 30 tons of herbicides, insecticides and mercury compounds to be released into the Rhine
1976

Adoption of the Birds Directive (oldest EU environmental legislation)
1979

Entry into force of the Montreal Protocol to protect the ozone layer
1989

Entry into force Single European Act
1987

Adoption of the Single European Act with Article 25 including environmental protection as an EU objective
1986

Passage of the Seveso Directive
1982

Adoption of the Habitats Directive and creation of the Natura 2000 network
1992

Entry into force Treaty on European Union (Maastricht Treaty); creation of the European Environment Agency
1993

Entry into force Treaty of Amsterdam; creation of Eurozone
1999

Adoption of Water Framework Directive
2000

Adoption of Waste Framework Directive
2008

Creation of the European Union Emissions Trading Scheme (EU ETS)
2005

Entry into force Treaty of Nice
2003

Commission Communication on the Precautionary Principle
2000

Commission Communication "20 20 by 2020: Europe's Climate Change Opportunity"
2008

Adoption of REACH Regulation
2009

Entry into force of Treaty of Lisbon
2009

Industrial Emissions Directive
2010

EU Action Plan for a Circular Economy
2015

2030 Framework for Climate and Energy
2014

Seventh Environmental Action Programme
2013

Creation of the Energy Union
2015

EU Ratification of Paris Agreement
2016

Revised Waste Framework Directive
2018

Adoption of European Green Deal
2019

Membership of the EU

Figure A2.A. In 1958, Belgium, France, Germany, Italy, Luxembourg, and the Netherlands joined.

Figure A2.B. In 1973, Denmark, Ireland, and the United Kingdom joined.

Figure A2.C. In 1981, Greece joined.

Figure A2.D. In 1986, Portugal and Spain joined.

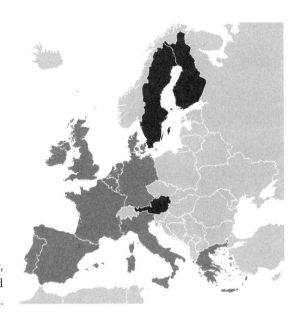

Figure A2.E. In 1995, Austria, Finland, and Sweden joined.

Figure A2.F. In 2004, Cyprus, Czech Republic, Estonia, Hungary, Latvia, Lithuania, Malta, Poland, Slovakia, and Slovenia joined.

Figure A2.G. In 2007, Bulgaria and Romania joined.

Figure A2.H. In 2013, Croatia joined.

Additional Resources

The purpose of this book is to present an accessible introduction to, and over-view of, the environmental law of the European Union. In many cases, readers may now wish to know more about particular environmental laws, or to research primary source material. This section is intended to point readers toward helpful additional resources for further study.

ACCESSING EU ENVIRONMENTAL LAWS

Throughout the book, we have referred to a number of different sources of law, including the EU treaties, EU legislation in the form of regulations and directives, and judicial decisions.

EUR-Lex is a comprehensive database of all EU legislation organized by type. It covers the treaties (past and present), legislation, international agreements, as well as preparatory documents to legislation. Moreover, it provides a portal to all case law. Searches can be done through case names and/or keywords.

EUR-Lex is maintained by the EU and is accessible via https://eur-lex.europa.eu /homepage.html. Most materials are available in all official languages of the EU.

EUR-Lex also features an e-learning module that helps you navigate the website and its more complex search functions (https://eur-lex.europa.eu/e-learning /index.html).

FINDING POLICY DOCUMENTS AND
OTHER USEFUL MATERIALS

The following resources provide further context for EU legislation:

> Every directorate-general (DG) of the European Commission has a dedicated
> website that provides a wealth of information regarding every EU policy,
> including fact sheets, historical overviews, and links to the main legal acts in
> every policy area. The Commission's general website is https://ec.europa.eu
> /commission/index_en; the website for DG Environmental is http://ec
> .europa.eu/environment/index_en.htm; the website for DG Climate Action
> is https://ec.europa.eu/clima/index_en. Each website is available in every
> official language of the EU.
>
> The European Environment Agency maintains significant information about
> environmental problems in the EU, including several databases on emissions,
> water pollution, and other environmental information, at www.eea.europa.eu/.
>
> The Institute for European Environmental Policy is an independent think tank
> with a well-resourced website on EU environmental law and policy: https://
> ieep.eu/. This includes its "Manual on EU Environmental Policy," which is
> accurate up to 2012.

FURTHER READING ON EU LAW

The EU legal system is complex and fascinating. For readers who want more
information on the overarching legal system, the following resources may be
helpful:

> Stephen Weatherill, *Law and Values in the European Union* (Oxford University Press,
> 2016)
>
> Paul Craig and Gráinne de Búrca, *EU Law: Text, Cases, and Materials* (6th ed.,
> Oxford University Press, 2015), one of the most-used textbooks on the
> subject
>
> Catherine Barnard, *The Substantive Law of the EU: The Four Freedoms* (4th ed., Oxford
> University Press, 2013), with a particular focus on the laws of the internal
> market
>
> Robert Schütze, *European Union Law* (2nd ed., Cambridge University Press, 2018),
> which includes some coverage of Brexit

FURTHER READING ON EU ENVIRONMENTAL LAW

For readers seeking additional legal writing on EU environmental law, there
are several textbooks on the subject. We particularly like the following:

Suzanne Kingston et al., *European Environmental Law* (Cambridge University Press, 2017)

Maria Lee, *EU Environmental Law, Governance and Decision-Making* (2nd ed., Hart, 2014)

Elizabeth Fisher et al., *Environmental Law: Text, Cases and Materials* (2nd ed., Oxford University Press, 2019)

NATIONAL ENVIRONMENTAL LAW

In many cases, national and local laws (often implementing by EU law) play a critical role in shaping the EU environment. Resources related to these national laws are country specific and tend to be in the official languages of the relevant Member State. There are, however, some non-national resources that provide a good starting point:

EUR-Lex provides a (non-exhaustive) overview of the national transposition of important European laws.

The European Environment Agency provides information on each of its members (including some cooperating countries that are not EU Member States) at https://www.eea.europa.eu/countries-and-regions.

COMPARATIVE RESOURCES

For readers interested in comparative environmental law, we recommend the following:

Arden Rowell and Josephine van Zeben, A *Guide to U.S. Environmental Law* (University of California Press, 2021), the companion to this volume, designed to allow for easy comparison between the environmental laws of the United States and the EU

Emma Lees and Jorge E. Viñuales (editors), *The Oxford Handbook of Comparative Environmental Law* (Oxford University Press, 2019), a recent resource on comparative environmental law, directed toward comparative legal scholars

Glossary

ADAPTATION Adjusting to expected or experienced changes to reduce the damage they cause.

ADMINISTRATIVE LAW Law that governs governmental bodies, such as administrative agencies.

ADMINISTRATIVE PROCEDURE Rules that govern procedures used by agencies and in agency proceedings.

AIR POLLUTION Higher-than-normal concentrations of materials, including chemicals, that are out of place in air.

BEHAVIORAL INSTRUMENTS Instruments for regulating behavior that build on social science research, particularly in psychology and economics.

BIODIVERSITY The variety of life in a habitat or ecosystem.

CAP-AND-TRADE SYSTEM A regulatory instrument that sets a maximum cap on a certain activity (e.g., emitting activities) and allows participants to trade permits with each other to engage in more or less of that activity.

CHECKS AND BALANCES A model of governance that limits the concentration of power by giving each of the branches of government the authority to limit the power of the other(s).

CHOICE ARCHITECTURE Purposeful structuring of decision-making contexts to shape people's behavior toward selected ends.

CIVIL LAW A legal system that codifies core principles into referable systems, such as statutes.

CIVIL PROCEDURE The rules that must be followed in noncriminal judicial courts.

CLIMATE CHANGE Changes in global climate patterns, specifically those occurring since the late twentieth century, that are attributable largely to increased levels of atmospheric carbon dioxide produced by the use of fossil fuels.

COLLECTIVE ACTION PROBLEM A situation in which people are disincentivized to pursue a joint or common goal.

COMMAND-AND-CONTROL REGULATION A group of regulatory instruments that rely on standard setting in order to permit or ban certain types of behavior.

COMMON AGRICULTURAL POLICY (CAP) A European policy creating a system of subsidies and support programs for agriculture. The CAP has environmental impacts but was not designed specifically to manage those impacts.

COMMON LAW Law made by judges, published in the form of judicial opinions, which gives precedential authority to prior court decisions (can be both public and private law).

COMPENSATORY MITIGATION Allowing for the degradation of one habitat, such as a wetland, in exchange for improving (or even creating) a different habitat.

COMPETENCE The EU's authority to act within a certain policy area in order to achieve set objectives. This authority can be exclusive (i.e., the EU is the only actor empowered to legislate), shared (i.e., subject to the subsidiarity principle), or supportive (i.e., the EU can facilitate and coordinate action between Member States but cannot legislate or take any independent actions).

COMPLEX IMPACTS Environmental impacts that are obscure, technical, and/or interactive. These can be difficult to measure, understand, and regulate.

COMPLIANCE COST The cost of complying with a regulatory standard.

CONSERVATION The protection of a natural environment or species.

CONSTITUTIONAL LAW Law that provides for the structure and functioning of a government—for how the government is "constituted"—and how the government is supposed to interact with individuals (a form of public law).

CONTRACT LAW Law that governs how promises between individuals are enforced (a form of private law).

COST-BENEFIT ANALYSIS A decision procedure for quantifying (and typically monetizing) the expected positive and negative impacts of a proposed policy.

COUNCIL OF MINISTERS The EU legislative body composed of government ministers of the Member States (its formal name is the Council of the European Union).

COURT OF JUSTICE OF THE EUROPEAN UNION The EU's judicial body and ultimate authority on the interpretation of EU law, made up of the General Court and the Court of Justice.

CRIMINAL LAW Law that governs the punishment and behavior of those who commit crimes—behaviors that are considered so socially damaging that they are punishable by law (a form of public law).

CRIMINAL PROCEDURE Rules that govern criminal legal procedures.

DEFAULT RULES A preset course of action that takes effect automatically, unless decision makers provide an alternative specification.

DIFFUSE IMPACTS Environmental impacts that are geographically and/or spatially distant from the human actions that caused them.

DIRECTIVE A type of EU law aimed at achieving a certain effect, leaving open to Member States how to implement and achieve that effect.

DIRECTORATE-GENERAL A branch of the European Commission responsible for the drafting, implementation, and enforcement of EU law in a specific area.

DISCOUNTING The process of making future (monetary) amounts comparable to current amounts.

DOSE-RESPONSE Relationship between the amount of a substance an organism is exposed to and the harm and response the exposure causes.

ECONOMIC INSTRUMENTS Regulatory instruments that rely on economic incentives in order to achieve compliance.

ECOSYSTEMS Geographic areas where living entities (plants, animals, and other organisms) and nonliving entities (water, air, and soil) interact in mutually interdependent ways.

ENERGY EFFICIENCY The process of reducing energy consumption by using less energy to achieve the same amount of useful output.

ENVIRONMENT The surroundings or conditions in which humans, plants, and animals function.

ENVIRONMENTAL ACTION PROGRAMME (EAP) An articulation of the EU's goals for environmental policy development.

ENVIRONMENTAL IMPACTS Consequences (generally of human actions) for the surroundings or conditions in which humans, plants, and animals function.

ENVIRONMENTAL JUSTICE Concerns about the fair distribution of environmental impacts.

ENVIRONMENTAL LAW The use of law to regulate human behaviors with environmental impacts.

ENVIRONMENTAL PRINCIPLES Principles on environmental policy that are listed in the Treaty on the Functioning of the European Union, which provides that such policy "shall be based on the precautionary principle and on the principles that preventative action should be taken, that environmental damage should as a priority be rectified at source and that the polluter should pay."

EUROPEAN COMMISSION The EU institution responsible for proposing legislation, implementing decisions, and managing the day-to-day business of the EU.

EUROPEAN COUNCIL The EU institution that sets out the general political direction of the EU. Consists of heads of states or government of the Member States, as well as its President and the President of the European Commission.

EUROPEAN PARLIAMENT The elected EU body that exercises legislative and budgetary powers.

EXCLUSIVE COMPETENCE Areas in which the EU is the only actor empowered to legislate.

EXPOSURE REDUCTION Amending behaviors so that there is less exposure to pollution and, thus (hopefully), less harm.

EXTERNALITIES Costs and benefits related to an activity that are experienced by someone other than the person engaged in the activity.

FRAMING A behavioral instrument that uses small changes in how contextual cues are presented to strategically shape people's behaviors.

FREE-RIDER PROBLEM A situation that occurs when those who benefit from resources, public goods, or other actions do not pay for them, resulting in the underprovision of such goods or actions.

GENETIC MODIFICATION The manipulation of an organism's genes using biotechnology, typically to augment desirable traits or delete undesirable ones.

GREENHOUSE GAS A gas that contributes to the greenhouse effect.

GUIDELINE A type of EU law that is not binding on third parties (i.e., it is binding only on the party issuing the guidelines).

HABITAT The natural home of an animal, plant, or other organism.

IMPLEMENTING/DELEGATED ACTS Type of delegated EU law adopted by the European Commission.

INFRINGEMENT PROCEDURE A procedure aimed at establishing and ensuring that an EU Member State fulfills its obligations under EU law.

INSTRUMENT CHOICE Selection among different types of regulatory instruments with a view to create the "best" fit between the regulated behavior and the method of regulation.

INTEGRATION PRINCIPLE A principle that provides that environmental protection requirements should be taken into account in defining and implementing EU policies and activities, particularly with a view to promoting sustainable development.

INTERGOVERNMENTAL LAW Processes and laws that are created by states and aimed at states (e.g., international law).

JUDICIAL REVIEW The power of a court to review actions taken by the other branches of government, often by testing those actions against constitutional norms.

JURISDICTION The authority to make legally binding decisions within a given territory or subject area.

LEGAL PERSONALITY The capacity to have legal rights and duties within a certain legal system.

LEGISLATIVE PROCEDURE The process through which legislative proposals (or "bills") are made into binding laws (or "acts").

ORDINARY LEGISLATIVE PROCEDURE In the EU, a procedure involving several actors, most importantly the European Parliament and the Council of Ministers.

SPECIAL LEGISLATIVE PROCEDURE In the EU, this legislative procedure can vary but typically excludes the European Parliament and involves only the Council of Ministers.

LIFE PROGRAMME A financial instrument for funding environmental, nature conservation, and climate change projects.

MARKET-BASED REGULATION A regulation that makes use of economic incentives created by markets.

MEMBER STATE A nation-state that is a signatory (or "member") of the EU treaties.

MITIGATION Attempts to limit the magnitude and rate of long-term climate change, primarily through reducing anthropogenic greenhouse gas emissions.

MULTILEVEL GOVERNANCE A regulatory system in which several levels of authority compete and coordinate with each other.

NATURAL HAZARDS Naturally occurring physical phenomena caused by either rapid- or slow-onset events, such as earthquakes, avalanches, droughts, or floods.

NONHUMAN IMPACTS Environmental impacts that relate primarily or exclusively to nonhuman animals, plants, and processes.

NONPOINT SOURCE WATER POLLUTION Water pollution that originates from multiple diffuse sources, as from agricultural runoff or drainage through urban streets.

NORMATIVE Relating to or deriving from a standard or norm.

NUDGE A behavioral instrument that is meant to alter people's behavior in predictable ways, without forbidding any options or significantly changing economic incentives.

OPINION A nonbinding policy document aimed at clarifying the interpretation of legal acts and/or other policy documents.

PATH DEPENDENCY A phenomenon whereby people continue existing practices even where better ones could be adopted, because of the costs associated with shifting to new "paths" or practices.

POINT SOURCE WATER POLLUTION Water pollution that originates from a single identifiable source, such as a pipe or ditch.

"POLLUTER PAYS" PRINCIPLE A principle that aims to ensure that costs are internalized by those engaged in polluting activity.

PRECAUTIONARY PRINCIPLE An EU principle related to risk management, which provides that if there is the possibility that a given policy or action might harm the public or the environment, and there is an absence of scientific consensus, the action should not be pursued.

PREEMPTION A process whereby the law of one level of government displaces the law of another. In the United States, this is most commonly preemption of state law by federal law.

PREVENTATIVE PRINCIPLE A principle that seeks to minimize harm from known environmental problems.

PRIMARY EU LAW Foundational EU law, such as the EU treaties, resulting from an intergovernmental process between the Member States (a type of intergovernmental law).

PRINCIPLE OF CONFERRAL An EU legal principle stipulating that the EU has only those competences that are explicitly conferred to it by the Member States via the EU treaties.

PRINCIPLE OF PROPORTIONALITY An EU legal principle aimed at limiting the EU's exercise of competence to that which is strictly necessary to achieve the EU's objectives.

PRINCIPLE OF SUBSIDIARITY An EU legal principle meant to regulate the division of competence between the Member States and the EU in areas of shared competence.

PRIVATE LAW Law that governs relationships between individuals (e.g., contract law, tort law, and property law).

PROPERTY LAW Law about the relationships between people and things.

PUBLIC LAW Law that governs issues that affect the general public or state (e.g., constitutional law, administrative law, and criminal law).

QUALIFIED MAJORITY VOTING The method of voting within the EU, whereby both a majority of countries and a majority of the EU's population has to vote in favor of a legislative proposal in order for it to pass.

RECOMMENDATION A legally nonbinding act from the EU.

"RECTIFICATION AT SOURCE" PRINCIPLE The idea that pollution is best addressed at the source rather than at the site of pollution (if geographically and/or temporally distinct).

REGULATION A type of EU law that is binding in terms of both its substance and its objective; Member State implementation is restricted to translating the regulation into national law.

REGULATORY INSTRUMENT A tool that a regulator uses to achieve regulatory goals.

REPRESENTATIVE DEMOCRACY Democracy exercised through elected officials representing a group of people.

RISK ANALYSIS A systemized method for identifying, assessing, quantifying, and evaluating risks.

RISK ASSESSMENT The scientific and technical first "stage" of risk analysis where the probabilities and magnitudes of hazards associated with particular behaviors and policies are identified and quantified.

RISK COMMUNICATION The communication of risk with the goal of enabling people to make informed decisions and exchange information on risk.

RISK MANAGEMENT The second "stage" of risk analysis, in which policy-based decisions are made about which and how risks will be reduced or tolerated.

SECONDARY EU LAW Supranational law resulting from the legislative process between the EU institutions.

SEPARATION OF POWERS An organizational principle of government whereby the legislative, executive, and judicial functions of the government are assigned to separate actors.

SHARED COMPETENCE Areas in which the EU and its Member States share the responsibility to legislate.

SOCIAL COST OF CARBON A monetized estimate of the expected impact (either globally or domestically) of emitting a set quantity of carbon dioxide.

SOIL POLLUTION Higher-than-normal concentrations of materials, including chemicals, that are out of place in soil.

SOVEREIGNTY The power to make laws and impose police power on people within a certain territory.

STANDING The legal right to bring a case before a court.

STRATEGIC IMPACT ASSESSMENT A type of environmental impact assessment that applies to plans and programs proposed by state actors.

SUPPORTIVE COMPETENCE Areas in which the EU can act only when explicitly requested to do so by the Member States.

SUPRANATIONAL LAW Processes and laws that are made by international bodies that can bind states (e.g., EU law).

SUSTAINABILITY The use of natural resources in a way that is economically, socially, and environmentally viable in the long term.

SUSTAINABLE DEVELOPMENT PRINCIPLE A principle that seeks to balance economic, social, and environmental development in managing global natural resources.

TECHNOCRACY A bureaucracy that is run by technologists and/or is heavily reliant on technical expertise.

TORT LAW Law that governs how people can use law to receive compensation for harms or injuries that other individuals have caused them (a form of private law).

WATER POLLUTION Higher-than-normal concentrations of materials, including chemicals, that are out of place in water, including drinking water.

WETLANDS A transitional ecosystem that forms a link between land and water.

WILDLIFE Undomesticated animals that live in their natural habitats.

Index

abatement, 216
acidification, 103, 106
acid rain, 158, 214–15
acquis, 41–42
actors, key, 12–35
adaptation, climate change, 194–98,
    229–31; definition, 237; key
    approaches, 231–32
administrative law, definition, 50–51
Agenda for Sustainable Development,
    235
agriculture: EU Common Agricultural
    Policy (CAP), 185–87; regulating,
    183–85, 213; soil pollution, 122,
    123–24; water quality, 114
air pollution: acid rain, 158, 214–15; Air
    Quality Framework Directive
    (AQFD), 102–5; from contaminated
    soil, 123; costs, 94; definition, 99,
    148; distinctive challenges, 99–101;
    distribution, 8; EU role in
    regulation, 95; incineration of
    waste, 135, 142; Industrial Emissions
    Directive, 108–10; IPPC permits,
    108–9; key legal approaches, 101–2;
    National Emissions Ceilings
    Directive (NECD), 106, 108;

Ozone-Depleting Substances
    Regulation, 107; quality thresholds,
    104–5; pollutants, 100–101
Air Quality Framework Directive
    (AQFD), 102–5
allowances, emissions, 61–62, 214–23;
    allocation methods, 218–20; credits,
    221–22; EU role, 219–21; scope,
    217–18, 231; summary, 215–16. *See also*
    EU ETS
aluminum: under EU Emissions
    Trading Scheme, 218; soil-based, 158
ambient air quality standards, 88, 101, 111
ammonia (NH_3): in agriculture, 187; as
    air pollutant, 101, 103, 106
animals: agriculture, 183–84; animal
    products, 170; ecosystems, 158–59;
    effects of pollution, 93;
    environmental impacts, 5–6;
    habitats, 177; wildlife, 169–70;
    zoos, 167
anthropogenic climate change, 194;
    mitigation, 209–210; Paris
    Agreement, 206; UN Framework
    Convention on Climate Change,
    203–4
aquatic ecosystems, 158

assessment: impact assessment, 86–87; definition, 89; impact assessment, 124, 179–82; risk assessment, 83, 84–85, 132; air pollutants, 83; definition, 89, 132
aviation, 199, 213, 218

bans: hazardous waste export, 142; leghold traps, 170–71; market-distorting measures, 226; regulatory instruments, 60, 64; seal trade, 161; Single-Use Plastics Directive, 139
Basel Convention, 142–43
Bathing Water Directive, 82, 118
BAT standard, 109–110
batteries, 135, 141
behavioral instruments, 60, 62–64; definition, 71
benchmarks, 104–5
benzene, 102, 103, 104
Best Available Techniques standard (BAT), 109–110
bilateral agreements, 97, 114
biocides, 133
biodiversity, 156, 159–60, 163–68; definition, 188
biofuels, 226
birds, 133; Birds Directive, 160–61, 170, 171–74
branches of government, 13–14
Brazil, 198, 218
breach, 21–22, 23, 44; Air Quality Framework Directive (AQFD), 104
breeding, birds, 174
bubble provision, 27
budget, EU, 46, 94, 166, 186
Bulgaria, 203, 221, 233, 255
bureaucracy, 83–84. See also technocracy
byproducts: further use, 138; industrial, 107; definition, 138; waste, 93, 129

cadmium, 103
CAP, 126, 161, 185–87; definition, 51

cap-and-trade systems, 61, 66, 68; definition, 71
capture, regulatory, 70
carbon: capture, 126; carbon dioxide (CO_2), 194, 213, 221, 237, 238; carbon monoxide (CO), 102, 103; leakage, 219, 220; market, 220; tax, 127
carbon tax, 217
carrots and sticks, 58, 222, 227
Cartagena Protocol on Biosafety, 165
checks and balances: definition, 23, 29; EU, 13–14
chemical substances: challenges of regulating, 101, 129; definition, 129; EU role in regulation, 75, 95; impacts on nonhuman environment, 104; key legal approaches, 130–31; REACH Regulation, 130–31; registration, 130–31; water quality, 117
children, distribution of impacts, 8
China: EU Emissions Trading Scheme, 218, 221–22; CO_2 emissions, 198–201
choice architecture, 62; definition, 71
circular economy, 137
CITES Regulation, 161, 171, 174–76
citizen initiatives, 120–21
civil law: definition, 51; systems, 37–38
civil procedure, 37; definition, 51
civil service, 7, 16
CJEU, 13–14, 17, 27–28, 37–38; Air Quality Framework Directive (AQFD), 105–6; definition, 29; infringement procedure, 21–22; reviewing acts, 23–25
Classification, Labelling and Packaging of Substances and Mixtures Regulation (CLP), 130, 132–33, 143
Clean Air Act of 1970, U.S., 69
Clean Development Mechanism, 214, 217, 221–22
Clean Water Act, U.S., 69
climate change, 91, 121; adaptation, 194–98, 229–31; definition, 237; key

approaches, 231–32; agenda, 151; anthropogenic, 194–96; carbon leakage, 220; challenges, 148; Climate-ADAPT platform, 233; Climate and Energy Policy Framework, 224; Common Agricultural Policy (CAP), 186; definition, 191; emissions: EU Emissions Trading Scheme, 214–23; EU Member States, 197–99; EU snapshot, 208; historical emissions, 197–98; human causes, 194–96; impacts, 199–201, 202; international agreements, 203–6; Kyoto Protocol, 27; mitigation, 209–213; public attitudes, 201–3; UNFCCC, 203–4; U.S., 197–98; water quality, 114

Closing the Loop, 137

CLP regulation, 130, 132–33, 143

coastal areas: beaches, 82; ecosystems, 159; habitats, 181; water, 103, 116

codes. *See* civil law

collaborative approach, 96, 109–10

collective action, 196; definition, 237

command-and-control regulation, 60–61, 64–65; definition, 71

commercial value, 138

Commission, European, 20–24, 42–47, 83–85, 97; agriculture, 186–87; definition, 30; enforcement, 21–24, 97, 105; legislation, 42–47, 120; structure, 13–14, 15–17; technocracy, 83–84

Common Agricultural Policy (CAP), 126, 161, 185–87; definition, 51

common law: definition, 51; legal systems, 37–38

Community Framework, 144–45

compensatory mitigation: definition, 188

competence, 18–19, 20; climate change, 205, 232; definition, 29; exclusive, 18, 20; definition, 30; shared, 26; definition, 31; supportive, 32; wildlife, 170

complaint procedure, 21–23

complex impacts, 9, 87

compliance, 97; cost, 69–70; definition, 71; EU environmental laws, 41–42, 44; gaps, 96; Member States, 97, 120–21; private actors, 59, 64–65, 97

composting, 142

conferral, 18, 21; definition, 31

consequences, unintended, 65, 80–81, 84, 104–5, 119, 157

conservation, 185; Birds Directive, 160–61, 170, 171–74; definition, 188; Natura network, 171–73; Special Areas of Conservation, 180; trends, 181–82

constitutional law, definition, 51

constraints, 66–68

construction, 136

contract law, 38

Convention on Biological Diversity, 164–66

Convention on International Trade in Endangered Species of Wild Fauna and Flora (CITES), 161, 171, 174–76

cost-benefit analysis, 69; definition, 88; use in U.S., 86

Council of Ministers, 13–15, 86, 115, 125, 203; definition, 29

Court of Auditors, 13

Court of Justice of the European Union (CJEU), 13–14, 17, 27–28, 37–38; Air Quality Framework Directive, 105–6; definition, 29; infringement procedure, 21–22; reviewing acts, 23–25

criminal law, 51

criminal procedure, 51

cross-media pollution, 94, 96, 108, 126

Cyprus, 37, 221, 254

Czech Republic, 221, 254

decarbonizing, 212–14, 225

decomposition, 5, 123

default rules, 63–64; definition, 71

deforestation, 209, 210

delegated acts, 42, 45; definition, 52
delegated powers, 67, 264
deterrence, 58
DG CLIMA, 158, 212
diffuse impacts, 4; definition, 10, 88
direct effect, 21, 39, 40–41, 105
directives, 20, 24, 44–45, 96; Air
    Quality Framework Directive
    (AQFD), 102–5; Bathing Water
    Directive, 82; birds, 172–173; Birds
    Directive, 160–61, 170, 171–74; direct
    effect, 41; Drinking Water
    Directive, 114, 115, 119–20;
    Environmental Liability Directive,
    29; Groundwater Directive, 114, 115,
    117; implementation, 69, 82;
    Industrial Emissions Directive, 108,
    110, 142; Marine Strategy
    Framework Directive, 115, 161, 173;
    Priority Substances Directive, 116,
    117; Soil Framework Directive, 100,
    101; waste management, 136–37;
    water, 115–16; Zoos directive, 161, 167
Directorate-General, 15, 258; definition,
    29, 263
Directorate-General for Climate
    Action (DG CLIMA), 158, 212
Directorate-General for European
    Civil Protection and Humanitarian
    Aid Operations, 235
disaster management, 226, 234–35
disclosure, 60, 62, 64, 132
discounting, 211; definition, 88
disposal: hazardous waste, 142–43;
    radioactive waste, 145; waste, 109,
    111, 115, 135–39; definition, 111;
    long-term, 116
dose-response, 93; definition, 148
drinking water, 112–115, 119, 121;
    Drinking Water Directive, 114, 115,
    119–20
droughts, 121, 199, 229–231, 234

EAPs, 46, 78; definition, 51
ECHA, 131–32

economic instruments, 60–64;
    definition, 72
Economics of Ecosystems and
    Biodiversity Initiative (TEEB), 166
ecosystems: aquatic, 158; biodiversity,
    163–66; birds, 171–74; CITES,
    174–76; invasive species, 166–68;
    management, 156–62; wildlife,
    169–71; zoos, 166–68
efficiency, energy, 201, 210, 212–14, 225,
    227–28; definition, 263
EIA, 62, 86–87, 99, 124, 179; definition,
    89; strategic impact assessments, 89
elderly, distribution of impacts, 8
elections, Parliament, 14
electricity generation, 143–44. *See also*
    renewable energy
emissions: expected impacts, 199–201;
    historical, 194–98; by Member
    States, 197–201, 212–21; EU
    Emissions Trading Scheme, 61; EU
    legislation, 101–2; greenhouse gases,
    65–66; Industrial Emissions
    Directive, 108–110, 126; Kyoto
    Protocol, 27; National Emission
    Ceilings Directive, 106–8; public
    attitudes, 201–3
emoticons, 63–64
employment, Commission, 16
endangerment, 169–71, 178
End of Waste, 138
energy: efficiency, 201, 210, 212–14, 225,
    227–28; emissions, 199; Energy
    Union, 225; initiatives, 210, 212–14;
    renewable, 223–24, 226
enforcement, 19, 21–25, 27, 40–42, 59, 82;
    air pollution, 102, 105; CITES, 175–6;
    climate change, 204–5, 219–20;
    Member States, 38, 83, 96–97;
    regulatory instruments, 64–65
environmental acquis, 41–42
Environmental Action Programmes
    (EAPs), 46, 78; definition, 51
environmental competence. *See*
    competence

Environmental Council, 124, 203
Environmental Impact Assessments
    (EIA), 62, 86–87, 99, 124, 179;
    definition, 89; strategic impact
    assessments, 89
environmental impacts, 66;
    characteristics, 4–9; complication
    of regulation, 8; definition, 10, 71;
    distribution, 7–8; human action, 4;
    regulation, 3
environmental justice, 88; definition,
    88
environmental law, 10, 71
Environmental Liability Directive, 29
environmental principles, 47–50;
    definition, 48
environmental quality standards, 87
environmental values, 6–9, 49
erosion, 125–26
Estonia: EU Emissions Trading
    Scheme allocation, 221; EU
    membership, 254; per capita
    emissions, 164, 198–99
EU ETS, 61, 214–23
EU legal system, 13, 37; development,
    38; enforcement power, 39;
    relationship to national laws, 37, 38
EU principles, 7, 13–14, 36–38; legal
    principles, 47–50; theoretical, 84
Euratom Treaty, 144–45
Eurobarometer on Climate Change,
    201
Eurojust, 176
European Central Bank, 13, 24
European Charter on Hunting and
    Biodiversity, 170
European Chemicals Agency (ECHA),
    17, 131–132
European Commission: circular
    economy plan, 137; climate change
    plan, 212–14; composition, 7;
    enforcement, 97, 105; as executive,
    13, 15–16; infringement process,
    21–24; Joint Research Centre, 110,
    195; legislative process, 41–43;

secondary law, 83; soil strategy,
    124–25, 127; water law, 115, 120
European Council, 13–14; definition,
    24, 30
European Environment Agency
    (EEA), 8, 17; climate science, 195,
    233; Report, 118, 126
European Parliament, 13–14, 16, 19, 86,
    139, 186; definition, 30, 33; elections, 14
European Pollutant Release and
    Transfer Register (E-PRTR), 62
European Union Emissions Trading
    Scheme, 61, 214–23
European Union External Action
    Service, 176
European Union Strategy on Climate
    Change Adaptation, 233–34
European Union Waste Hierarchy,
    137–40
Europol, 176
eutrophication, 103, 106
exclusive competence, 18, 20;
    definition, 30
executive, EU, 13–14, 23
exposure reduction, 92–93; definition, 148
External Action Service, 26, 176
external competence, 26, 205
externalities, 20, 60, 71, 81–82, 195–196,
    209; definition, 10, 72, 88
externalization, 81–82, 195

farming, 183–87; effects on biodiversity,
    167; EU Common Agricultural
    Policy (CAP), 185–87; regulating,
    183–85, 213; soil pollution, 122; soil
    pollution, 122; threat to soil, 123–24;
    threat to water quality, 114
Financial Instrument for the
    Environmental Regulation (LIFE),
    46, 126; definition, 48, 52
fisheries regulation, 160–61
fit, 56, 57, 59, 65–66, 70
Flaminio Costa v. ENEL, 39
flexibility, 44, 64, 68, 216; in impact
    assessments, 70

floods: climate change, 199, 230–31; ecosystem services, 159; mapping, 195; soil sealing, 127; Water Framework Directive, 116
food: processing, 119; scraps, 135; security, 183–84, 185
forest fires, 195, 231
forestry, 167, 178, 213
fossil fuels, 194, 210, 223–24
framing, 62–64; definition, 72
free movement, 78, 130
free-rider problem, 196; definition, 237
French (language), 16, 17
funding, 165; Common Agricultural Policy, 186; Emissions Trading Scheme, 220–22

gains, valuing, 61, 69
Ganga river system, 159
garbage. *See* waste
genetic modification, 7, 184–85, 188; definition, 144, 188
geographic diffusion, 6, 19; beyond EU, 25; climate change, 230; definition, 10, 88; ecosystems, 158; habitats, 178; soil pollution, 123; subsidiarity, 80–82
Germany, 15–16, 144, 198, 252
glyoxylic acid, 218
GMOs, 7, 184–85, 188; definition, 144, 188
goals: biodiversity, 166–67; climate, 205, 207, 212, 214; Common Agricultural Policy, 185, 186, 187; Habitats Directive, 181; Kyoto, 219–21, 223–27; Paris Agreement, 231–32, 235; Waste Framework Directive (WaFD), 137, 140
Gothenburg Protocol, 106, 111
grandfathering, 164, 218–19, 221
Greece, 113, 233, 253
greenhouse gases: EU Emissions Trading Scheme, 61, 194–208; definition, 178; delay of effects, 156; emission reduction, 164; EU Emissions Trading Scheme, 214–17, 221, 227, 237; mitigation, 152, 209–14; per capita, 149; relationship to climate change, 146; sequestration, 158
green leadership, 25, 205
Greens/European Free Alliance, 14
ground-level ozone pollution, 101, 103, 106
groundwater, 93–94, 114–17; Groundwater Directive, 114, 115, 117

habitats, 69, 156, 160–67, 171–73, 177–78, 180–82, 183
harm: chemical substances, 129–30; from climate change, 211; distribution, 8; to ecosystems, 157–59; from emissions, 106; environmental, 7–8, 58, 61, 92; EU principles, 49; from invasive species, 167; from pollution exposure, 93, 94, 100
harmonization, 79, 226
hazardous air pollutants. *See* air pollution
hazardous waste, 135–37, 140, 142–43
health, human, 3–5, 8; chemicals, 95, 129–30; climate change, 202, 209, 230; effect of plastics, 5; effect of pollution, 99–100, 103–6; hazardous waste, 131; impacts of waste, 202; ozone risk, 93; policy balance, 66; water quality, 119, 121
heavy metals, 101, 122, 150
heuristics, 63
household waste, 136, 140
human behavior: adaptation, 177; agriculture, 122; climate change, 194–96; environmental impacts, 4–6, 80–81, 156–59; regulation, 3, 6, 86, 112
humanitarian aid, 226, 234–35
Hungary, 113, 221, 233; EU membership, 254

hunting, 169–70, 174
hurricanes, 231

impact assessment, 48, 86, 89, 99, 124, 179; link to risk analysis, 70
implementation: inadequate, 16, 23–24; Member States, 36–38, 82, 96; EU Strategy on Climate Change adaptation, 234; REACH Regulation, 17; regulations, 20; regulations and directives compared, 46; supervising, 44–45
import restrictions, 131–34, 217
incentives, 58, 222, 227
incineration, 94, 135, 142
India, 149, 159, 175, 198, 199, 200, 201, 218
indigenous traditions, 161, 170
Industrial Emissions Directive, 108, 110, 142
Industrial Revolution, 194, 197
industry: agriculture, 183; collaboration, 131–32; emissions, 199, 215–16; energy, 96, 223, 226; pollution control, 99, 108–10, 112, 119, 122; waste management, 136
information-based instruments, 60, 62, 64
infringement procedure, 21–23; definition, 30
initiatives, citizen, 120–121
inland surface waters, 116
innovation, 64, 216, 222, 225, 227; Innovation Fund, 222
instruments, regulatory, 205, 207, 216; common purpose, 50; definition, 61; instrument choice, 65–71; definition, 72; mechanisms, 58–59; types, 60–65
integration: EU and national laws, 38–39, 78–80; integration principle, 46, 48–49, 80, 84; definition, 52
interdependencies, 158
intergovernmental law, 13; definition, 30, 48, 52; Intergovernmental Panel on Climate Change (IPCC), 195

internal market, 19, 78–79; agricultural policy, 185; chemical substances, 130; climate change, 208; climate policy, 212; pollution control effects, 95; tensions, 226; waste, 138; water resources, 120; wildlife, 170, 174
International Civil Aviation Organization (ICAO), 218
international law, 24, 27 28, 40, 107, 114; climate change, 193; compared to EU law, 82; relationship to EU law, 37–38, 97
international treaties: air pollution, 101; Basel Convention, 142–143; Cartagena Protocol on Biosafety, 165; CITES, 161, 171, 174–76; climate change, 205; complex network, 114; Convention on Biological Diversity, 164; Euratom, 144–45; European Union, 7, 26; subsidiarity, 20–21; Gothenburg Protocol, 106, 111; implementation, 160; Kyoto Protocol, 27, 204–8, 214, 221; Maastricht, 22; Member State involvement, 26; Montreal Protocol, 106–7, 207, 250; Nagoya Protocol, 165; Paris Agreement, 25, 205–7, 225, 231, 232, 235; preexisting, 97–98; timeline, 250; Treaty of Lisbon, 26–27; Treaty on European Union (TEU), 20, 42–43, 80; Treaty on the Functioning of the European Union (TFEU), 42, 48–49, 80, 96, 130; UN Framework Convention on Climate Change (UNFCCC), 32; Vienna Convention for the Protection of the Ozone Layer, 107
intrinsic commercial value, 138
invasive species, 166–68, 202; Invasive Alien Species Regulation, 128, 161, 167
IPCC, 195

Joint Implementation, 214, 221
Joint Research Centre, 110, 195

judicial review: CJEU, 23, 25; definition, 30
jurisdiction: definition, 30; exclusive, 78; geographical, 81

Kissinger, Henry, 26
Kyoto Protocol, 27, 204–8, 214, 221

labeling, 62, 64
landfills, 136, 137, 139, 140, 141, 142
land use, 43, 122, 124, 125, 136, 160, 183, 213
languages: Commission, 16, 17; Court of Justice of the European Union, 16, 17, 258, 259
leaching, 122–23, 158
lead, 103
legal personality, 26, 159; definition, 30
legal principles, 47–50
legal structures, 7
legal systems, 36–39, 159
legislation, EU: chemicals, 130, 131; European Commission, 16–17, 41–43, 47–69, 83; European Parliament, 13–14; soil, 126; water, 114–115
levels. *See* thresholds
LIFE Programme, 46–47, 126; definition, 52
limitations: emissions, 104, 109, 204, 214, 222; EU competency, 67; instrument choice, 61, 66–68; rationality, 59
Lithuania, 221, 254
local initiatives: climate change, 208, 233–34
loss, economic, 210, 234; loss aversion, 60–61; no net loss, 166–67; welfare loss, 199–202
loss aversion, 52
loss of habitat, 177–78, 181, 184
Lower Assessment Threshold (LAT), 104

malaria, 230
mandates, 15, 60, 115
manufacturing, 131, 132, 140

marine policy, 161, 171, 172; Marine Protected Areas, 173; Marine Strategy Framework Directive, 115, 161, 173
market-based regulation, 64, 214, 217, 221; definition, 72
Market Stability Reserve (MSR), 222–23
Members of Parliament (MEPs), 14–15
Member States, 12, 16; competence, 9, 18–19, 26–27; definition, 33; enforcement of EU law, 21–23, 76; implementation, 95–98, 102, 104; implementation of EU laws, 67, 76; interests, 14–15; jurisdiction, 66; laws, 36–37, 38–39, 44–47; private enforcement, 24; relationship to EU, 20, 26, 81–83
microplastics, 4–5. *See also* plastics
mining, 122, 123, 136, 140
mitigation, 196, 198, 201, 203, 204, 205–12, 231; definition, 238
Modernisation Fund, 222
monoculture, 183
Montreal Protocol on Substances that Deplete the Ozone Layer, 106–7, 207, 250
moral objections, 62, 64
multilateral agreements, 80, 97, 114, 165, 193
multilateralism, 25, 28, 82, 237
multilevel governance, 9, 77, 80–81, 87; definition, 71, 88
municipal waste, 136, 140–42

Nagoya Protocol, 165
National Adaptation Strategies, 232–33
national air pollution control programmes, 108
National Emission Ceilings Directive (NECD), 101, 106, 108, 111
national interests, 43, 115, 208
national laws, 36–37, 38–39, 44–47
National Renewable Energy Action Plan (NREAP), 224, 226

Natura 2000 Network, 160, 171–73, 180
Natural Capital Financing Facility, 166
natural hazards, 229, 231, 234
Nature Protection and Environmental
    Impact Assessment procedure, 62
NECD, 101, 106, 108, 111
negative impacts, 129, 139
Netherlands, 198–99
New Zealand, 159
nickel, 103
NIMBY, 136
nitric acid, 218
nitrogen, 123. *See also* ammonia (NH$_3$)
nitrogen dioxide (NO$_2$), 102, 103
nitrogen oxides (NO$_x$), 101–3, 106, 158
nitrous oxide (N$_2$O), 187, 217
noise pollution, 99
noncompliance, 97, 121, 139, 216. *See also*
    compliance
no net loss principle, 166
nonhuman impacts: assessment, 86–87;
    climate change, 196, 230; definition,
    88; ecosystems, 157–59; pollution,
    92–94; air pollution, 100; chemical
    substances, 129; soil pollution, 122;
    water pollution, 112
non-methane volatile organic
    compounds, 106
nonpoint source water pollution,
    118–19, 188
norms: definition, 10; EU, 27–28;
    international legal norms, 27;
    normative choices, 3–4, 7–9;
    normative decisions, 7; normative
    values, 4, 6, 8, 13, 26, 94; social, 59, 68
nuclear power, 135–36, 143–46
nudge, behavioral, 57, 60, 62, 65;
    definition, 72

oil, 194, 213, 218, 225
ombudsman, 21
opinions: Commission, 22–23;
    definition, 52; EU act, 41, 45–46;
    judicial, 37; recommendations, 41,
    45–46; definition, 53

ordinary legislative procedure, 42–43;
    definition, 30
organic compounds, 101, 106, 218
organic matter, 123, 125
oxides of nitrogen, 101–3, 106, 158
ozone, 93; ground-level, 101, 102, 103,
    106; atmospheric, 103; ozone-
    depleting substances, 107, 133

packaging: hazardous substances, 130,
    133, 178; labeling, 62, 64; waste, 63, 135.
paper products, 135
Paris Agreement, 25, 205–7, 225, 231,
    232, 235
Parliament, European, 13–14, 16, 24, 43,
    45, 115, 186; definition, 30
particulate matter, 80, 101–3, 106;
    definition, 82
path dependency, 68–69; definition, 72
penalty, pecuniary, 21–22, 23
perception, public, 59, 64
perfluorocarbons (PFCs), 217–18
permits, 60, 61, 64, 71, 176, 221;
    Integrated Pollution Prevention
    and Control (IPPCC), 108–9
PESETA II, 195
pesticides, 122, 126, 129, 133, 184
petroleum hydrocarbons, 122
plastics, 4–5, 139, 141
point source water pollution,
    definition, 189
Poland, 231, 233, 254
politics, 3, 14, 21, 45, 83, 210, 224;
    controls, 19; EU, 208; pressure, 7;
    solutions, 22
Pollinators Initiative, 170
pollutants, 47–49, 84; air, 100–103, 106;
    cross-media, 94
polluter pays principle, 7, 49, 84;
    definition, 52; water law, 116, 178
pollution: air, 94–95, 99–108; definition,
    99, 148; distribution, 8; control, 69,
    92–97, 99–100, 108; effects on
    animals, 93; soil, 122
population density, 198–99

positive incentives, 58–59
power plants, 100, 112, 143, 215, 221
precautionary principle, 7, 47, 48, 49, 84, 85, 87, 132, 245; definition, 10
precedent, 37, 38
precipitation, 193, 230
preemption, 19; definition, 31
present value, 211
preventative action, 47, 48
prices, 60, 217
primacy, 39–40, 43
primary EU law, definition, 31, 52
primary pollutants, 100
principles: constitutional, 13–14; environmental: definition, 51; EU legal, 36–38, 47–50, 84; polluter pays, 7; precautionary, 7, 130; proportionality, 81; subsidiarity, 81, 102
priorities, 7, 27, 66, 78
prioritization, 7, 47, 70, 129, 137, 164, 168, 183, 225
Priority Substances Directive, 116, 117
privacy laws, 110
private actors, 21, 24, 43–44, 97, 105–6
private enforcement, 24, 41, 64, 97, 105
private law, 38; definition, 48, 52
property law, 39, 160; definition, 52
proportionality, 20–21, 47, 81, 102
protectionism, 136
psychology of behavior, 58–59, 64
public actors, 21, 38
public enforcement, 97
public law, 38; definition, 53

qualified majority voting, 15–16; definition, 31
quality standards, 109; air, 102, 111; water, 113, 116–17, 119
quarrying, 140

radioactive energy generation, 143
radioactive waste, 135, 137, 143–45; storage, 143–44; transport, 145
REACH, 16–17, 130, 131–34

recommendations, 41, 45–46; definition, 53
rectification at source principle, 47–49, 84; definition, 88
recycling, 63, 135–37, 140, 142
REFIT, 166
Registration, Evaluation, Authorisation, and Restriction of Chemicals (REACH), 16–17, 130–34
regulation: agriculture, 4, 5, 183; biodiversity, 166–67; chemical substances, 130–34; definition, 267; ecosystems, 160–61; emissions, 213; hazardous waste, 135, 137, 142–43; industry, 135; radioactive waste, 145; solid waste, 141; wildlife, 169, 171, 174–75, 180
regulatory capture, 70
Regulatory Fitness and Performance Programme, 166
regulatory instruments, 205, 207, 216; common purpose, 50; definition, 61; instrument choice, 65–71; definition, 72; mechanisms, 58–59; types, 60–65
renewable energy, 201, 210, 212, 213–24, 226
repositories, 145
representative democracy, 31
Reserve, Market Stability, 222–23
resolutions, 46
reuse, 137, 140
reward, 58
Right2Water, 120–21
risk analysis, 84–87; definition, 88
risk assessment, 84–85, 132; definition, 89
risk communication, 84–85; definition, 71, 89
risk management, 84–85, 232, 234–35; climate, 176; definition, 71, 89
river basins, 113, 116
river pollution, 113, 116, 158–59
Roma, 136
Romania, 113, 140, 220, 221, 255

safety, 30, 144, 184; biosafety, 165; data sheets, 132; water, 113
science: behavioral research, 62; greenhouse gases, 146; climate change, 194–95; versus policy, 85
secondary EU law, 20, 31, 40, 42, 49, 83
secondary pollutants, 100
separation of powers: definition, 39; EU, 13–14
sequestration, 210
Seville process, 110
shared competence, 18–19, 26, 43, 66; definition, 31
shipment, 141–45
Single European Act, 80
single-use plastics, 139, 147
Sites of Community Importance (SCI), 172, 179–80
Social Cost of Carbon (SCC), definition, 238
social norms, 59, 68
social value, 57, 169
socioeconomic status, 8, 46, 197, 198, 206, 221
soft law, 41, 45–46, 127
soil: sealing, 123, 126, 127; treatment, 86, 108, 123, 127
Soil Framework Directive, 100, 101
soil pollution, 92–93, 95; challenges, 122–23; definition, 122, 148; EU role, 99; key approaches, 123–24
solid waste, 134–135, 140, 141; definition, 268. *See also* waste
solvents, 103, 122, 129
source reduction, 92, 100
sovereignty, 13, 18, 20, 39, 125, 175; definition, 31
Special Areas of Conservation, 172, 180
special ecosystems, 136, 177–82
special legislative procedure, 15, 42–43, 125; definition, 30, 33
Special Protection Areas (SPAs), 172–74
species: agricultural, 183–84; biodiversity, 163–64; birds, 161, 170, 171, 172, 174–75; conservation, 262;

decline, 160; endangered, 169–70, 171, 175–76; extinction, 230; habitats, 177–80; invasive, 161, 166, 167–68, 202; protection, 167
standing, 25; definition, 25, 32
stare decisis, 37
sticks, 58
Rio+20 Conference on Sustainable Development, 78
storage: carbon, 210, 213; nuclear fuel, 143, 144, 145; underground tanks, 122; waste, 135, 142
Strategic Environmental Assessments (SEAs), 179
strategic impact assessment, definition, 89
stringency, regulatory, 63, 70, 94; Birds Directive, 171; climate change, 196; drinking water, 119; National Emissions Ceiling Directive (NECD), 106
structural funds, 46, 166
subsidiarity, 19–21, 25, 47–48, 94–95, 102, 267; definition, 31
subsidies, 64, 184, 226
sulphur oxides, 101, 102, 103, 106, 158
Sunstein, Cass, 62
supportive competence, 18, 19; definition, 32
supranational law, 13–14, 20, 21, 31, 82; definition, 32, 53
supremacy. *See* primacy
surface water, 116, 117
sustainability, 7, 158; definition, 144, 189
sustainable development, 48–49, 78, 96–97, 232, 234–35; definition, 53, 268

taxes, 60–61, 64, 66–68
technocracy, 77, 80, 83, 87, 245; definition, 89
TEEB initiative, 166
temperatures: climate change, 193, 198, 206, 232; extreme, 8, 199
temporal diffusion, 84
Thaler, Richard, 62

thresholds, 25; air pollution, 99–100, 102; Air Quality Framework Directive (AQFD), 104–5; Bathing Water Directive, 82; dose-response, 93–94; EU Emissions Trading System, 61; integrated pollution prevention and control (IPPC), 109

tipping points, 157

tort law, 38; definition, 53

tourism, 178, 195, 202

toxic metals, 103

trade-offs: agriculture, 184–185; biodiversity, 164; climate change, 229–30; policy choices, 157; soil additives, 123

trading: EU Emissions Trading Scheme, 61, 102, 205, 213–22; trading space, 68

transboundary effects, 21; air pollution, 45, 95, 101, 106; EU geography, 94–95; hazardous waste, 143; preexisting treaties, 97; water pollution, 113–14

transitional waters, 116

transportation: emissions, 199, 212–13; energy use, 224, 226; hazardous waste, 142; radioactive waste, 145; waste, 135

transposition, 20, 22, 24, 44–45, 259

trash, 135

treaties: air pollution, 101; climate change, 205; complex network, 114; Convention on Biological Diversity, 164; Euratom, 144; European Union, 7, 26; subsidiarity, 20–21; implementation, 160; Kyoto Protocol, 25; Maastricht, 22; Member State involvement, 26; Montreal Protocol, 107; Paris Agreement, 25; preexisting, 97–98; timeline, 250; Treaty of Lisbon, 26–27; Treaty on European Union (TEU), 20, 42–43, 80; Treaty on the Functioning of the European Union (TFEU), 42, 48–49, 80, 96, 130

Treaty of Lisbon, 26, 250

Treaty on European Union (TEU), 20, 42–43, 80

Treaty on the Functioning of the European Union (TFEU), 42, 48–49, 80, 96, 130; Common Agricultural Policy (CAP), 185; environmental competence, 80, 130; environmental principles, 47–49; integration principle, 96

UAT, 104

UN Framework Convention on Climate Change (UNFCCC), 32

uniformity, 42

United Kingdom: climate skepticism, 202–3; EU Emissions Trading Scheme, 217, 220; EU membership, 37, 252; industrialization, 197–98; nuclear energy, 144

urbanization, 123, 127

Urgenda case, 208

U.S. National Environmental Policy Act (NEPA), 62

values: competing, 94, 156–57, 164; biodiversity, 165; normative, 6–7; systemic, 47–49; wildlife, 169. See also thresholds

van Gend en Loos case, 40

Vienna Convention for the Protection of the Ozone Layer, 107

volatile organic compounds, 101, 106, 149

voluntary agreements, 170

waste: chemical, 129; consumer, 5, 63; Council Directive, 45; disposal, 136; Framework Directive, 137–39; hazardous, 135–36, 142–43; history, 95; industrial, 92, 96, 108, 136–37; legal definition, 138; management, 134–35, 136, 137, 140; municipal, 136,

140–42; nuclear, 136; plastic, 5, 139; prevention, 137; radioactive, 143–45; solid, 134–35, 140–42; toxic, 58

Waste Hierarchy, 117, 137, 140

water: Bathing Water Directive, 82, 118; Groundwater Directive, 115–16; pollution, 112–22; quality, 82, 114–18, 123; wastewater, 133; water bodies, 93; Water Framework Directive, 114–18, 126

waters, transitional, 116

weather patterns, 114, 230

wetlands, 187; definition, 189

Whanganui river ecosystem, 159

wildfires, 231

wildlife, 159, 163, 169–71, 174, 176; definition, 189

World Health Organization, 106

Yamuna river system, 159

Zoos directive, 161, 167